Citizenship and Vulnerability

Citizenship and Vulnerability

Disability and Issues of Social and Political Engagement

Angharad E. Beckett
Durham University, UK

First published 2006 by
PALGRAVE MACMILLAN
Houndmills, Basingstoke, Hampshire RG21 6XS and
175 Fifth Avenue, New York, N.Y. 10010
Companies and representatives throughout the world

PALGRAVE MACMILLAN is the global academic imprint of the Palgrave Macmillan division of St. Martin's Press, LLC and of Palgrave Macmillan Ltd. Macmillan® is a registered trademark in the United States, United Kingdom and other countries. Palgrave is a registered trademark in the European Union and other countries.

ISBN 13: 978–1–4039–9236–9   hardback
ISBN 10: 1–4039–9236–3   hardback

This book is printed on paper suitable for recycling and made from fully managed and sustained forest sources.

A catalogue record for this book is available from the British Library.

Library of Congress Cataloging-in-Publication Data
Beckett, Angharad E., 1976–
    Citizenship and vulnerability : disability and issues of social and political engagement / Angharad E. Beckett.
        p. cm.
    Includes bibliographical references and index.
    ISBN 1–4039–9236–3 (cloth)
        1. People with disabilities–Government policy–Great Britain.
2. Citizenship. 3. Social movements. I. Title.

HV1559.G7B43 2006
323.3–dc22
                                                          2005055563

10   9   8   7   6   5   4   3   2   1
15   14   13   12   11   10   09   08   07   06

Printed and bound in Great Britain by
Antony Rowe Ltd, Chippenham and Eastbourne

For my parents

Contents

List of Figures   ix

Acknowledgements   x

1 Introduction   1

Citizenship and vulnerability   1
Key questions   4
Introduction to the research   5
Practical issues: subject information, data collection and   9
   analysis
Key definitions   13
Overview of chapters   19

2 Citizenship   22

Introduction   22
Ancient and classical theories of citizenship   24
Modern/social-liberal theories of citizenship   34
Contemporary accounts of citizenship   46
Conclusion: future developments?   61

3 Social Movements   65

Introduction   65
Phase 1 theories   67
The 1960s 'watershed'   73
Phase 2 theories   74
Conclusion: the future for social movement theorizing?   87

4 Issues in Disability   90

Introduction: a brief history of theorizing on disability   90
Experiencing disability   99
Conclusion   117

5 The Views of Disabled People   118

Structural issues   118
Disabling attitudes, empowering identities?   129
Disability culture   143

	The disability movement	145
	Deafness and disability	153
	Conclusion	161

6   Reconsidering Theorizing on Citizenship and Social Movements in the Light of Disability   **162**

	Introduction	162
	Social-Liberalist accounts	163
	Pluralist accounts	169
	Beyond the pluralist accounts	179
	Implications for social movement theorizing	183
	Conclusion	190

7   Conclusion   **192**

| | The future for citizenship theorizing | 192 |
| | Concluding comments: implications for future research and theorizing | 196 |

Notes	200
References	203
Index	213

List of Figures

Figure 2.1   The changing nature of citizenship theorizing   23
Figure 3.1   Social movement theories   66

Acknowledgements

I acknowledge the financial support of ESRC Postgraduate Studentship Award Number: R00429934031 in carrying out the research upon which this book is based.

I would also like to express my thanks to the following people: all of the research respondents. David Phillips for giving me intellectual freedom whilst gently 'steering' my more 'exuberant' writing tendencies and for all of his advice. Richard Jenkins and Nick Ellison – both of whose work has influenced me greatly – for their encouragement and comments on an earlier draft of this book. Alan Walker for his comments.

Finally, thank you to those friends, especially Claire Fleming, who 'cheered me along' and, most importantly, my parents for their support and interest.

1
Introduction

Citizenship and 'vulnerability'

In recent years, the concepts of *citizenship* and *social and political engagement*, especially the involvement of individuals in what have come to be termed the *new social movements*, have become major issues for academics from a wide variety of perspectives. The reason why citizenship has returned to centre stage probably rests, as Kymlicka and Norman (1994: 352) have written, upon the notion that the *'stability of a modern democracy depends, not only on the justice of its basic structure but also on the qualities and attitudes of its citizens'*. Connected with this upsurge of interest in 'citizenship' is a growing support for the idea that *'the institutions of constitutional freedom are only worth as much as the population makes of them'* (Habermas, 1992: 7). Such thinking may explain the increased interest in social movements since in many respects they can be seen to be the major sites of struggle and negotiation between the individual members of society, albeit working *en masse*, and the chief 'institution of constitutional freedom' in the form of the *state*.

At the same time, academic concerns with a range of forms of social exclusion have also reached centre stage. High on the current agenda for social science are matters relating to the ever increasing 'vulnerability' of individuals in relation to a range of factors and there is a growing agreement that 'personhood' is now best understood as fragile and contingent. Some of these factors are already well recognized, for example people around the world continue to face the 'risks' associated with changing labour markets and poverty, ill-health or 'traditional' forms of discrimination and associated disadvantage such as racism, sexism etc. Other factors, however, are being newly identified and understood. For

1

example, there is now an increasing awareness that the information flows associated with globalization and new technologies are leading to new forms of polarization between the information 'rich' and 'poor'. Concerns are also being raised about the potential for new forms of prejudice and discrimination arising out of new 'medical' technologies, for example in relation to genetics. Concerns surrounding the impact on the 'person' of new 'threats' associated with the environment and international terrorism are also starting to be voiced widely. Finally, changes to the life-course in terms of vastly increasing life-expectancy around the world, but especially within the advanced capitalist countries, are not only placing an increasing burden upon welfare states and working-age family members in relation to taxation and caring responsibilities, but are also resulting in an increased number of vulnerable elderly people within society.

In the light of concerns such as these, it would therefore seem timely to begin the process of theorizing citizenship and social movements in relation to these new and continuing forms of 'vulnerability' and this is the motivation behind this book. In seeking to achieve this 'theoretical' goal, it is also a concern of this book, however, to ground any theorizing in empirical evidence and in particular to allow some 'bottom-up' views of non-academics to become part of academic discourses in this area. For this reason, the starting point for the argument presented in this book is the absence of consideration within theorizing on citizenship of the position of one of society's particularly 'vulnerable' groups – disabled people – and the lack of adequate consideration by social movement theorists of the concerns of the UK disability movement. The book therefore seeks to provide a platform for disabled people to voice their opinions on issues relating to citizenship and the UK disability movement. Within this book, 'disability' is then used as a *case study*, contextualized by an interest in the manner in which an understanding of the *vulnerability* associated with the experience of 'disability' may impact on citizenship and social movement theorizing.

At this point it is important to make clear the basis on which I am 'classifying' disabled people as being 'vulnerable' since it is my argument here that the term 'vulnerable' does not, at present, possess particularly positive or empowering connotations for anyone so described. The use of the term by the media, for example, appears to have rendered it synonymous with groups who lack 'ability' in one respect or another. Like the equally unpopular term amongst many disabled people – 'sufferer' – the unfortunate connotations that develop around certain terms can, however, distract and detract from the genuine uses of such terms. Thus, whilst many disabled people have stated that the term 'sufferer' has negative and patronizing associations with 'charitable' attitudes towards disabled people, equally the term does, for example, aptly describe the experiences of many disabled individuals who experience pain as part of their impairment. To deny the appropriateness of the term as a description of the experiences of certain individuals would be, therefore, tantamount to ignoring the plight of these individuals. Applying this argument to the term 'vulnerability', and in order, I hope, to avoid any misunderstanding, I think that it is therefore important to state the following.

Firstly, I am keen that the term 'vulnerable' should not be imbued with notions of competency/ability. In other words, in describing disabled people as a 'vulnerable' group I am not questioning the abilities of disabled people. On the contrary, I am in fact suggesting that one of the ways in which disabled people are 'vulnerable' is with regard to negative assumptions made about their abilities by some non-disabled people. The second issue that I think is important to mention is that the definition of 'vulnerability' employed within this book is not one that is particularly or exclusively associated with physical limitations of the body – although the risks people face and experiences they may have of what might be termed *bodily vulnerability* are key to understanding contemporary personhood.

In this book, 'vulnerability' is used as a way to describe the fragile and contingent nature of personhood. Thus, we are all 'vulnerable' in some respect and most people are potentially, or actually 'vulnerable' with regard to a very wide range of 'risks' and new forms of social exclusion. 'Disability' is one of the 'risks' facing every individual in society and understanding that we are all physically vulnerable and interdependent at some point in our lives should be a central part of understanding the late modern condition. Not only this, however, 'disability' as opposed to 'impairment' (the straightforward description of the physical limitations of the body) is defined as being the experience of a range of 'disabling practices' and attitudes within society that further disadvantage, devalue and attack the 'personhood' of individuals who are already living with difficulties associated with their physical 'differences'. In this respect, therefore, since we are all vulnerable with regard to acquired disability, we are also all vulnerable with regard to experiencing the 'disabling society'.

Having stated that one of the primary goals of this book is to begin the process of bringing together theorizing on citizenship, social movements and 'vulnerability', it is equally important, at the outset, to state that the argument put forward here is as yet only tentative and represents only an initial attempt to explore these matters. Further, the discussion within this book represents only 'one piece of the jigsaw'. It is clear that a great deal more empirical research and associated theorizing will need to be carried out before it is possible to understand the 'whole picture' with regard to citizenship and 'vulnerability'.

Key questions

Whilst the development of a 'uniting' theory that brings together understandings of citizenship, political engagement and issues of 'vulnerability' is clearly going to involve asking a very wide range of questions and to involve numerous investigations from a range of different angles, consideration of three key issues sets the parameters of this book's contribution to theorizing in this area. These issues are as follows:

Issue 1

How might it be possible to reconsider citizenship in the light of the experiences of disabled people?

Issue 2

What do disability organizations believe to be the basis of their 'struggle'? Authors such as Shakespeare (1993), Oliver and Zarb ([1989] 1997) have made tentative claims that the disability movement is a 'new' social movement, but how accurate is their assessment? Is the disability movement currently acting within a broadly defined socio-cultural sphere, or does it remain concerned largely with persistent issues of social inequality?

Issue 3

Thirdly, drawing upon a consideration of the first and second issues, how might we reconsider current theories of social movements and 'citizen engagement' in the light of disability and the concerns of the UK disability movement?

Focusing upon these three questions, it is hoped, will allow for an exploration of current theorizing on citizenship and social movements in the context of 'disability' and subsequently of 'vulnerability'.

Introduction to the research

This book draws upon the findings of a UK Economic and Social Research Council (ESRC) funded study carried out in 2000–2001 at six disability organizations based in the UK, and run *by* disabled people, *for* disabled people. In order to achieve one of the key aims of this research – to inject the voices of disabled people into citizenship and social movement theorizing – a methodology was chosen that owes much to the abductive and critical/emancipatory research paradigms. Blaikie (1993: 176) has most recently defined the sociological version of abductive research thus:

> (...) the process used to produce social science accounts of social life by drawing on the concepts and meanings used by social actors and the activities in which they engage.

This is an approach, therefore, that gives a central place to the views of the 'insiders' and as such has clear ontological implications for it rests upon an understanding of the social world as being that which is perceived and experienced by its members from the 'inside'. It is an approach that also has clear epistemological implications for it is a method that begins by seeking to encourage actors to reflect upon their activities and thus 'give accounts' for their actions. For Blaikie (1993) the role of the researcher is then to transfer these accounts into 'social science descriptions', at which level, he claims, it is perfectly legitimate to conclude the research. Equally, however, much abductive research will go on to a second level, to form social theories from the data or to relate the findings to existing perspectives.

The process of this research echoed Blaikie's model, advancing to the second level, for it sought to compare the empirical findings with existing perspectives on citizenship and social movements. The important point about abductive theorizing, however, is that even when theorizing at the second level, the aim is to avoid developing overly abstract terms for recurring themes lest the resulting theories should prove to be inaccessible to the social actors in question. Ensuring that the conclusions of this research were accessible to the research participants was central to this project and to the claim that the research has 'emancipatory properties'.

This having been stated, however, it is important to make a clear distinction between the approach taken in this research and the form of 'emancipatory research' often employed within Disability Studies. Critical theory has greatly influenced Disability Studies and has led to a preference in this field for social theory that is so interlinked with social practice, that the truth or falsity of the theory can be partially determined by whether it can be transformed into action – particularly of the kind that leads to important shifts of power (Oliver, 1992). In other words, according to this model, emancipatory disability research must affect praxis within the marginalized group and researchers must espouse engagement with the struggles of disabled people over object-ivity. As Barnes (1996: 110) has stated: *'researchers can only be with the oppressors or with the oppressed'*.

This model of emancipatory research has not, however, gone unchal-lenged. Shakespeare, for example, writes with candour about his own research and admits to engaging in research practices and to possessing certain views that many within Disability Studies would find 'challeng-ing'. He begins by questioning the notion that there needs to be a formalized connection between Disability Studies and the disability movement. He highlights the fact that in the case of lesbian and gay studies the connection between the discipline and the lesbian and gay political movement has been much less formalized, and indeed that there has been dissent amongst some academics in the field from the 'orthodoxy' of the movement. What has been vital, however, to the development of lesbian and gay studies, is, according to Shakespeare, that whilst commitment has been clear, accountability has been more diffuse. Relating this to Disability Studies, Shakespeare (1996a: 249) states that in his opinion *'there is a difference between accountability to one's research subjects, and accountability to the disability movement or specific organizations within it'*. Further, Shakespeare (1996a: 252) states that:

> I have major reservations with the concept of emancipatory research (...) I am cynical about the possibility of research achieving major change (...) Ideas clearly have a role, but actions decide the day, and while it is possible to make the research process more balanced, grandiose claims for its revolutionary potential seem to me to be over-optimistic. Furthermore, whilst few would now argue in terms of objectivity, a notional independence and balance is still seen as critical to the academic endeavor. Given the political context, there is little point in developing progressive research which is rejected out of hand by government and media alike as being contaminated by ideological prejudice (...) academics cannot be perceived to have axes to grind.

At first glance this statement might appear to be a rejection of the emancipatory approach to research on the basis of some fairly practical concerns, i.e. that research that is perceived to be partisan will not have as much influence upon policy-makers. In fact, Shakespeare clearly has some more profound difficulties with the notion that praxis must always be an essential part of disability research. He comments that he does not think that all research should be judged on instrumental grounds. Whilst he does not believe that researchers should have *carte blanche* to '*parasite disabled people's experiences and develop careers on the back of disabled people's lives*' (Shakespeare, 1996a: 253), he nevertheless defends the rights of researchers to undertake research and to develop theory for its own sake. Equally, he also rejects the idea that for research to have emancipatory outcomes, the findings must be accessible and immediately comprehensible to disabled people. According to Shakespeare, if Disability Studies is to engage properly in a sociological understanding of disability, it will have to make use of complex ideas and analyses which may be quite difficult to grasp. It is important, he believes, to acknowledge within theory the '*often complex, nuanced and difficult*' (Shakespeare, 1996a: 252) nature of social reality. Social research cannot always, therefore, be simple and transparent in order to facilitate praxis. In arguing thus, Shakespeare is clearly at odds with Barnes and Oliver who have suggested that the only legitimate role for disability research is to produce knowledge that can easily be used by disabled people to challenge disablism within society and bring about positive changes in their lives.

With regard to this research, considerable effort was made to follow the guidelines for good research practice as set out by authors such as Barnes and Oliver. For example, this research did consult seriously with disabled people and aimed to represent their views fairly; the respondents were given the opportunity to ask questions about the research and to identify key issues that they wished to discuss; feedback was given at each stage of the research to provide respondents with the opportunity to revise, or add to their existing comments; a more informal and less tightly structured interview technique was utilized in order that respondents could be enabled to speak out, truly, about issues in their lives; the comments of respondents have been reproduced in this book *verbatim* and have been given a prominent position within the findings chapter (Chapter 5); and I have remained accessible and accountable to research respondents throughout the research.

Finally, with regard to the nature of the theory generated by the research, as previously stated, and in contrast to Shakespeare's view, a stance was taken that as far as possible, the majority of respondents should be able to understand the theories resulting from the research and even more importantly, how the theories were generated. It was thought that the first stage of this process was to ensure that all participating organizations received a record of their meeting. This was important because it allowed respondents to consider what had been their responses to the research questions, and to draw their own conclusions about how their views might inform the research. In the second document sent to each organization, in which the findings of the whole research were outlined and in which verbatim quotations from many respondents had a prominent position, it was hoped that each respondent would be able to see how their views 'fitted into' the overall conclusion.

Despite these important aspects of the research, however, certain aspects of this project do not seem to fit directly within the emancipatory approach as set out by Barnes and Oliver. Whilst in the initial stages of this research this was a matter of some concern, by the end of the research this concern was less about the potential for criticism of the research and more about the need to question some of the existing research 'orthodoxies'. As has already been stated, this research does not have the clear emancipatory outcomes as described by Oliver (1992), since it is not tied into policy-making structures. In the light of what might be viewed by authors such as Oliver as a failing on the part of this research, Tom Shakespeare's reservations concerning the emancipatory approach to disability research and his subsequent defence of research which seeks to 'develop theory for its own sake' is, at first glance, reassuring, for he appears to offer a way out for researchers who are finding it difficult to identify clear emancipatory outcomes in their work. My argument here, however, is that it is not always necessary to seek this way out. Indeed, whilst I share Shakespeare's unease concerning the orthodoxy within disability research, it is possible to argue that his analysis of the alternative is not entirely convincing. Arguably, no sociological theory is, or should be, only of value in itself.

Sociologists have long prided themselves on their critical role in society. As Giddens (1993: 23) has commented:

> No sociologically sophisticated person can be unaware of the inequalities that exist in the world today, the lack of social justice in many social situations or the deprivations suffered by millions of people. It would be strange if sociologists did not take sides on practical issues (...)

The history of sociology demonstrates that understanding differences, concern with social inequalities and/or the potential for social change, are major and honourable parts of what sociology is *about*. Whilst much of this sociology is not tied directly to the formulation of a particular policy, this is not to say that sociological theory has no influence upon society. Within Disability Studies itself, to deny the importance of the development of theory that is not policy related, would be to deny the important influence of such theories as Goffman's *Stigma* and Douglas' *Purity and Danger* to understandings within this field. It can be argued that with knowledge comes understanding and having a clearer understanding of the *status quo* must surely provide a more solid basis from which to seek change. Arguably, therefore, much social theory is 'emancipatory' or possesses 'emancipatory properties'. In relation to this research, a central aim of the project was to ensure that the disabled people involved in the research should emerge from the process in a more powerful position, in that they would, hopefully, be able to use the understandings and knowledge gained from the research to both define and then act upon their own objectives. It is the argument here that this research can legitimately be termed 'critical/emancipatory' on this basis.

Practical issues: subject information, data collection and analysis

Subject information

In order that this research encompassed disability organizations from a variety of different areas within England, all groups that met the criteria of being run by disabled people, for disabled people, and that were located in one of the following locations, were contacted: London; the cities of South Yorkshire, Lancashire and Manchester Region; and Cumbria. In all, 19 organizations were contacted, but only six organizations were found either to be suitable (i.e. had a membership that met regularly) or were willing to become involved in the research. Additionally, it was a sad reflection upon the state of funding for many disability organizations that several groups that were contacted were either in the middle of major upheaval due to changes in funding, or had ceased to exist due to complete lack of funds.

In the case of those organizations not willing to be involved in the research, a form of 'stalling' often took place, in which groups never finally agreed to becoming involved, no matter how many times they were contacted. Sometimes it was suspected that this stalling may have been due to the effect of gatekeepers. One group, however, – The Greater Manchester Coalition of Disabled People – did directly respond to the research letter and explained that they were not willing to participate in the research because, as an organization, they had decided not to support research being carried out by non-disabled people.

The direct and indirect refusal by some organizations to becoming involved in the research did, of course, raise an important question for the research: *to what extent were those organizations that agreed to become involved in the research representative of the feelings of all groups within the disability movement?* In answer to this question I would like to state the following: whilst acknowledging that there are shortfalls associated with 'opportunity sampling', it is hoped that readers will note that in focusing upon *micro-representativeness*, this research was not seeking to be 'definitively representative' of the entire disability community. Thus, the research remains accountable only to the groups and individuals involved. At the same time, however, it was also considered that the groups who had agreed to becoming involved in the research were not so atypical that insight gained from working with them would be of *no relevance* to understanding the disability movement as a whole. Indeed, since all six organizations involved in the research matched the definition of groups that make up the disability movement as set out by Oliver (1997), in other words they were run *by disabled people for disabled people,* it was concluded that the resulting data would allow for tentative generalizations to be made.

The participating organizations:

South Yorkshire groups
1. S1: A 'politically' orientated group of disabled people.
2. S2: A self-advocacy group of people with learning disabilities.

Lancashire group
3. L1: An organization acting as a resource for other disabled people.

Cumbria groups
4. C1: A support group of predominantly young/middle aged people living with chronic arthritis.
5. C2: An organization acting as a resource for other disabled people.
6. C3: An organization acting as a resource for other disabled people.

Data collection and analysis

In-depth semi-structured interviews or focus groups were held at each organization. In all of the interviews/focus groups, respondents were encouraged to choose which questions from the interview schedule they wished to discuss at length and to identify any further issues relating to the research topic that they considered important. Each interview/focus group lasted between 1–2 hours. The decision to utilize 'focus groups' as the central method of data collection in this research was made on the basis that this interview technique is of considerable value where there are inherent power differentials between the researcher and the researched, as was the case in this research between the non-disabled researcher and disabled respondents. This is because a large degree of control of the discussion is devolved to the respondents.

Full transcripts of all interviews and focus groups were sent to each participating group for their approval. Transcripts were subsequently analysed using a process of informal or open coding. The purpose of this analysis was to ensure that the voices of respondents remained undistorted and to avoid fracturing the text. Feedback was given to all participating organizations in the form of a report on the research findings.

Two further aspects of the data collection must also be mentioned. Firstly, since all groups were sent a set of proposed questions for consideration within the focus groups before the focus groups took place, some respondents chose to write additional responses to questions. These responses were considered along with the transcripts of the focus groups. Secondly, as has already been discussed at some length, data was also collected *via* the web-based mail group 'Deafmail'. The data took the form of a series of emails that had been sent between a number of participants in the mail-based group and me, and the text of these emails was saved. It must be acknowledged, however, that one of a number of key dilemmas associated with the use of web-based communication within research (see British Sociological Association's Ethical Guidelines for further details), is the problem that it is often impossible to ensure that respondents are who they say they are. For example, in the case of this research, it was necessary to accept as a matter of trust that the respondents to the questions posted on 'Deafmail' were truly Deaf/deaf people. There are, however, some key benefits to this method of data collection, which I consider to have out-weighed the limitations. Firstly, the use of the mail-base enabled me to contact a very large number of Deaf/deaf people, rapidly. Secondly, there are benefits to the use of email where respondents may have difficulties with verbal communication. In such cases, email provides a way of interacting with the researcher that is more like a conversation than more formal, written correspondence.

Ethical statement

It has long been acknowledged that when research is being carried out with/on oppressed groups, there must be transparency with regard to the position of the research/er. This was a particularly significant issue within this research because, as previously mentioned, of my position as a non-disabled researcher carrying out research with disabled people. Whilst it is not the intention here to consider the continuing debate within Disability Studies surrounding the role of non-disabled researchers in this field within the confines of this methodological summary, a statement regarding the position taken during this research in relation to this issue follows.

An ethical stance was taken to this research that involved self-reflection on my part, as researcher, and that echoes the theoretical position taken within this research towards the idea of citizenship and vulnerability. As will be discussed in the final chapter of this book, a more fluid and dynamic understanding of citizenship as 'personhood', in which the identity of every individual is seen to be vulnerable and contingent, may provide the best way forward for understanding and changing attitudes towards many historically oppressed groups. It is my argument here that the methodological implication of this theoretical stance is that what is needed on the part of the researcher is not necessarily to possess the identical experience of oppression to their research subjects, but rather to be constantly aware of the vulnerability of their own personhood. In acknowledging and attempting to transcend one's own fairly 'conditional' identity it is therefore possible to add to calls for the end of a range of oppressions without directly experiencing those oppressions. Thus, echoing much of the anti-racist and feminist approaches to research, a researcher does not have to be black to recognize and deplore the injustice of apartheid or more widespread racism, and following the same argument, the non-disabled researcher does not need to be disabled to appreciate the 'second-class' citizenship experienced by disabled people. My argument, therefore, is that non-disabled people can and should engage in disability research so long as they maintain reflexive at all times with regard to their motives, their own identities and their research practices.

Additionally, this research abided by the British Sociological Association's (BSA) ethical guidelines for research with vulnerable adults and guidelines for the use of non-disablist language. Permission for involvement of respondents in the research and the recording of their views on audio-tape was sought from the respondents themselves. The confidentiality and anonymity of respondents has been ensured at all times throughout the research and within this book.

Key definitions

Before providing an overview of the various chapters of this book it is important to acknowledge the position taken in this book with regard to a number of key issues.

Defining disability

According to the Social Model of Disability, disability is defined separately from impairment – the straight forward description of the effects of a physiological 'condition' – as a form of oppression, the focus being upon the manner in which 'society' increases the dependency of disabled people and prevents them from participating equally within the economic and social sphere. According to key proponents of the approach such as Finkelstein (1996), to consider *impairment* as part of the explanation for the experiences of disabled people is to dilute the effectiveness of the Social Model. It is my admittedly somewhat controversial assertion in this book, however, that this definition of 'disability' provided by the Social Model of Disability is no longer entirely adequate, for it perpetuates a *disembodied* notion of disability. As will be discussed in Chapter 4, more contextualized understandings of personhood are now emerging that acknowledge the part that the physiology of *embodied persons* plays in determining life experiences (see Butler, 1993, Turner, [1996] 2000). Proponents of this understanding of personhood claim, however, that to understand fully the effects of physiology a *social* framework must be employed.

Applying this approach to attempts to understand the experience of 'disability', it is the argument here that the Cartesian compartmentalism that has led to the separation of impairment and 'disability' should be abandoned in favour of establishing a social framework with which to understand the experiences of disabled people. This framework would be based upon the *'realignment between body, self and society'* (Bendelow and Williams, 1995: 156).

Whilst the fears expressed by many within Disability Studies – that considering 'impairment' in this way 'fudges' the issue of causality and the source of disability – may be understandable, nevertheless, apply-ing Butler's theorizing, to challenge successfully the discourses of power that *'disable'* individuals, it is important to understand that 'impairment', whilst having an undeniable, basic, biological definition, is also imbued with diverse social meaning. It is for this reason that this book rests upon a definition of disability that allows for the 'reversibility of impairment and disability' and an understanding of the effect on the lives of disabled people of the simultaneous experi-ences of pain or debility *and* associated oppression by a 'disabling' society.

Why talk about citizenship not social exclusion?

In recent years, the term social exclusion has become something of a 'buzz word' both in academic and non-academic circles in the UK. The importance currently being given to the idea is demonstrated by the Government's commitment to its *'Social Exclusion Unit'*, for example. Whilst the term may have become a 'buzz word' that is not, however, to deny its value, for it is a powerful way of expressing the fact that practices can exist in a society that have major consequences in terms of disadvantage for some of the people in that society. For some authors such as Jordan (1996), to talk about 'social exclusion' is arguably preferable to discussing citizenship since the past 20 years have witnessed the development of a dominant definition of citizen-ship that is highly individualist. He dismisses citizenship as a way of analysing social exclusion because the term has become all too associ-ated with individual rights and duties, *'at the expense of interdependency and collective action'* (Jordan, 1996: 85). For Byrne (1999: 24) this problem with the term 'citizenship' has arisen because it *'(...) has been formulated as a concept almost entirely in terms of abstract philosophical discussion rather than by reference to the real historical social politics (...)'.* He goes on to argue, convincingly, that this overly philosophical approach to theorizing on citizenship has allowed for the appropri-ation of the concept by the New Right and other proponents of 'possessive individualism'.

It is certainly true that during the 1980s the term citizenship became linked in the minds of many with the writings of people such as Charles Murray (1990, 1994) and his notion of the 'underclass'. In this way, 'citizenship' as a concept became a political tool with which to categorize certain individuals and groups as 'failed citizens'. The term thus became far 'narrower' in definition than had historically been the case, and its transformative and collectivist properties appeared to have been largely forgotten.

As the end of the 20th century approached, however, 'citizenship' again became fashionable and continues to be so. The reason for this resurgence in interest in citizenship is not entirely clear. One possible reason may be that sufficient time has now elapsed, since the hey-day of the New Right, for citizenship now to have lost some of its individualist connotations. Many authors are now returning to the concept of citizenship as a way of explaining and mediating the changing relationships between the state and its population. Concern with governance, with the nature of the rights that form part of citizenship and with the extent to which the role of citizen is an 'active' one, have become 'hot-topics' again both inside and outside of academia.

Despite the resurgence of interest in the idea of citizenship, however, the risk that new work in this area may continue to be predominantly abstract and philosophical, remains. Whilst this philosophical work is of considerable value, research is also required, however, that is more empirically grounded in real social politics. Complementary research such as this is starting to be carried out, and is an important new step in the history of citizenship theorizing. Dwyer (2000) for example, has moved discussions about social citizenship away from the purely theoretical level by making the practical concerns of citizens an integral part of current debates. Dwyer's work is just one example of a growing trend towards injecting the voices of presently marginalized groups into citizenship theorizing.

The new approach to citizenship theorizing, of which, it is hoped the arguments put forward in this book with be considered a part, is not, therefore, an alternative to theorizing on 'social exclusion' but is instead about placing citizenship at the heart of discussions surrounding social inclusion and exclusion. It is my argument here that the 'ideal form of citizenship' is one in which each citizen is socially, politically and legally *included*. Evidence of disadvantage amongst those who are, officially, '*legally*' included suggests however, that many people are not being '*socially*' or '*politically*' included. In other words when we talk about people being socially excluded, we are talking about people being excluded from important parts of citizenship. This having been said, the question facing theorists within this field must then be: what is the *basis* of the *social/political inclusion* dimension of citizenship? It is hoped that a consideration of the first question of this research will contribute to some degree to answering this question.

Why talk about 'late modernity'?

When I use the term 'late modernity' it is with awareness that it is a contested concept. The debate surrounding the term, however, appears to focus less upon the idea that there has been a 'crisis in modernity' and more upon questions surrounding what epoch has come in its place. In other words the debate surrounds the relative appropriateness of the terms 'late modernity' and 'post-modernity'. Whilst it is not the intention here to engage with this debate in any great depth, since it warrants a fuller consideration than is possible within the confines of this book, it is important to explain why the term 'late modernity' is used here in preference to 'post-modernity'.

As previously stated, it is now widely, if not unanimously, accepted by sociologists that the past 50 years have witnessed such significant social, political, economic and cultural change as to render the concept of *modernity* increasingly problematic. Opinions tend to differ, however, surrounding the extent to which there has truly been a movement *beyond* modernity. Many theorists favour the idea that what has occurred is a transition from modernity to late modernity, two factors being referred to most frequently as having brought about the greatest change. Firstly, there is what Ellison (1997, 2000) has referred to as changing patterns of social and political 'belonging' characterized by the disruption of 'traditional' social divisions. Secondly, there is the impact of globalization and the so-called demise of the nation state, factors considered in some depth by Roche (1995). The threat that such changes pose to the coherency of societies has become the chief concern of those who favour the notion of 'late modernity'. The concept of 'late modernity' does not, however, imply that at the current time the nation state has declined beyond importance, nor does it imply that there has been a total decline in the importance of older social divisions such as class.

In other words, to talk about 'late modernity' is to remain cautious about claiming an 'end to history', and to be sceptical about claims such as those made by one group of post-modern authors that the 'world is being remade' in such a way as to see the growth of mobility and internationalization or the end of such things as mass production and the 'big-brother state' (Hall *et al*, 1988). It is the argument here that the world post-11 September 2001 is not being *remade* in this way. The threat of global terrorism has, arguably, brought about the reinforcing of the power of certain nation-states, as demonstrated by the decision of the USA and the UK to go against the wishes of the UN in the recent war in Iraq. Such a climate of fear has also led to the further control of migration, as demonstrated by the current UK refugee 'crisis'. At the same time as this 'crack down' on global mobility is occurring, within the UK continuing problems of social exclusion suggest that despite rises in absolute social mobility, relative social mobility remains a problem. These issues, amongst others, suggest that it may be premature to suggest that a post-modern era has arrived and that it may be better to utilize instead the idea of 'late modernity'.

What is the disability movement?

In his well-known introduction to sociology, Giddens (1993: 746) has provided a useful 'broad-brush' definition of social movements as:

> A large grouping of people who have become involved in seeking to accomplish, or to block, a process of social change.

In addition to his definition, drawing upon the work of Blumer ([1951] 1995) it is the argument here that the activities of social movements may not always be about social change, but may also be 'expressive' in nature. The combination then of these two broad definitions has provided the basis, within this book, of categorizing the various *episodes* of collective action by disabled people as the 'disability movement'. As will become apparent within the subsequent chapters of this book, however, a certain degree of diversity in terms of aim and action between the various constituent groups and individual members of the disability movement is something that characterizes this movement. On the basis of such diversity some might question the idea that a social movement of disabled people truly exists. It is the argument here, however, that many widely recognized social movements are equally diverse, the women's movement being a prime example. Total homogeneity in terms of all aims and forms of action is not, therefore, something that needs to be considered as a defining feature of a social movement.[1] There does, however, need to be some common ground between the various individuals and groups that comprise a movement. Just as the various strands of the women's movement can be seen to be united on the basis of such things as a shared understanding of the need to challenge pre-conceived ideas about women, so the various strands of the disability movement are united in their view that we live in a 'disabling society' in which many people with impairments are socially excluded in a number of ways.

Having established this fairly loose framework within which to define the 'disability movement', determining a *coherent* body of disability groups or disabled individuals who can be considered to be a part of this movement is more difficult. This difficulty arises because many groups who might easily be categorized from an 'outsider' perspective as being a part of a movement network do not appear to see themselves as firmly connected to the disability movement. It is at this point that it should be stated that it was not the intention of this research to consider the history of the disability movement, but rather to provide a 'snap-shot' of the contemporary movement and the position taken in this book is that in order to remain focused on the central issues of concern as set out above, emphasis should be given to a comparison between the definitions of the contemporary movement provided by key academics in the field and the evidence collected within this research relating to the nature of the movement.

This is not to deny that a consideration of the development of the disability movement over time is an interesting one, or that this history is of no relevance to this research. The history of the formation and subsequent tensions between the Disablement Income Group, the Disability Alliance and the Union of Physically Impaired Against Segregation (UPIAS), for example, has, however, been well-documented by authors such as Oliver (1990, 1996). The important point about the history of the disability movement, in relation to this research, is that in the UK the development of the Social Model of Disability by organizations such as UPIAS has been closely linked to a range of disability rights campaigns carried out by the movement. It is precisely such campaigns that, amongst other issues, have called for the funding of organizations *of* rather than *for* disabled people.

Oliver's (1997) definition of the disability movement as being constituted *only* by organizations *of* disabled people, not organizations *for* disabled people, therefore reflects the campaigns of the disability movement of the past and present.[2] In the light of this tension, and on the basis of Oliver's definition, it was therefore decided that only groups run by disabled people themselves would be contacted about this research. As a final point, however, it is important to state that this research did not take as its starting point Oliver's tendency to equate the disability movement with the constituent member groups of the British Council of Disabled People (BCODP). This decision was made on the basis of my pre-existing links within the field that informed me that the BCODP does not encompass all groups run *by* disabled people, *for* disabled people and that there is considerable debate amongst disabled people surrounding the importance of this organization.

Overview of chapters

Chapter 2   Citizenship

This chapter aims to provide a critical outline of those theories of citizenship that relate most clearly to the focus of this book. It is also the aim of this chapter to introduce the most contemporary debates within the field that will then be considered in more depth as they relate to the findings of the research referenced here, in Chapter 6. The chapter begins with a critical appraisal of the ancient and classical theories of citizenship. Particular attention is given within this section of the chapter to the work of Hobbes, Locke and Rousseau since the influence of their ideas upon subsequent theorizing has been profound. The discussion then moves on to consider the Conservative Neo-Liberalism of Nozick and Hayek, and the Neo-Republicanism of authors such as Arendt, Barber and Oldfield.

The second section of this chapter considers the modern or Social-Liberal theories of citizenship provided by Rawls, Marshall and Berlin. This section highlights the importance of Berlin's work to citizenship theorizing and argues for greater consideration of his work by sociologists working in this field. The final section of this chapter provides a critical outline of the most contemporary theories of citizenship. The pluralist accounts of Kymlicka and Young are considered in this section of the chapter, as is Habermas' reflexive approach and Mouffe's more post-structural account. The chapter concludes with a reflection upon the future of citizenship theorizing – an issue that is then discussed in greater depth within Chapters 6 and 7.

Chapter 3   Social Movements

This chapter begins by considering the most important early, or first phase, social movement theories. This 'first phase' can be divided into an American and a European tradition. The first phase of the American tradition centred on the Collective Behaviour approach to social movements, and is best exemplified in the work of Herbert Blumer. The first phase theories in the European tradition are less clearly associated with particular theorists but can be broadly termed a Social Democratic tradition and can be sub-divided into Weberian and Marxist approaches. These approaches will be discussed briefly before a consideration of what is meant by the notion of the '1960s watershed' and what effects it has had upon subsequent theorizing.

The second section of this chapter then aims to provide the reader with an overview of the 'second phase' theories. This second phase of theorizing can also be divided into American and European traditions. In the American tradition, post-1960s theorizing has been dominated by the Resource Mobilization theories. It is argued within this chapter that the Political Process theories should be considered as being a part of this resource mobilization approach and, therefore, these theories are also considered at this point. In post-1960s Europe a number of related theories emerged based around notions of identity, defence of the 'lifeworld', values and culture. These approaches can be rather loosely termed as the 'new' social movement theories and the work of the key authors in this field, Touraine, Habermas and Melucci are considered in turn within this section.

The chapter concludes by considering the future for social movement theorizing and proposes that there are two important interrelated questions that are, as yet, unresolved within social movement theorizing. The first question relates to the appropriateness of the idea of '1960s watershed': *what was so fundamentally different about the movements that came after this 'watershed' in comparison to those that came before?* The second question relates to understanding the nature of 'unrest': *has the nature of unrest really moved so significantly away from older concerns with structural inequalities as to render the older social movements theories largely redundant?* Possible answers to both of these questions are proposed within the concluding section of this chapter. An even more critical analysis of certain theories introduced within this chapter is then made in relation to the findings of this research, within Chapter 6.

Chapter 4   Issues in Disability

This chapter aims to provide an overview of the position of disabled people in UK society today and of the theorizing that has sought to explain the experience of disability. The first section of this chapter presents an overview of the current state of theorizing on disability. The work of Parsons and Goffman is considered as an important precursor of more contemporary theorizing. The somewhat different theoretical approaches taken by Medical Sociology and Disability Studies are then discussed. Having introduced the main theoretical approaches to disability within the first part of this chapter, the aim of the second section is to consider the empirical evidence to support the widely accepted notion that disabled people occupy a position in society that is characterized by discrimination and disadvantage. Given the extent of this empirical evidence, however, it would be impossible within the confines of this chapter, or book, to consider all issues, adequately. For this reason, two key areas have been chosen, and it is hoped that these will, when considered together, provide the reader with an overview of the current position of disabled people within society. These two areas are: equal opportunities and the 'coming out' of disability.

Chapter 5   The Views of Disabled People

This chapter sets out the key findings of the research cited in this book, as they relate to the following issues: structural issues; disabling attitudes-enabling identities; disability culture; and the disability movement. As previously stated, one of the central aims of this research was to provide a platform for the voices of disabled people and it is in this chapter that these voices are most apparent, for respondents are quoted extensively. The analysis that forms part of this chapter then forms the basis for the more theoretical consideration of the findings in Chapter 6.

Chapter 6   Reconsidering Theorizing on Citizenship and Social Movements in the Light of Disability

This chapter considers the appropriateness of the modern/contemporary theories of citizenship in the light of the findings of this research and proposes that a consideration of the 'struggle' faced by disabled people can illuminate useful links between citizenship theorizing and current approaches to social movements. Particular attention is given in this chapter to the important links between the work of Berlin, Habermas, and Mouffe; and to the value of Ellison's ideas about 'proactive and defensive engagement'.

Chapter 7   Conclusion

In this chapter an argument is presented in support of a new approach to citizenship that builds upon a synthesis of a number of ideas discussed in this book, together with a new focus upon the notion of 'universal vulnerability'. It is proposed that this may provide the starting point for a model of citizenship conceived as a process of 'proactive engagement', and according to an understanding of 'vulnerable personhood'.

In the concluding comments some implications of this model of citizenship are briefly considered in relation to educational and social policy and with regard to the future of protest within the UK.

2
Citizenship

Introduction

> A modern notion of citizenship gives rights but demands obliga-
> tions, shows respect but wants it back, grants opportunity but
> insists on responsibility.
>
> (Blair, 1996: 218)

> Citizenship involves providing for family members, being a
> loving parent, playing by the rules or looking out for a neigh-
> bour in need. It's about having a sense of responsibility, obliga-
> tion and duty.
>
> (Duncan Smith, 2002: quote from speech given at
Toynbee Hall on Iain Duncan Smith's
first anniversary as Party Leader.)

As the above quotations demonstrate, the rhetoric of 'Citizenship' is a
favourite tool of politicians. Clearly, for the concept to be so utilized,
'citizenship' must be widely accepted to be a *good thing*! Centuries of
theorizing have, however, demonstrated the difficulty in establishing
a widely agreed definition of what exactly the notion of citizenship
entails. In writing this overview of some of the central academic theorizing on citizenship, it became clear, for example, that it is difficult, if
not impossible, to separate out discussions of citizenship from wider
debates surrounding notions such as *democracy; liberty; justice; human
rights discourses; the nature of the polis; the nature of the 'self'; identity;
'difference'; and 'struggle'*. It is not possible within the limits of this
chapter to consider each of these areas in-depth, as they each warrant

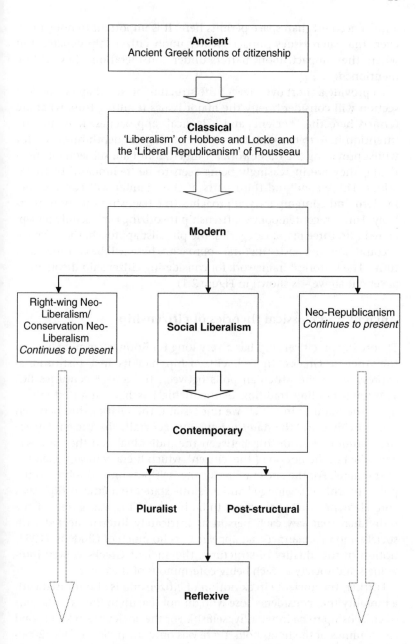

Figure 2.1 The changing nature of citizenship theorizing

a fuller account than space permits here. It is important to note, however, that such issues impact greatly upon citizenship debates and
where they impact upon matters under consideration, they will be
mentioned.

To provide a short overview of the structure of this chapter: the first
section will consider briefly the major issues resulting from what are
termed here the 'Ancient' and 'Classical' approaches. It is not the
intention here to consider these theories in great depth however, for
whilst providing the framework for much, if not all, subsequent theorizing, they are increasingly being seen to be 'redundant' in themselves. The second and third parts of this chapter will consider the
modern and contemporary approaches to citizenship theory respectively. Further, contemporary citizenship theorizing can usefully be separated into three major categories: the pluralist approach; the reflexive
account: and the post-structural approach. These will be considered in
turn. (The historical framework for considering citizenship theorizing –
as set out above – is shown in Figure 2.1)

Ancient and classical theories of citizenship

Theorizing on citizenship has a very long tradition, stemming back to
the Ancient Greeks. Indeed, citizenship had its first institutional
expression in the Athenian polis between the 5th–4th centuries BC.
This long-standing tradition of theorizing has had profound effects
upon the manner in which we understand the relationship between
the individual and the state/society more generally. In Ancient Greece
the optimum relationship between the individual and the state was
embodied in the notion of the 'citizen', which literally meant 'member
of the state'. For the ancient Greeks, the 'self' was only as robust as the
polity to which it belonged and Aristotle stated that citizenship was a
core element of what it means to be human. This was a view of the
individual that saw each person as intricately interconnected with
society and in a manner that appears to echo much of Giddens' (1984)
notion of the 'duality of structure', the ancient Greeks viewed individuals and society as each being coterminous of the other.

Further, the ancient Greek notion of citizenship is also infused with
a morality that considers those who do not live up to the expectations
of citizenship to be inherently 'selfish'. For the ancient Greeks, beyond
the confines of the household, there was only the polis. McAfee (2000)
highlights this fact by noting that the Greek word for someone who is
uninterested in public life is 'idiôtês' i.e. an 'idiot', thus the word 'idio-

syncratic', which literally means to hold only to one's own self. Aristotle echoed this sentiment when he famously argued that to refuse to take part in the running of a community is to be either a beast or a God! Meier (1990) has also concluded that this sense of morality is key to understanding the ancient Greek notion of citizenship. Meier has questioned why it was that the citizens of ancient Greece worked so hard in their duties as citizens, often in a military capacity, but for so little in return. He concludes that the activity on the part of citizens was partly due to social pressures but also because fulfilling the duties of a citizen was also thought to make one a better person and to be the opposite of acting out of self-interest.

The context in which the notion of citizenship was born, therefore, was the small-scale, organic community of the ancient Greek, and in particular, the Athenian polis. The content and 'depth' of this citizenship was greatly influenced by the fact that it was not a purely public matter. For the ancient Greeks, the values of active citizenship should be internalized within the individual citizen. In many respects, this ancient view of citizenship is diametrically opposed to much subsequent theorizing, perhaps most acutely to the classical liberal approaches of Hobbes and Locke. For the ancient Greeks, the self is '*"fleshed out" by the city – that is, the polis brings about a richer subjectivity – and politics is the collective search for the good life*'. (McAfee, 2000: 6) Classical theorists, however, considered 'selves' to be substances of sorts, which may or may not, according to their desires, engage in the polis. Thus whilst the ancient Greeks considered citizenship to be about the combined struggle by citizens for the good life, for the classical, liberal theorists, politics is a struggle *between* citizens in a climate of scarce resources, and is, therefore, an essentially antagonistic process.

Although it is often stated that the classical theories of citizenship mark the clearest opposition to earlier, ancient theorizing on citizenship, this process of change within citizenship theorizing in fact began during the medieval period. It is not the intention here to consider this period in any great depth, but it would be wrong to overlook the contribution that Machiavelli, for example, has made to thinking within this field. For Machiavelli, citizenship was not a *manner of being*, but rather it was a process, or a method, by which those individuals deemed to be citizens could assert their interests, yet his notion of protective republicanism was designed to ensure that public order was maintained (Faulks, 2000) and in this respect his work reveals a preoccupation with social order. Such a preoccupation continued to characterize later theories.

The classical models of citizenship did not, therefore, emerge out of a vacuum. Chief proponents of this classical approach to citizenship, Hobbes and Locke, were, however, writing in a context that varied greatly from that experienced by previous theorists. One key point about the nature of the ancient Greek citizenship that has not been previously mentioned here, is its inherently *exclusive nature*. Ancient Greece was an agrarian, slave-based society in which inequality had been naturalized: *'citizenship was valued in part because of its exclusive nature and as a mark of superiority over non-citizens whether they be women, slaves or "barbarians"'*. (Faulks, 2000: 18) It was only with the development of the liberal state, the beginnings of which emerged in the late 16th century, that citizenship became infused with egalitarian and/or inclusive notions.

From the 17th century onwards, most of the key liberal philosophers who contributed to the classical theories of citizenship were concerned not with notions of self-governance, but with the 'social contract' between each individual citizen and the state. There are a number of different strands of thinking that can be encompassed within this 'social-contractual' tradition, ranging from the *'essentially authoritarian prescriptions of Hobbes to the essentially libertarian prescriptions of Rousseau'*. (Dean *et al*, 1999: 74) The essential element characterizing all theories within this tradition, however, is an understanding of what is meant by a 'social contract'. At its core this notion rests upon the idea of a 'contract' as a formal agreement between two or more parties, and that by entering into a contract, moral and legal obligations come into play. As Heywood (1994: 148) has stated: *'A "social contract" is an agreement made either amongst citizens, or between citizens and the state, through which they accept the authority of the state in return for benefits which only a sovereign power can provide'*. Amongst the classical theorists, however, there was little agreement surrounding the basis of this contract or the obligations involved.

For Hobbes (1973) and Locke (1965), the major question facing citizenship theory was how political authority could arise out of a society composed of morally free and equal individuals. In short, they concluded that the right to govern rested upon the consent of those being *governed*. Without such agreement between rulers and ruled, Hobbes and Locke feared a barbaric 'state of nature' would result. The pursuit of power and wealth could not go unchecked or the result would be a war of all against all. In the light of such risks, 'rational' individuals would *wish* to enter into a social contract in which an agreed authority would be established and order achieved.

From what might be considered to be a somewhat authoritarian position, Hobbes argued in *Leviathan* (1973) that individuals are faced with the bleak choice between anarchy and absolutism. His central contention, upon which this rather gloomy conclusion is based, is that humans are fundamentally self-interested. The social contract that he envisaged involved the complete surrender of individual sovereignty to a powerful political authority. For Hobbes, whose writing is likely to have been greatly influenced by his experiences of the chaos of the English Civil War, the existence of a state, no matter how oppressive it may be, was preferable to the instability and disorder of the 'state of nature'.

It has been suggested, however, that in so theorizing the relationship between the individual and the state, Hobbes in effect nullified citizenship. Critics of Hobbes such as Clarke (1996) have argued that in defending the right of a monarch to possess absolute power, Hobbes' theory terminates citizenship and politics. Instead of providing a model of the relationship between the citizen and the state, Hobbes was in fact producing a model of the relationship between the *subject* and the state. Further, in relation to rights and obligations, Hobbes' view of the citizenship is rather 'thin'. For Hobbes, the state had only one major obligation to the individual citizen – to maintain social order. Equally, the individual citizen was obliged to obey the state, but had few rights beyond that of living in a socially ordered society.

This is not, however, to negate Hobbes' contribution to theorizing in this field. In many ways his approach marked an important transition in theorizing on citizenship and his work has been highly influential. Faulks (2000) identifies four key ways in which Hobbes' work has influenced later theorists. Firstly, unlike the medieval notions of citizenship in which rights were extended to groups, in Hobbes' account it is the individual who is seen to be in a direct relationship with the state. Secondly: *'Hobbes believed that in terms of their abilities, as well as in their powers to upset the basis of social order, individuals were equal'*. (Faulks, 2000: 22) This line of argument provided the basis for the link between citizenship and equality that has characterized subsequent liberal thinking. Thirdly, although Hobbes had a personal preference for a monarchical system, this is not to say that his theory perceives the state and the sovereign as indivisible. Finally, by arguing for the concentration of power in the monarch, Hobbes was arguing for the concentration of the means of violence. This was important because Hobbes was suggesting a break from the feudal notion of divided sites of power.

Whilst acknowledging, however, the importance of Hobbes' contribution to theorizing in this area, an alternative, and some would argue, more balanced view of citizenship is to be found in the work of Locke. Locke's conception of the relationship between the individual and the state involved two 'contracts'. The first was essentially Hobbes' 'social contract', in which individuals agreed to sacrifice a degree of their personal freedom in order to ensure social order. The second contract was a 'contract of trust', between a society and its government, in which the government became authorized to protect the natural rights of its citizens. The important point to note here is that for the first time in citizenship theorizing there emerges, within Locke's work, a sense of the reciprocal nature of the relationship between citizens and state, for he implies that obedience to the state is conditional upon the state fulfilling its side of the bargain.

As was previously discussed, however, this classical liberal approach, with its fairly *passive* view of citizenship as a series of rights possessed by the individual, stands in contrast to the more ancient approaches which saw citizenship as being a more *active* process engaged upon by citizens as part of a republic. At this point it is interesting to consider the work of Rousseau (1913) because his Liberal Republicanism is often considered to stand apart from the liberalism of Hobbes and Locke on precisely this basis, that his is a view of a more *active* citizenship. At first glance, Rousseau's theories do seem to be somewhat more optimistic than those of Hobbes and Locke, particularly with regard to his views on human nature, for he believed, in contrast to the views of Hobbes and Locke, that government should be based upon active citizenship – what he termed the 'general will' – which reflects the common interests of society over the selfish desires of each individual. Rousseau's work is also often considered to represent an important first step away from the classical liberal tradition's individualistic construction of citizenship, since he is clearly concerned with the process by which the desires of the individual can be melded with the needs of the community.

The extent to which Rousseau's theorizing should be considered to be an important part of the communitarian/republican tradition, however, needs to be considered carefully. Importantly, Rousseau did not manage to resolve convincingly the issue of conflicting interests. He acknowledges that the individual will have 'selfish desires' and admits that there will be some degree of conflict between the individual's desires and that of the 'general will' and yet he side-steps the question of how this conflict will be resolved by arguing that the 'general will' is synonymous with each individual's 'real' interests. Thus for Rousseau in fulfilling their duties and responsibilities according to the 'general will', citizens are obeying their own 'higher' selves. The problem with his theorizing in this regard is that in his quest to meld the desires of the individual with that of the community, Rousseau arguably negates individual rights.

Further, in his famous dictum Rousseau states that ignorance or selfishness might blind individuals to the fact that the 'general will' embodies the desires of their 'higher selves'. Under such circumstances, he argues, it would become necessary to be 'forced to be free'. Critics have pointed to the fact that such ideas seem to be at odds with the notion of government by consent. Ultimately, therefore, despite the apparently optimistic start to Rousseau's theorizing, his conclusions point to a much more pessimistic perception of human nature. When Rousseau states that a 'higher' body or intellect, in the person of the 'lawgiver', must determine the rules of a society, he is essentially mistrustful of the individual's capacity to determine the future democratically. This last point must bring into some doubt the extent to which Rousseau was really proposing an 'active' form of citizenship.

In essence then, what a consideration of both the classical 'liberal' model of citizenship and Rousseau's Liberal Republicanism provides is a view of a *passive* citizenship. As Burchell (1995: 541) comments:

> (...) with the rise of market society in early modern Europe the (...) 'active' civic ideal was progressively replaced by a (...) 'passive' or 'liberal' ideal which crucially weakened or distorted the vitality of the original civic impulse.

Even Rousseau's conception of the citizen, which was, in many respects, an attempt to rejuvenate the ancient model, was a corrupted version of the latter because, in the end, it relied upon an *enforced* return to ancient civic rectitude. Rousseau's model is thus essentially both anti-libertarian and utopian.

This utopianism in Rousseau's theorizing can be seen to have an interesting parallel in the work of Marx. Marx shared with Rousseau a utopian vision of a society in which each individual can achieve his/ her 'higher' self. Whilst he was heavily influenced by Rousseau, however, Marx did not agree the earlier theorist's work regarding how this 'fully developed' society could be achieved.

> On the one hand, he notes, Rousseau's version is founded on a conception of a civic space dominated by the sphere of public altruism; on the other hand, the stuff from which Rousseau's citizens had of necessity to be created is the privatised bourgeois self of market

society. Famously, Marx's solution to Rousseau's contradiction is the utopia without contradictions: the Communist societies in which the stunted and divided personalities of societies based on the division of labour have at last been overcome. (...) Of course, to replace a contradictory utopia with a utopia without contradictions may be accounted no solution at all.   (Burchell, 1995: 548.)

Marx can thus be criticized for providing an equally unrealistic utopian vision of society. His critique of Rousseau and the 'liberal' model of citizenship is, nevertheless, important because it highlights the classical theorists' failure to engage with the issue of the inequitable distribution of resources. For Rousseau, for example: '*the nature of the authority vested in the state by the general will should at best temper rather than redress the imbalance of power between the poor and the rich*'. (Dean *et al*, 1999: 75)

This thorny issue of the extent to which citizenship should aim to reduce social inequality has continued to plague citizenship theorists. Later, 'modern', theorists such as Rawls, Marshall and Berlin have followed on from the 'liberal' tradition of Hobbes and Locke, but have focused specifically upon this problem of social inequality. The general approach taken by these three theorists can usefully be termed Social Liberalism. For these thinkers, a distinction should be made between absolute destitution/poverty and social inequality. In effect, the Social Liberalist approach is an attack on poverty but a legitimation of inequality according to a system of meritocracy. That is not to say that all Social Liberals are concerned to the same extent with these issues and there are some important distinctions between their approaches. Rawls' work is essentially an attempt to re-work social contract theory, whilst countering the Marxist critique amongst other issues. The work of T.H. Marshall ([1963] 1998), on the other hand, also acknowledges the inherent tension between an egalitarian notion of citizenship and the economic inequality that is a recognized part of capitalism, but marks a more sustained shift away from the 'liberal' model of citizenship in search of solutions to this problem. It is the argument here and in Chapter 6, however, that it is Berlin's work that represents the most convincing and potentially most useful Social-Liberal approach because implied in his work is the need for resource systems to facilitate active citizenship and on a somewhat different basis, because he also demonstrates a concern with issues of *pluralism*.

Whilst the Social-Liberalist approach to citizenship has proved to be the most influential in terms of contemporary theorizing, precisely because of its focus upon the issue of inequitable outcomes, that is not to say that all 'modern' citizenship theories rest upon the notion that social inequality should be a concern of citizenship. Indeed, almost at the same time as the Social-Liberal approach was being developed, two rival approaches emerged, the first being Conservative Neo-Liberalism and the second being Neo-Republicanism. It is not the intention here to go into any great depth on either of these approaches since they have had significantly less impact than Social Liberalism, but it would be wrong to overlook these theories completely for they both provide interesting arguments in opposition to the idea that social issues should be allowed to impact on the civil sphere.

Conservative Neo-Liberalism is to be found in the work of authors such as Hayek (1944) and Nozick (1974) and whilst it is tempting to suggest that this approach has not been of long-term significance theoretically, some theorizing in this vein does continue to the present day in the form of discussions about 'consumer citizenship' and it would be wrong to suggest that there have been no real consequences of the approach on peoples' lives. For example, the UK government of the 1980s, led by Margaret Thatcher, was highly influenced by what might be considered to be the more 'populist' form of this Conservative Neo-Liberalism, namely the 'New Right' theories.

The dominant characteristic of the Conservative Neo-Liberal approach is an intense opposition to the idea of social rights. Hayek (1944) believed that inequalities affecting an individual's private life are both inevitable and desirable within a free-market economy. Democracy, he believed, has certain useful properties but it should only be allowed to function in those areas of life that are not determined by the market. Nozick (1974) took this one step further, stating that any attempt to seek social justice *via* democratic means is an infringement of civil rights. The state should act only as a 'night-watchman', providing security, but in the most inconspicuous way possible and it should not be directly concerned with the material welfare of its citizens since this would inevitably mean that it was interfering in relation to the market's role as distributor of resources.

Despite this less than 'full-hearted' embrace of democratic ideals by Conservative Neo-Liberalism, it is nevertheless often claimed by those who adhere to the principles of this approach that it is based upon a form of citizenship akin to Rousseau's vision of 'active citizenship'.

Setting aside the whole issue of whether or not Rousseau's model is really one of active citizenship, there are also reasons to question Conservative Neo-Liberalism's credentials in this regard. As previously mentioned, successive Conservative administrations of the 1980s and 1990s in the UK drew heavily upon Conservative Neo-Liberalist ideas. Repeated attempts were made by the government at this time to reduce the state's role in the funding and provision of welfare for its citizens in an effort to redefine the state in accordance with Nozick's 'night-watchman' principle. Further, the idea of an 'active citizen' who was both individually and socially responsible and for whom state help was only a 'last resort' was an idea favoured by Margaret Thatcher ([1988] 1989) and Douglas Hurd (1988). The 'active citizen', it was claimed, would take responsibility for him/herself and for their families. Beyond this, philanthropic activities were also encouraged in order to reduce the need for the state to provide for the welfare needs of the less fortunate (Hurd, 1988, Thatcher, [1988] 1989). At the same time, active citizenship also became associated with the consumer culture. To be an active citizen meant asserting one's rights within the market as a *consumer*, with such an ideology applying even to public services.

The central problem with this approach, however, was that it both ignored and at the same time exacerbated the problem of material inequality. Individuals who failed to live up to the ideals of active citizenship were increasingly stigmatized as being either 'work-shy' or part of Charles Murray's (1994) 'underclass' if they failed to take responsibility for their own welfare, or 'second order' citizens if they failed to act in a philanthropic manner for the welfare of all (Dwyer, 2000). The Conservative Neo-Liberals overlooked the fact that many disadvantaged groups did not have the resources to fulfil the responsibilities of 'active citizenship'. As will be discussed later in this chapter, this approach stands in stark contrast to the approach taken by the Social-Liberals who, whilst not proposing an entirely egalitarian system of equality of outcome, certainly envisaged a considerably larger role for the state in guaranteeing those universally held rights that make inequalities more tolerable and which *enable* active citizenship.

In comparison to the Conservative Neo-Liberal approach, however, a truer sense of 'active citizenship' is perhaps to be found in the Neo-Republican approach. This approach also draws upon Rousseau's republican ideas as inspiration and its proponents believe in the importance of commitment and participation in public life. The main difference between Conservative Neo-Liberalism and the Neo-Republican approach, however, is that the Neo-Republicans reject the idea of the private pursuit of interest that so characterizes the 'New Right' accounts of citizenship. For authors such as Arendt (1958), rather than self-interest, what is actually at stake is public interest. At the heart of this approach is a fairly radical theory of citizenship as participation in the public domain of civil society, the challenge being to '*preserve as much of the autonomy of the political field as possible, to prevent politics from becoming privatistic or statist*'. (Delanty, 2000: 33) Further, in relation to the issue of social inequality, what this approach argues is not that social inequality does not exist, but rather that this 'social issue' should not intrude upon what must be a purely political domain.

'Active citizenship', for the Neo-Republicans, is about participation not just rights and duties. This was the central idea of authors such as Arendt (1958) and later Oldfield (1990) and it was most powerfully expressed in Barber's (1984) idea of 'strong democracy'. Democracy, Barber (1984: 151) claims, must be taken out of the hands of the elites and given back to citizens: '*(...) strong democracy transforms conflict. It turns dissensus into an occasion for mutualism and private interest into an epistemological tool for public thinking*'. A similar, if slightly less radical approach is taken by Putnam (1993) who claims that the value of participation in civil society is not connected with the ability to the overcome conflict, but is instead to promote the values of trust, commitment and solidarity that allow democracy to flourish (Delanty, 2000).

Critics of this approach have suggested, however, that the problem with all of the Neo-Republican theories is that they underestimate the level of conflict that occurs within civil society on the basis of different identities and social inequalities and which must bring into some doubt the idea that solidarity is something that can be achieved easily. To this extent this approach may be somewhat utopian. It can be argued, however, that there are more profound difficulties with this approach. The first problem is that in stressing the need for citizens to commit to participation, some Neo-Republicans advocate fairly authoritarian measures to ensure that citizens actually do participate. Oldfield (1990: 47) states that it may be necessary for the citizen to be '*shamed, disciplined and sometimes terrorized into living "civic virtue" (...)*'. By arguing thus, Oldfield opens himself up to the same criticisms that have been directed at Rousseau for negating the rights of the individual.

The second problem is that the Neo-Republicans tend to prioritize the actual process of participation over the substance of the common goal. Thus, whilst it is undoubtedly true to say that this approach represents an important precursor of later models of citizenship as a deliberative process of 'engagement' (see for example Habermas, 1998, Ellison, 1997, 2000), unlike some of these later theories, the Neo-Republican view of citizenship does not theorize adequately the nature of the rights being actively sought. The reliance upon somewhat substantive rationality within not just the Neo-Republican approach but also wider citizenship theorizing, is something that is only now being reconsidered seriously. As MacLeod (1998: para. 1) has commented from a philosophical perspective:

> The typical noninstrumentalist position, by contrast, would be that for the action in the conclusion to be one it is rational for the agent to perform, it must serve an objective it is rational for the agent to pursue (...)

As will be discussed at some length later within this chapter and in Chapter 6, understanding the nature of *contested citizenship* is key to understanding the nature of citizen participation.

Modern/social-liberal theories of citizenship

Rawls

Since the publication of his work entitled *A Theory of Justice* in 1971, John Rawls' ideas have inspired many subsequent theorists, whether they are sympathetic towards, or critical of his theories. Rawls' credentials as 'torch-bearer' of the liberal tradition of citizenship theorizing stems from his continuing use of the classical liberal theorists' idea that the 'social contract' is at the heart of social order. Rawls' work differs significantly from earlier theorizing, however, in two regards. The first relates to the extent to which he considers achievable the liberal concept of a society based upon a shared state of 'higher being', in which true happiness for all is the desired goal. The second relates to his concerns with social justice and egalitarianism.

To understand Rawls' notion of citizenship it is vital to consider his discussion upon the rights of free and equal individuals that forms the central part of his theory of social co-operation. The central aspect of his theory is the idea of 'justice as fairness':

> In justice as fairness, social unity is understood by starting with the conception of society as a system of co-operation between free and equal persons. Social unity and the allegiance of citizens to their common institutions are not founded on their all affirming the

same conception of the good, but on their publicly accepting a political conception of justice to regulate the basic structure of society. (Rawls, [1985] 1998: 70)

There are several key points arising from the previous quotation. Firstly, for Rawls, the notion of 'justice as fairness' is not intended to be a comprehensive moral doctrine, but rather a method for achieving an over-lapping consensus. Rawls ([1985] 1998) rejects the earlier liberal idea that all rational and well-informed individuals will have the same sense of what constitutes the 'good'. 'Justice as fairness' he argues: *'must allow for a diversity of doctrines and the plurality of conflicting, and indeed incommensurate, conceptions of the good'*. (Rawls, [1985] 1998: 54) Having said this, however, Rawls then faces the problem of how such diverse goals could be attained through co-operation and yet still benefit all.

To solve this problem Rawls employs a somewhat abstract political theory of democratic citizenship in which 'political justice' is the desired goal. To begin with, Rawls hypothesizes a situation in which people have to assume a 'veil of ignorance' in which they must not know the true nature of their position in the inherently unequal society. Having assumed this 'veil of ignorance', and an imaginary position of equality, individuals will *'evolve from their basic intuitive ideas of cooperation in a democratic society a framework of political justice'*. (Shafir, 1998: 7) The resulting concept of political justice, or 'social contract', is made up from two principles:

(1.) Each person has an equal right to a fully adequate scheme of equal basic rights and liberties, which scheme is compatible with a similar scheme for all. (2.) Social and economic inequalities are to satisfy two conditions: first, they must be attached to offices and positions open to all under conditions of fair equality of opportunity; and second, they must be to the greatest benefit of the least advantaged members of society. (Rawls, [1985] 1998: 56)

Rawls also states that (1) takes priority over (2). Thus, the first stage of 'justice as fairness' will always be to ensure that the basic liberties of all have been safeguarded and that the rights of the least advantaged are always the main consideration in a just society. After this, principle (2) can be viewed as the 'difference principle' and amounts to a call for a meritocratic society in which there is equal opportunity to be *unequal*, providing that any resulting inequalities work to the advantage of the least advantaged members of society. This may represent Rawls' response to criticisms directed towards the earlier liberal thinkers in respect of their failure to take sufficient account of the inequalities that characterize capitalist societies.

The second part of Rawls' political theory of democratic citizenship is concerned with the notion of identity. As Shafir (1998: 8) has noted, Rawls makes a distinction between an individual's private and public identities:

> Since rights are attached to an individual's public identity as a free and equal citizen and not to one of the features that determine her identity, such as religion or nationality, she is free to change her view of the good life (eg. convert from one religion to another) without being deprived of these rights.

Rawls clearly believes that this distinction between public and private identities allows for the toleration of diversity and for the emergence of an overlapping consensus, despite oppositional doctrines. Here again, however, Rawls' theory rests upon his notion of the *reasonable* individual, for in order for this over lapping consensus to be sustained, he states that citizens must take into account the need for co-operation and must not make excessive demands.

It is this final point that has proved to be the basis for much of the criticism that has been directed against Rawls' theory. Most critics of Rawls have highlighted the normative nature of his theory and have questioned his faith in the ability of *rational* individuals to co-operate on the basis of mutual respect. Rawls himself acknowledged this problem with his approach in later work (see Rawls, 1993), but by the time he came to reconsider his position, the issue had been 'taken over' somewhat by the more pluralist/multiculturalist perspectives. To highlight a further problem with Rawls' approach, his definition of co-operation also appears to rely upon a notion of *competency*, a term that is far from un-problematic:

> (...) since we wish to start from the idea of society as a fair system of co-operation, we assume that persons as citizens have all the capacities that enable them to be normal and fully co-operating members of society.   (Rawls, [1985] 1998: 60)

The implications of this notion of competency will be reconsidered in Chapter 6.

Marshall

Although it is not my intention to say much more about the notion of competency at this point, it is interesting to note that competency also underpins much of the theorizing of T.H. Marshall. T.H. Marshall was greatly influenced by the writings of Alfred Marshall, the economist, who provided a very similar definition of citizenship to that of Rawls, in the respect that he regarded citizenship to be a status that expressed the ability, or the competence, to be a member of society. This definition was greatly to influence the writings of T.H. Marshall ([1963] 1998: 102) who wrote that:

(...) societies in which citizenship is a developing institution create an image of an ideal citizenship against which achievement can be measured and towards which aspiration can be directed.

Turner (1986) has pointed out that in many respects T.H. Marshall's work fits comfortably into a liberal democratic tradition, particularly with regard to his emphasis upon equality of opportunity, whilst at the same time promoting universally held rights as the way of making the resulting inequalities of outcome more tolerable. Evidence for this is to be found within his essay *Citizenship and Social Class* in which Marshall ([1963] 1998: 109) makes clear his faith in the concept of an 'educational meritocracy':

The right of the citizen in this process of selection and mobility is the right to equality of opportunity. Its aim is to eliminate hereditary privilege. In essence it is the equal right to display and develop differences, or inequalities; the equal right to be recognised as unequal. (...) the final outcome is a structure of unequal status fairly apportioned to unequal abilities (...)

Further, he states that the status differences that result from this educational meritocracy can be regarded as legitimate in terms of citizenship, provided that 'they do not cut too deep'. In relation to this last point, however, it is this level of concern for those experiencing poverty that marks out his theory as being significantly different from earlier liberal theories.

In the work of Marshall, the concept (citizenship) was developed to answer a problem in liberalism. In capitalism, liberal values were successful in emphasising freedoms and individualism, but there

> was no easy answer to critics who pointed out that the classic free-
> doms (...) were ineffective tokens for the majority of the population
> who lived in poverty.   (Turner, 1993a: 176-7)

Marshall was, therefore, concerned with protecting individuals from the vicissitudes of capitalism. He believed that by developing the concept of citizenship at both a practical and a theoretical level, it might be possible to remove or reduce some of the inequalities generated by the capitalist market system. As authors such as Mead (1997) and Dwyer (2000) have highlighted, however, what clearly indicates that Marshall was not a social democrat, as he is often claimed to be, is that he was not 'about' social reform in a Marxist respect. Marshall's intention was only to moderate the worst excesses of capitalism through the promotion of the idea of citizenship and in so doing only to modify, rather than remove, the social class system. As Mead (1997: 198) has commented, for Marshall: *'In part, equal citizenship compensates for social inequality and makes egalitarian social reform less imperative'*.

Further, in relation to Marshall's overall aim, the question of how he thought that his notion of citizenship would achieve the goal of protecting individuals from the vicissitudes of the capitalist system, also remains. Marshall began his theorizing with an historical analysis of the development of citizenship. Based upon this analysis, he claimed that there are three major components of citizenship, namely civil, political and social rights. In his essay *Citizenship and Social Class*, Marshall ([1963] 1998: 95) demonstrated how over the centuries these three elements of citizenship have developed at their own pace, and often disproportionately, to the extent that *'it is only in the present century (...) that the three runners have come abreast of one another'*. Thus, the 18th century, according to Marshall, was characterized by the development of *civil* rights; the 19th century by the development of *political* rights; and the 20th century by the development of *social* rights.

It is not the intention here to go into very great depth surrounding Marshall's definitions of civil and political rights, since his understanding of these rights did not differ from widely held understandings of these terms. In brief, however, civil rights, according to Marshall, included such things as liberty, freedom of speech, equality before the law and the right to own property. Political rights amounted to universal suffrage and, more vaguely, the right to access the decision making process. It was his concept of 'social rights', however, that really represented his contribution to citizenship debates and moved citizenship theory beyond more 'historical' definitions.

According to Marshall ([1963] 1998: 99–100) then, the basis of his definition of social rights stemmed back to the older Poor Law (pre-1834) which was the:

(...) last remains of a system which tried to adjust real income to the social needs and status of the citizen and not solely to the market value of his labour...[But] by the Act of 1834 the [new] Poor Law renounced all claim to trespass on the territory of the wages system, or to interfere with the forces of the free market.

So, the 19th century had actually marked a backwards step with regard to social rights. In fact, according to Marshall, the Workhouse and the minimal social rights that remained post-1834 became detached from the status of 'citizenship' because paupers forfeited their civil right of freedom (in practice), and, by law, they lost their political rights on entering the Workhouse. In addition, according to Marshall ([1963] 1998: 100), a profound sense of 'stigma' clung to poor relief and *'expressed the deep feelings of a people who understood that those who accepted relief must cross the road that separated the community of citizens from the outcast company of the destitute'*.

For Marshall, then, the advent of proper social rights, which began to emerge in relation to education in the late 19th century and with the 20th century welfare state, were vital steps in countering the attack upon social rights that had occurred in the 19th century, and an important advancement in the notion of citizenship. Indeed, his vision is somewhat utopian in this regard for, to use his much quoted comment, Marshall ([1963] 1998: 94) believed that social rights represented: *'the whole range from the right to a modicum of economic welfare and security to the right to share to the full in the social heritage and to live the life of a civilized being according to the standards prevailing in the society'*.

This definition of social rights, however, has been criticized for being rather 'woolly' and for lacking clarity with regard to the actual levels of economic welfare and security envisaged. At a later date, Marshall (1972) did explain his position by stating that a distinction should be made between absolute destitution/poverty and social inequality. In effect, he argues, his approach is an attack on poverty but a legitimization of inequality according to a system of meritocracy. Arguably, however, it is not the 'woolliness' of Marshall's definition of social rights that is the problem, but rather the manner in which he apparently overlooks major power differentials within society that affect individuals' chances of success and which, therefore, bring into some doubt the idea that we live in a meritocracy.

Equally importantly, however, Marshall's theory has also been criticized for having normative connotations – for the notion of a 'civilized being' carries implications for an image of an 'ideal citizen'. This point will be considered in more depth within later sections of this chapter and within Chapter 6. In addition, Delanty (2000) has identified five major challenges to Marshall's concept of citizenship. Firstly, there is the challenge of cultural rights. Writers such as Kymlicka ([1995] 1998) and Young ([1989] 1998, 1990), to name but two, have highlighted types of exclusion that cannot be accommodated within a model of social rights. Such discussions have led to the development of 'the politics of difference'. Secondly, there is the challenge of globalization and 'multiple modernities'. As Delanty (2000: 18) comments, drawing upon Mann (1987): *'(...) there is no singly developmental logic by which citizenship unfolds along a historical trajectory'*. The worldwide experience of citizenship has been very diverse.

For example, in the USA social rights have been slow to develop, whilst in the former USSR there was a strong recognition of social rights. As Delanty highlights, the irony is that totalitarianism is not incompatible with social rights, for example, as was the case in Chile under the rule of Pinochet. Marshall's framework for considering the development of civil, political and social rights can, therefore, be considered to be flawed once applied outside the UK. Further, as Roche – drawing upon Rhodes (1996) – highlights in relation to this point, whilst not rejecting out-of-hand the continuing relevance of Marshall's analysis as a point of reference, globalization can be seen to have led to the current crisis in a number of national welfare states, thus bringing into question the manner in which Marshall's notion of social rights can be sustained:

> (...) globalisation tends to generate unemployment, and thus simultaneously raise the cost of welfare while undermining the tax base necessary to pay for it. Secondly, although globalisation depends to a significant extent on nationally and internationally based social compacts, arrangements and cohesion (particularly between classes associated with power in the realm of the state and the economy and their hegemonic influence over subordinate classes and groups), nonetheless it stimulates forces which are destabilizing and destructive of these national and international social orders.   (Roche, 2002: 82)

Thirdly, Marshall largely omitted to consider the importance of participation as a dimension of citizenship. Citizenship, it has been argued, is not simply a strategy of the ruling classes by which to control the masses. Citizenship can be an empowering concept and indeed, has come about precisely due to centuries of popular protest and mobilization. Giddens (1982: 171) has also criticized Marshall on this point stating that: *'The extension of citizenship rights in Britain as in other societies, was in substantial degree the result of the efforts of the under-privileged to improve their lot'*. This is an important point because it suggests that on many occasions the notion of citizenship may underpin/form the basis of social movement activity and as such must be considered as a 'contested concept'. This issue is one of considerable current interest and will be considered in more depth in Chapter 6.

Fourthly, there is the challenge posed by the de-coupling of citizenship and nationality. Marshall's notion of citizenship was dependent upon a firm link existing between the nation and the state. For Marshall, the state provides and guarantees rights, whilst the nation is the focus of identity. Today, according to Delanty, we live in a 'global age' in which this link can no longer be assumed. The development of regional governments has caused a shift in sovereignty downwards, whilst simultaneously, trans-national developments such as the EU, have shifted governance upwards, away from the nation-state. The need to re-think the 'social' aspect of citizenship, in particular in the light of these changes to the national, trans-national – and in the British case, most centrally the European dimension – has been identified clearly by a number of authors, but most notably by Roche (1987, 1992, 1995, 2002) and Turner (1993a) – Turner particularly focusing on the issue of international human rights.

As an additional point here, it has been argued that Marshall did not acknowledge that an explicit link between citizenship and the nation state has also impacted negatively upon many ethnic groups and has, in the case of the UK, led to a racialized notion of 'Britishness'. Tariq Modood (1992: 54) has commented on this point:

> The more distant an individual or group is from a white upper middle class British, Christian/agnostic norm, the greater the marginality of exclusion.

Finally, Delanty points to the confluence of public and private spheres. Marshall assumed that there would be separation between these two zones, equating as he did the 'private' with social class and 'public' with the state. For Delanty (2000: 20) this was a highly reductionist stance for:

> (...) there is more to civil society than the culture of entitlements and the administrative welfare state does not entirely absorb the public sphere, which also contains informal networks of organisation and mobilization.

Further, Lister (1997a/b), has argued that in maintaining a false public/private dichotomy, Marshall's work has been a factor in the continuing oppression of women. Marshall's concept of citizenship relies upon the ideal of full *male employment*. He appears to have overlooked the important role women play in the labour market and in supporting the welfare system and the market economy *via* unpaid domestic work and the provision of care for many groups in society, such as elderly people and children.

To Delanty's and Lister's challenges to Marshall's theory can also be added the argument put forward by Offe (1984), that Marshall's 'social rights' of citizenship, as they are embodied within the welfare state for example, have acted to buy off dissent and as a form of crisis management for capitalism. Whether this is a correct interpretation of the intentions underpinning the welfare state is unclear. It would certainly seem that the welfare state has not alleviated inequalities to the extent that Marshall may have envisaged. Further, authors such as Oliver and Heater (1994) have highlighted the conflict between social rights and civil/political rights. For Oliver and Heater, civil and political rights are 'first generation rights', being residual in nature. As such, they do not conflict with the underlying values of the capitalist system, indeed they have at times been vital to the success of this system. Social rights, however, are seen as being 'second generation rights' and ensuring that the necessary financial resources are made available to meet the costs of these rights is largely a matter of political will. Barbalet (1988) has argued similarly, pointing to the conditional nature of social rights and questioning whether such rights can truly be regarded as citizenship rights at all.

Having stated these criticisms, however, it is only right also to note that 20 years after writing *Citizenship and Social Class*, Marshall (1981) did respond to at least some of his critics, acknowledging problems with his notions of both political and social rights. In this later lecture he focused upon power and rights and was essentially concerned with establishing which types of rights would best prevent the rise of authoritarianism. To summarize his argument briefly: he states that political rights can be easily undermined, and that social rights have not been designed for the exercise of power at all, but instead reflect the strong individualist element in society in which individuals are best viewed as consumers and not as actors. It is only civil rights that, according to Marshall, truly relate to the individual as 'actor'. Such rights, Marshall argues, are internalized by each individual at the early stages of socialization. These civil rights then permeate the social body making them very difficult to attack and they can then be used to create groups, movements, associations and as the basis of social and political pluralism (Isin and Wood, 1999).

Marshall then goes on to theorize usefully power in relation to the civil rights movement in the USA and concludes that the powerlessness of Black people in the USA was not only due to lack of rights, but was also due to the fact that the manner in which Black people possessed power, despite the apparent contradiction in terms, actually made them powerless. According to Marshall then, what the leaders of the Civil Rights movement were calling for was '*not for power over or redistribution but rather an effective share in the total power of society, which we may now call the politics of recognition*'. (Isin and Wood, 1999: 31) According to Marshall (1981; 150): '*The goal is a new kind of society, truly multiracial or, should that prove impossible, then, some would say, composed of independent and equal racial communities*'. In this way, Marshall appears to have anticipated much of the debate over multiculturalism and the politics of difference – themes taken up by a wide array of authors, but perhaps most notably by Kymlicka ([1995] 1998) and Young (1990).

Berlin

Marshall's later thinking with regard to the US Civil Rights movement resonates clearly with a lesser-known aspect of Isaiah Berlin's work. It seems strange that the work of Berlin (1958) is only very occasionally considered by sociologists, considering that his 1958 lecture *Two Concepts of Liberty* has very clear implications for citizenship theorizing. Berlin's (1958: 7) first form of liberty he defines as *negative* liberty:

I am normally said to be free to the degree to which no human being interferes with my activity.

His second form of liberty he terms positive liberty, and he defines this as deriving from the *'wish on the part of the individual to be his own master'*. (Berlin, 1958: 16) Although at first glance this form of liberty may not sound very different from Berlin's definition of negative liberty, his subsequent discussion of the two concepts results in a more distinct account. It becomes clear that in using the term 'positive liberty' Berlin was implying the need for resource systems that enable social actors to engage in active citizenship where they would otherwise be constrained. This point is of considerable importance because for the first time within the liberal tradition, Berlin acknowledges fully that such things as lack of material resources can radically reduce the ability of individuals to engage in active citizenship. It is easy to see, therefore, how it can be argued that Berlin's concept of positive liberty both requires and underpins the idea of a welfare state and advances considerably beyond Marshall's quite minimal social rights.

The aspect of Berlin's work that is the most interesting, however, is not one of his two famous concepts of liberty, but a lesser known concept that he defines at the end of his work *Two Concepts of Liberty*, albeit somewhat indistinctly, as *'the desire for recognition'*. (Berlin, 1958: 43) In part VI of this work Berlin considers the 'search for status' and the following discussion, it would seem, represents Berlin's theorizing upon the 'self'. Curiously, Berlin's (1958: 41) theorizing here is highly reminiscent of the symbolic interactionist perspective of authors such as G.H. Mead:

> (...) I am a social being in a deeper sense than that of interaction with others. For am I not what I am, to some degree, in virtue of what others think and feel me to be? (...) My individual self is not something that I can detach from my relationship with others, or from those attributes of myself that consist in their attitude towards me. Consequently, when I demand to be liberated from, let us say, the status of political or social dependence, what I demand is an alteration of the attitude towards me of those whose opinions and behaviour help to determine my own image of myself.

What Berlin (1958: 42) appears to be arguing here is that what oppressed individuals are demanding is not simply freedom of action, or equality of social and economic status/opportunity, the importance of which he does not overlook, but the right to be regarded as *'fully human'*. In a very interesting article on the writings of Berlin, Gary Reed (1980: 371) discusses the importance of this third, somewhat 'hybrid' form of freedom and uses the idea of the 'stranger' to explain the concept:

> A free person is then one who is a member of the kin; not a stranger. A second metaphor introduces the idea of liberation, of making free, by speaking of a person born a stranger as if he had grown up with the kin. This metaphor enables people to do by choice what at first only nature could do by birth: make a person free. A liberated person is one who is no longer a stranger, whether a stranger within (a slave) or without (an enemy). At this stage simple release of a stranger from captivity is not yet called liberation, making free; a former captive remains a stranger unless by admission to membership he is made free.

Although this terminology may seem somewhat removed from present day concerns, the idea that an *'unappropriated stranger is simply a slave without a master'* (Reed, 1980: 372) can, it is argued here, be employed usefully when considering the position of many disadvantaged, stigmatized or exploited groups within society.

The other useful aspect of Berlin's theorizing on this third form of liberty is the manner in which he critiques the normative and monistic tendencies of other neo-liberal thinkers such as Rawls. Berlin considered other neo-liberals to have relied too heavily upon universalistic definitions of *'what is right/good'* and in so doing to have failed to resolve the dilemma of what happens when people disagree about what constitutes the *right or good*. For writers such as Gray (1995) and Galipeau (1994), it is precisely this rejection of the universalistic philosophies favoured by other liberal thinkers that is the basis of Berlin's unique and important contribution to the field.

For Berlin, the idea, as found in the work of both Rawls and Marshall, that there can be a universally accepted image of 'ideal citizenship' against which *'all human projects should contribute or tend, and against which they might be evaluated'* (Gray, 1995: 8) is flawed, for as Kenny (2000: 1028) has written: *'The principle of incommensurability suggests that there is no external standard, no "super-value", according to which values can be rationally ranked'*. It is in this way that Berlin introduces the idea of 'value-pluralism' and, because of this, it is the argument here that his work should be seen to be – to an even greater extent than that of the later work of Marshall – an important precursor of more contemporary accounts of citizenship. Berlin's work will be considered again as it relates to the findings of the research cited in this book, in Chapter 6.

Contemporary accounts of citizenship

The pluralist/multicultural accounts

In the traditional liberal conception, as has already been discussed, citizenship is seen to be the embodiment of universalist ideals. In this conception of citizenship, all individuals who can legitimately claim to be citizens of a state are supposed to possess equal rights and equal responsibilities. For pluralist thinkers, however, this notion of citizenship can act as a '*powerful exclusionary discourse*' (Faulks, 2000: 83), and needs modifying if it is to be sustained within plural societies. The general approach taken by the pluralist thinkers is, therefore, that in addition to individual rights of citizenship, special group rights are also required. What is less clear is the extent to which some of the chief proponents of this approach to citizenship theorizing agree about the form that this pluralist citizenship should take.

The chief pluralist thinkers are probably Will Kymlicka and Iris Marion Young and, for this reason, the focus of attention in this section is upon their work. This is not to say, however, that they are the only pluralist theorists. Even more recent pluralist accounts can be found in the work of Pakulski (1997) and Stevenson (1997a/b) and in the writings of a number of authors from a variety of perspectives, for example from feminism, the sociology of 'race' and of sexuality (see the edited collection – Stevenson (2000) – for a selection of chapters from a range of perspectives). Whilst these accounts are of importance, Kymlicka and Young are nevertheless widely held to have made the most powerful contributions to this branch of citizenship theory. Both Kymlicka and Young take as the basis of their theorizing a critical stance towards the universalist notion of citizenship. Both authors perceive that in pluralist societies it is essential to consider group rights within the citizenship framework. Despite proposing a relatively similar critique of universalist notions of citizenship, there are differences, however, between the models of citizenship employed by Kymlicka and Young. The next section of this chapter will provide a critical appraisal of their separate approaches.

Kymlicka's defence of group rights is, he claims, firmly rooted in a liberal conception of citizenship. In support of this statement he has developed a multiculturalist perspective that requires social institutions to be reformed in a manner that allows for the '*accommodation of the cultural distinctiveness of multiple ethnic groups in a single state*'. (Shafir, 1998: 18) Such a perspective demands that the rights that have previously been bestowed only upon the individual citizen, as in liberalism, be extended to groups as well. This, Kymlicka claims, would lead to a *differentiated citizenship* and should be seen as an extension of, rather than a threat to, the liberal conception of citizenship.

To this end, Kymlicka proposes that there are three types of differentiated citizenship: in particular he states that it is important to distinguish between the closely related *representation rights* and *polyethnicity* and the altogether different, *self-government rights*. For Kymlicka ([1995] 1998: 169), group representation rights generally take the form of a demand for inclusion by disadvantaged groups:

> Groups that feel excluded want to be included in the larger society, and the recognition and accommodation of their 'difference' is intended to facilitate this. (...) It has always been recognized that a majoritarian democracy can systematically ignore the voices of minorities. In cases where minorities are regionally concentrated, democratic systems have responded by intentionally drawing the boundaries of federal units, or of individual constituencies, so as to create seats where the minority is in a majority. Proponents of special representation simply extend this logic to nonterritorial groups who may equally be in need of representation (for example, ethnic minorities, women, the disabled.)

Similarly, according to Kymlicka, demands for polyethnic rights most often take the form of requests for special rights to facilitate the participation of certain groups within the mainstream of society. Kymlicka cites, as an example, the case of Sikhs who wished to join the Royal Canadian Mounted Police but who faced problems because they were not allowed to wear turbans as part of their uniform. Modifying an institution such as the Royal Canadian Mounted Police in order to allow Sikhs to integrate into it as fully as possible is, according to Kymlicka, an important step in preventing Canadian Sikhs from withdrawing from mainstream society. Further, according to Kymlicka ([1995] 1998: 170): '*the fact that these men wanted to be a part of the national police force or the national military is ample evidence of their desire to participate in and contribute to the larger community*'. Thus, in Kymlicka's opinion, group representation and polyethnicity can promote social integration and political unity.

His third form of differentiated citizenship, however, *self-government*, poses, he believes, a more '*serious challenge to the integrative function of citizenship*' (Kymlicka, [1995] 1998: 174). The basis for his fear is that demands for self-government suggest a desire to weaken the notion of a permanent, unitary, 'macro' level political community. In other words, demands for self-government are very different from demands for representation rights, in which it is seen that certain groups are disadvantaged within the political community, or polyethnic rights, where there is a need to see the political community as culturally diverse. Instead, calls for self-governance suggest that there is more than one political community within one state. Such multination states, Kymlicka argues, are inherently unstable, since the tendency towards secession will always be strong.

This is not to say that Kymlicka is entirely opposed to secession, however, for he believes that where it is viable it may be desirable. In this he draws upon J.S. Mills' argument that a stable liberal democracy will be based upon a nation-state, with a single national culture. Nevertheless, he claims that secession may not always be desirable where the minority group would have problems developing a viable nation-state. In such cases, a way of holding such a multi-nation state together must be found. Unfortunately, as Kymlicka himself admits, it is not easy to find such a solution. He does consider, however, that the basis of unity within states is likely to be dependent upon the development of particular sentiments amongst citizens. These sentiments would take the form of a desire to be united, but at the same time to remain respectful of the deep diversity that constitutes their state. It must be said, however, that although Kymlicka claims that he is not proposing an overly legalistic definition of citizenship which neglects more socio-cultural factors, in calling for the development of certain 'sentiments' on the part of citizens, he does appear to be at risk of echoing, somewhat, the normative and monistic liberal notion of a *common citizenship* so usefully critiqued by Berlin.

It is proposed here that the problem rests upon Kymlicka's definitions of culture and identity. Although he begins his theorizing on differentiated citizenship by acknowledging that culture need not be tied to membership of a national group, as previously mentioned with regard to representation rights, his subsequent theorizing on the possible ways of maintaining unity in a multi-national state suggests that he is relying somewhat on the idea that the choices citizens make are meaningful only in the context of the nation (Faulks, 2000). There is a risk that such theorizing becomes too reductionist of the complexity of culture – for the idea of a national culture often stands in tension to social cleavages that can occur within one nation, such as class, gender, sexuality and so on.

Further, it can be argued that are a number of problems associated with Kymlicka's understanding of culture *per se*, for it is, perhaps, not as concrete a phenomenon as his theory suggests. The first issue is that he may be at risk of essentializing cultural *difference* between groups of people. There are undoubtedly differences between all people, but as has been highlighted by a range of authors, most notably, perhaps, from within feminism, the manner in which society manipulates the concept of 'difference' in an essentialist manner in order to categorize some groups as 'other', needs to be problematized. Where he talks about the idea of representational rights, Kymlicka appears to suggest that differences such as gender or dis/ability are necessarily based upon cultural differences. Whilst a shared sense of cultural identity may be the basis of the formation of *many groups*, it need not be the basis of *all groups*. Equally, to assume that any group exists on the basis of only one predominant identity trait, is both to essentialize the nature of group formation and to be reductionist of the complexity of 'identity'. As Fierlbeck (1998: 99) has commented:

(...) to assert that one simply knows that another person is defined predominantly by their culture or specific group traits rather than other factors seems as oppressive as refusing to believe that cultural characteristics are important at all.

Further, anti-essentialist understandings of culture and identity are gaining increasing ground within sociology more widely. These approaches conceive identity as either 'fragmented' or 'messy' depending upon the perspective (Ackelsberg, 1997). A further problem with Kymlicka's approach may, therefore, be that in proposing group rights in a differentiated citizenship, he does not adequately tackle the problem posed by complex identities and cultures. Where cultural groups *do* exist, they are not all perhaps as distinct and unified as Kymlicka appears to suggest. The culture itself may show differences according to such factors as class, or gender. This issue and Bourdieu's contribution to theorizing on this point will be considered in more depth in Chapter 6. Equally important, however, and only touched upon by Kymlicka, is the problem posed by 'illiberal' cultures that involve cultural practices that disadvantage particular members of the cultural group. It is the argument here that Kymlicka does not explain adequately how he believes it to be possible to achieve a multicultural unity based upon shared 'sentiments' when the cultural practices of one group are fundamentally in conflict with the practices of another.

As previously stated, in many respects the goal of Iris Marion Young is very similar to that of Kymlicka in that she seeks to critique those theories of citizenship that have tried to suppress group differences. She differs from Kymlicka, however, in that she does not seek to develop a modified liberalist approach to citizenship, but instead rejects the earlier approach entirely. Central to Young's approach is the argument that the universalistic sense of citizenship that had underpinned liberalism:

> (...) by separating the public sphere of 'reason' from the private realm of 'desire' and the body, elevates the dispassionate notions of 'collective interest' and 'equal citizenship' as expressed in the idea of the 'civic public' over and against the particularised interests that comprise the aspirations of groups and individuals.   (Ellison, 1997: 705)

The result of this liberalist approach to citizenship, Young claims, has been to suppress or deny the differences between groups in the public realm and instead to demand of each citizen the denial of their very identities when exercising their rights and duties. In other words, as Faulks (2000: 85) has commented, Young perceives liberalism as standing *'not for equality between different individuals but the domination of the ideal of equality over difference: the diversity that characterizes society is sacrificed in the name of an abstract and unattainable conception of citizenship'*.

According to Young this insistence on the part of the liberal thinkers that equality and liberation can only be achieved by ignoring differences has had three oppressive consequences. The first consequence of this liberal approach has been a focus upon a process of *assimilation*, in which formerly excluded groups are brought into the mainstream. So influential has this idea been, that it has gone largely unchallenged, even by other pluralist thinkers. For Young (1990: 164), however, assimilation *'always implies coming into the game after it has already begun, after the rules and standards have already been set, and having to prove oneself according to those rules and standards'*. Needless to say, it is the privileged groups that determine these standards. In so doing, however, they genuinely consider themselves to be determining a culturally neutral ideal of common humanity. This is clearly not the case, for norms determined by the dominant group will always be culturally biased.

This then, according to Young (1990: 165), is the second problem with the liberalist approach to citizenship for *'the ideal of a universal humanity without social group differences allows privileged groups to ignore their own group specificity'*. This, she states, leads to the final oppressive consequence of liberalism: the tendency to denigrate any groups that fail to live up to the supposedly neutral, but in fact culturally biased standards as set by the privileged group, in turn can lead to *'an internalized devaluation by members of those groups themselves. (...) The aspiration to assimilation (thus) helps produce the self-loathing and double consciousness characteristic of oppression'*. (Young, 1990: 165) The answer to these problems, according to Young, is to reject assimilationist ideals entirely and to embrace instead what she terms the 'politics of difference'. This new politics would, she argues, take the form of a rejection of the *'appropriation of a universal subject position by socially privileged groups'* by which they force *'those they define as different outside the definition of full humanity and citizenship'*. (Young, 1990: 169)

Further, echoing the ideas of Goffman and Mary Douglas, Young proposes that the root cause of this tendency on the part of the dominant group to essentialize difference is their fear of making the boundaries permeable between themselves and those they determine to be 'others'. For Young the alternative to this essentialized notion of difference is a notion of difference as 'variety'. In this way group differences can be seen to be merely functional means of comparison between groups, with dominant groups such as white people being seen to be just as *specific* as Black people, men as women, homosexuals as heterosexuals and so on. The other important aspect of this new form of politics, Young argues, is that it is also a contextualized understanding of difference. According to this argument, depending upon the groups compared and the context, differences may become more or less salient. Young (1990: 171) gives the following example:

> (...) in the context of athletics, health care, social service support, and so on, wheelchair-bound people are different from others, but they are not different in many other respects. Traditional treatment of the disabled entailed exclusion and segregation because the differences between the disabled and the able-bodies were conceptualised as extending to all or most capacities.

In many respects, therefore, the great value of Young's work is that it provides us with the basis for a more fluid and contextualized notion of difference. There are, however, some problems associated with the manner in which Young then sets about utilizing her understanding of difference to develop a model of democracy. She states that:

I assert, then, the following principle: a democratic public should provide mechanisms for the effective recognition and representation of the distinct voices and perspectives of those of its constituent groups that are oppressed or disadvantaged. Such group representation implies institutional mechanisms and public resources supporting (1) self-organization of group members so that they achieve collective empowerment and a reflective understanding of their collective experience and interests in the context of the society; (2) group analysis and group generation of policy proposals in institutionalised contexts where decision makers are obliged to show that their deliberations have taken group perspectives into consideration; and (3) group veto power regarding specific policies that effect a group directly, such as reproductive rights for women, or land use policy for Indian reservations.   (Young, 1990: 184)

Whilst this may at first glance appear to be an appealing notion of democracy, there are, however, some difficulties with this approach. Taking Young's second point first, since in some respects it is perhaps the least problematic, it is nevertheless the argument here that she is being overly optimistic about this matter. Many disadvantaged groups have already had experience of *decision makers (being) obliged to show that their deliberations have taken group perspectives into consideration*, but have found that this 'consultation' takes the form of mere 'rubber stamping'. This is a point that will be returned to later in Chapters 5 and 6 in relation to the findings of the research upon which this book is based. In defence of Young's ideas, however, it can be argued that there is nothing intrinsically wrong with her notion of consultation; it just needs to be put into proper effect.

Point (1) in the schema is more problematic, however, for it is clear that Young believes that the self-organization of group members in order that they achieve collective empowerment is both possible and desirable. Although the work of Bourdieu will be considered in more depth in Chapter 6, it is important to note at this point that much of his work on the nature of groups appears to contradict Young's work. Firstly, according to Bourdieu (1987), no matter how many resources are available to a number of individuals occupying similar positions, it does not necessarily follow that they will mobilize as a group. In other words, simply because a number of individuals can be identified by others as being 'similar' in some way, does not mean that they can be *categorized* as a group or a community. Secondly, although Bourdieu would probably agree with Young that where groups have mobilized, they gain collective empowerment, he perceives there to be risks associated with this process. He highlights the fact that in the process of becoming such a 'practical group', chief advocates or spokespeople emerge. He concludes that a paradox then arises, for whilst individuals who so identify themselves with a group become empowered and gain recognition, they are at the same time relegating their individual powers to those who claim to speak on behalf of the group. Collective empowerment may, therefore, mean individual disempowerment.

In relation to point (3), the problems associated with Young's schema echo those associated with Kymlicka's theorizing. Giving powers of veto to groups in relation to policies that directly affect them can be a positive step. It may, however, allow for the continuance of practices and behaviours on the part of minority groups that may be regarded as illiberal by the majority. It is the argument here that neither Kymlicka, nor Young, explain adequately how this potential conflict could be overcome. This may not be unintentional on their part, however, for ultimately, problems such as this must rest upon ethical dilemmas that are not easily resolved. For example, there is an important debate currently taking place in the world of genetics between geneticists who would like to find ways to eliminate congenital deafness, and some Deaf people who oppose the development of such technologies on the grounds that such moves are akin to genocide.[1] Whilst it is not the intention here to go into any depth on this matter since it warrants significantly greater attention than can be afforded here, it is nonetheless important to highlight how giving Deaf people the right to veto moves to eliminate congenital deafness, immediately sets up a dilemma in relation to the rights of the unborn child to *not be born deaf*. In the light of such continuing debates, it is the argument here that theories that 'bypass' ethical dilemmas need to be reconsidered.

Having stated the above there is, however, an even more problematic assumption underpinning the idea of the 'politics of difference'. The problem is that Young (1990), like Kymlicka, appears to rely somewhat upon the idea that social groups are culturally determined and whilst she does admit that other collectives can and do exist on the basis of other factors – these she terms interest groups and ideological groups – she argues that such groups do not require specific representation. Her tendency to focus primarily upon issues of cultural recognition – and in so doing to omit to give sufficient attention to groups who are concerned with issues of redistribution for example – has been highlighted by writers such as Nancy Fraser (1997) who states that social inequality must still be considered to be one of the key impediments to a true democracy.

Whilst Young (2000) has recently attempted to counter this criticism of her theorizing, by stating that it is not her intention to prioritize cultural issues over other special interests, her ongoing support for the idea of a 'politics of difference' continues to be examined critically. A growing number of other feminist authors, although recognizing the great importance of Young's contribution to feminist thought, are now expressing concerns about certain aspects of her work (see for example Lister, 2003). Phillips (1993) and Narayan (1997) also state that they have 'reservations' about certain aspects of Young's approach. Phillips (1993: 116) states that her concern surrounds: *'the difficult problems of group closure (people coming to define themselves politically through what is only one frozen single aspect of their lives); the question of who is to legislate on which groups qualify for additional group representation; and the almost insuperable obstacles to establishing what any group wants'*. Narayan (1997: 57 [original emphasis]) states that she shares Phillips' reservations, but adds that:

> Any serious consideration of the fact that oppressed groups are themselves internally heterogeneous with respect to identities, interests and political perspectives leads to worries about the problematic results of taking the policy proposals put forward by the leadership of these groups as definitive of the interests of <u>all</u> members of the group. (...) whilst Young's <u>analysis</u> acknowledges the internal heterogeneity of groups, her <u>proposals</u> run the risk of treating 'oppressed groups' as totalised unities, where all members are assumed to share common interests and policy perspectives simply by virtue of their being 'oppressed'.

These issues associated with Young's theorizing will be considered again in relation to the findings of this research in Chapter 6.

It is not entirely surprising, therefore, given the significance of some of these problems associated with the pluralist account of citizenship that alternative approaches have emerged. Two alternatives to the pluralist account are considered in the following section. The first approach is termed here a 'reflexive' account of citizenship, and is most clearly articulated in the work of Habermas. This theory has been developed to counter the tendency on the part of some pluralist thinkers, such as Kymlicka, to focus upon citizenship as being based upon nationally held, shared 'sentiments'. This approach highlights the effects that globalization/cosmopolitanism has had upon the notion of citizenship and calls for a more *'reflexive transformation of existing national conceptions of group membership'*. (Delanty, 2000: 65)

The second account is probably best termed 'post-structuralist' (although it is often termed 'post-modernist'), and arises from recent feminist critiques of the work of Young and of the pluralist account more generally. Although the work of Lister (1997a/b) and Yuval-Davis (1997), who both call for a more fluid understanding of citizenship, also forms part of this approach, it is proposed here that the post-structural model of citizenship is most notably found within the work of Mouffe (1992a, 1993). Mouffe's approach to citizenship has been developed to challenge the pluralist assumption that *'individual persons can have singular, integral, altogether harmonious and un-problematic identities'* or that *'collective identities as based on some "essence" or set of core features shared by all members of the collectivity'* (Calhoun, 1994: 13) do actually exist. Further, Mouffe states that unlike the pluralist account of Young, her model does not impede wider solidarities from forming across difference.

The reflexive account of Habermas

Habermas' contribution to the citizenship debates begins with his work on the political realm, where he distinguishes between the 'lifeworld' and the 'system'. Habermas develops the distinction between these two zones of action within the second volume of his *Theory of Communicative Action*. McAfee (2000: 85) usefully defines Habermas' notion of the 'lifeworld' and the 'system' thus:

> (...) the lifeworld (...) consists of the background assumptions, cultural norms, expectations, and meanings that we use to interpret and make sense of our experience and to co-ordinate our actions with others. The system on the other hand, is society conceptualised in terms of the division of labour and functions into separate spheres of actions and goals (e.g., the banking system, the political system, the educational system), each with its own predetermined ends and selected means for achieving them.

Habermas (1984: xxix) then integrates these two concepts into an analysis of society in which society is seen as both a *'system that has to satisfy the conditions of maintenance of socio-cultural lifeworlds'* and a *'systematically stabilized nexus of action of socially integrated groups'*. Even as he so theorizes, however, he identifies simultaneously an increasing trend towards the differentiation, or what he terms the 'de-coupling' of the lifeworld and the system. Habermas sees this as being the inevitable outcome of Modernity. In particular, he considers this passage to Modernity to be characterized by the move away from more traditional forms of society towards a society characterized by various aspects of life becoming increasingly independent of the normative structures in society, such as traditions, culture and kinship.

In some ways, Habermas perceives this move towards Modernity to be a good thing, for it ended the authoritarian traditions and conventions that had previously governed society and led to a more rational society of 'post-conventional' morality. Habermas does not consider this move to be without risk, however, for these changes render the lifeworld vulnerable to colonization by the system, as reasoning previously only appropriate to systems is applied to social life. The result, Habermas fears, is that Modernity has not made society more just. McAfee (2000: 88) summarizes Habermas' concerns thus:

> While the prerogatives of citizenship have been expanded to more and more people, the tasks of citizenship have been distorted into the role of consumer. Likewise, capitalism has not made the labor-for-wage relationship better in any real way, instead it has transformed the identity of worker into that of consumer. The colonization of the lifeworld turns citizens into clients and workers into consumers, thereby minimizing opportunities for overcoming capitalism's and Modernity's injustices.

Despite such theorizing, Habermas is not entirely pessimistic about Modernity, for he sees the rise in communicative rationality and the existence of the 'new' social movements as being precisely *about* challenging the manner in which the lifeworld is encroached upon by the system. In this respect Habermas' work appears to have had profound influence upon social movement theorizing, particularly upon the work of writers such as Touraine and Melucci.

In his work, subsequent to *The Theory of Communicative Action*, Habermas has sought to develop further the notion that certain mechanisms can prevent the system encroaching upon the lifeworld. He calls for the re-kindling of democracy, in which the will of the people guides public policy and, in particular, states the need for 'discursive democracy', which he perceives to be a deliberative process within public communication. In other words, Habermas believes that the solution to the previously stated problems of Modernity is to foster the right conditions so that public opinion can have public influence. In contrast to his earlier work, however, Habermas has now somewhat re-stated his position, for whilst he still largely locates discursive democracy within the communicative domain that is the public sphere, he also locates it in the *'partly institutionalized political culture of civil society'* (Delanty, 2000: 41).

The idea of a discoursive democracy has not gone unchallenged, however, for the question of how a consensus can be reached within a heterogeneous society remains. Feminists such as Meehan (1995), for example, have argued that the aim of consensus actually closes off many of the differences that characterize society. Habermas, on the other hand, has countered these criticisms by stating that such problems can be overcome by the 'public use of reason'. Delanty (2000: 42) has described Habermas' thinking about 'discursive democracy' thus, as seeking to:

> (...) render positions reflective. (...) To adopt the public perspective is to accept a third-person perspective, which is neither the perspective of the opponent nor one's own vantage point. The public perspective is the genuinely intersubjective perspective, reducible to neither self nor other.

Thus, Habermas' notion of consensus differs from that of Rawls, for example, because it does not rest upon the normative assumption that decisions can be made on the basis of an overlapping sense of the 'common good'. In fact, Habermas rejects this idea and states that in complex societies characterized by cultural pluralism, it cannot be taken for granted that a background consensus exists. In Habermas' (1998) notion of consensus, therefore, it is not assumed that different parties will necessarily reach an overlapping consensus, but rather that a reflexive position can be reached that looks for the critical appropriation of both positions.

It is the proposal here, however, that Habermas' position can be viewed as equally, if differently normative in approach, when compared with the work of more liberal thinkers such as Rawls. Many Feminist writers reinforce this criticism of Habermas' work, for example Fraser (1989) who has highlighted the fact that Habermas does not theorize adequately the notion of *power*. Differentials in the power possessed by different groups will affect the degree of autonomy they possess within the public sphere. Attention must, therefore, be paid to the 'pre-discursive' space. Thus, whilst Habermas' work has been highly influential within contemporary citizenship theorizing, particularly with regard to his theories of communicative ethics, other aspects of his work are more contentious. In particular, the question of the extent to which this reflexive position can realistically be achieved from within a society characterized by a large number of social cleavages and related power differences, continues to be a major issue within the citizenship debates.

Arguably, however, the great strength in Habermas' theorizing lies less with the fine details of how this discursive democracy could be made to work in practice. The strength of his theory lies instead in the manner in which he locates this discursive democracy largely within the state, whilst simultaneously rejecting the idea that this citizenship is in itself necessarily rooted in a particular cultural community. Habermas is clear when he states that since each individual possesses multiple 'selves', the idea that uniform cultural communities *ever exist*, must be placed into some doubt. It would also seem likely that he is right to reject the idea, to be found in the work of Kymlicka, that certain 'shared sentiments' need to/can be developed by citizens.

For Habermas, all that is needed is a shared sense of obligation between members of a polity that is solely political, and in no way cultural. This, he claims, would take the form of minimal shared identity, a kind of 'common denominator commonality' that is based only upon the legal frameworks as set out within the constitution of a state. In this way Habermas is paving the way for a more cosmopolitan notion of citizenship. Indeed, he states: *'Only a democratic citizenship that does not close itself off in a particularistic fashion can pave the way for a world citizenship (...)'* (Habermas, 1996: 514). Thus, borders at every level, between neighbourhoods, regions or states, are seen as only existing for administrative purposes, not as barriers between 'us' and 'them'.

By de-coupling the notion of citizenship from nationality or cultural heritage in this way, Habermas (1992, 1996) is thus providing a way of integrating states, as for example in the case of the EU, on the basis of a shared civil society, rather than a shared sense of culture. Further, by uncoupling nation-state and citizenship discourses, there is more of a chance that citizens will sense that their responsibilities reach beyond their immediate locality (Faulks, 2000), from the local to the global.

The post-structuralist approach of Mouffe

Again, in the work of Mouffe, the essential focus is democracy. Mouffe's vision of democracy is one that sees the tension between universalism and particularism, not as something that needs to be resolved, but rather as constitutive of the democratic process itself. As in the later work of Habermas, in which he proposes that the individual is best understood as having multiple selves, Mouffe perceives the social agent as an ensemble of subject positions. In other words, Mouffe's notion of 'citizenship' rests upon her understanding of the identity of the subject as being; *'always contingent and precarious, temporarily fixed at the intersection of those subject positions and dependent on specific forms of identification'.* (Isin and Wood, 1999: 11)

Since Mouffe is a feminist writer, she is essentially talking about feminist politics. Her thoughts can nevertheless easily be applied to other groups. Thus her rejection of what she regards to be the essentialist idea that certain qualities or functions that are commonly associated with women are central to women's identity as women, can be applied to many other groups engaged in 'struggle'. Equally useful is her idea that, ultimately, there is no need to hold to any kind of essentialist concept of identity in order to make political action possible or to support any kind of democratic politics. Indeed, according to Mouffe, what feminists should be doing is seeking to find a common cause with other groups that have been denied the democratic ideal of equal citizenship. Thus as McAfee (2000: 118) states: *'The goal, for Mouffe, is for such oppressed people to join together as a "we" to gain hegemony over "them", all those oppressors'.* In relation to her conception of citizenship, Mouffe is therefore suggesting that *'radical democratic citizens depend on a collective form of identification among the democratic demands found in a variety of movements: women, workers, black, gay and ecological as well as other oppositional movements'.* (Isin and Wood, 1999: 11)

In this way, she proposes that the way forward is to develop a 'radical and plural democracy', in which there is a non-essentialist conception of the subject, and identity is seen to be determined by identification with *groups* rather than as an essential property of the subject (Mouffe, 1993). Thus, for Mouffe, politics will always be a 'struggle', an antagonistic process between such groups. Focusing thus on groups, Mouffe does not support the idea of the 'self-regarding individual' of liberalism, nor does she believe that an allegiance to the 'common good' is possible, no matter how desirable it may be. This leaves her with the central problem, however, of how then to theorize a concept of citizenship that does not perceive individual liberty to be incompatible with the political community.

Mouffe's answer is to reconsider the *nature of the polis*. She draws upon the work of Oakeshott (1975), who makes the distinction between *universitas* and *societas*. In the former, the polity is composed of individuals with a shared *purpose*, in the latter, the polity is seen to be composed of individuals with shared *interests*. Mouffe proposes that her notion of a 'radical democracy' is best understood as a radical *societas*, in which conflict and antagonism play a crucial part. In other words, in Mouffe's view, individuals cannot be considered to be pursuing their interests peacefully, but should instead be considered to be engaging with each other over the meaning and definition of their common interests. There will never be, therefore, a homogenous unity in such a societas, for there will always be a need for an 'other'.

The form of citizenship arising out of this definition of a radical societas is one that is clearly opposed to the more classical approaches to citizenship theorizing. For Mouffe, the citizen is neither the passive possessor of rights, as in the work of Hobbes for example, or someone who agrees to submit to the rules prescribed by the 'general will', as Rousseau proposed. Instead, Mouffe (1992a: 237) proposes that this notion of citizenship is best understood to be '*not a unitary subject but as the articulation of an ensemble of subject positions, constructed within specific discourses and always precariously and temporarily sutured at the intersection of those subject positions*'. The existence of these multiple subject positions has already been documented in many movements demanding democratic, citizenship based rights, for example, in the Black, gay and ecological movements.

Mouffe's work has not gone un-criticized, however, particularly with regard to what some critics have perceived to be her tendency to label any theory that takes identity categories seriously, as 'essentialist'. In relation to Mouffe's attacks on what she regards to be essentialism within feminism, many feminist theorists counter her criticisms by stating that they are not talking about a supposed female *essence*, but rather about the manner in which women have been historically, socially and culturally *constructed*. McAfee (2000: 119) has stated that it is important to distinguish between essentialism and nominalism:

Are we talking about women de re or women de dicto? Is it a matter of what woman is in herself or of what she is called? Of how she is 'naturally' versus how she's been constructed socially? Many feminists are careful to make distinctions between, for example, what a woman is biologically and what she is taken to be culturally.

Nevertheless, it is proposed here that the importance of Mouffe's work lies, not so much in its attack on essentialism, but rather in the manner in which it highlights the inadequacies of any theory that takes a *particular aspect* of a person's identity and claims that it is more pertinent than any other.

Conclusion: future developments?

This chapter has sought to provide a critical overview of some of the key citizenship theories as they have developed over time, from ancient to more contemporary accounts. The aim of this chapter has also been to introduce the continuing debate surrounding the extent to which any of the existing models account for the nature *of*, or provide a realistic ideal *for*, the citizenship of 'Later Modernity'. In the complex and often unstable world of Later Modernity, whilst much cannot be said with certainty, it is the argument here that the following can be held to be widely apparent. Firstly, it is no longer possible to talk about a sense of citizenship that is 'universal'. Secondly, understandings of citizenship based upon the idea of 'national communities' must also be placed in some doubt. Thirdly, whilst rejecting universalistic understandings of citizenship, it is equally difficult to develop a convincing theory of citizenship that relies upon the recognition of a stable set of 'differences'.

Whilst the development of theory within this field must be ongoing, some existing models have gone further than others in providing the basis for future theorizing. Berlin, Habermas and Mouffe, in particular, provide us with a contemporary idea of citizenship that is still about social engagement, and, in particular, is still firmly linked to democracy and the struggle for a common goal. Yet what is common in the approaches, particularly of Habermas and Mouffe, is also an understanding of citizenship as being about the development of new forms of social and political practices that are themselves the result of the formation of new social alliances across a range of different 'communities'.

The idea that understanding these practices or *processes* of engagement is key to developing a new theory of citizenship, is something that is also proposed by Ellison (1997, 2000). Ellison, however, examines the reality of social and political engagement somewhat more critically, perhaps, than previous authors and proposes that it is impossible to understand citizenship as a process of engagement without considering the differential effects that power can have on the capacity and nature of citizen engagement. Ellison's approach is key to the model of citizenship proposed later in this book and further discussion of his ideas is made in Chapter 4 and then again in Chapter 6, along with further consideration of the work of Berlin, Habermas, and Mouffe.

There are, however, some new contributions to the citizenship debates that advance beyond the traditional parameters of citizenship theorizing and into realms that have not previously been considered by theorists in this field. The idea that has remained unquestioned for so long, that citizenship is connected with *competence*, is now being deconstructed by a number of authors (see for example Silver, 2002) and this marks an important step in terms of understanding the 'citizenship' experiences of many disadvantaged or stigmatized groups. More central to the argument in this book, however, Jenkins (1998) has also called for an understanding of the effects of socio-cultural models of the body in determining certain social groups as incompetent and ultimately, in some cases, denying personhood. Of course, in terms of 'bringing the body' back into sociology, Foucault's (1979) work has clearly been highly influential, for in writing about the body as a site of power, he grounded what may seem at first glance to be fairly esoteric theorizing on the body/materiality, in the actual, everyday processes of power. Such ideas have also been taken up usefully and modified by post-structuralist/post-modern feminists. Butler (1993: 2), for example, states that:

> (...) what constitutes the fixity of the body, its contours, its movements, will be fully material, but materiality will be re-thought as the effect of power.

As part of this re-thinking of materiality, Butler (1995: 37) calls for a questioning of the ways in which certain paradigms serve to disempower and erase that which they seek to explain, '*effecting a violent reduction of the field to the one piece of text*'. In relation to the case study considered in this book – disability – for example, such theorizing has clear implications in terms of challenging the social model of disability and the work of authors such as Finkelstein (1996), who as will be discussed later, consider the inclusion of 'impairment' in theorizing on disability as running the risk of diluting the social model's potential in terms of praxis. Using the arguments put forward by Butler, to truly challenge discourses of power in terms of disability, it is important to understand that 'impairment', whilst having an undeniable, basic, bio-logical definition, is also imbued with diverse social meaning (Fawcett, 2000).

In this respect Butler's views clearly resonate with those of a number of other authors from feminism and queer studies (Yeatman, 1994, Lister, 1997a, Weeks, 1998, Richardson, 2001 and others) who have shown how traditional approaches to citizenship have rested upon the premise of a public/private divide and in so doing have relied upon a *disembodied* notion of citizenship. For such theorists, the rights and responsibilities that are part of being a citizen cannot be divorced from an understanding of the importance of the body – not least in respect of the need to reject the unachievable practices of the 'imper-sonal, rational and disembodied' citizen (Yeatman, 1994: 84) and to embrace instead further domains of citizenship that are concerned with 'the body', its needs, pleasures and sexualized identities. In other words, this approach stresses the importance of challenging the assumption that there is a 'neat' divide between the 'personal' and the 'political'.

In terms of citizenship theorizing *per se*, however, it is the argument here that it is Turner ([1996] 2000) who has most famously developed this connection between a Sociology of the Body and citizenship. In order to break with this earlier theorizing he proposes a Sociology of the Body which requires consideration of the following:

1. an elaborate understanding of the basic notion of embodiment, which would be a method of systematically exploring the com-plexity of the body in terms of its corporality, sensibility, and objectivity;
2. an embodied notion of social agency in the theory of social action and a comprehensive view of how body-image functions in social space;
3. a genuinely sociological appreciation of the reciprocity of social bodies over time – that is, an understanding of the collective nature of embodiment;
4. a thoroughly historical sense of the body and its cultural forma-tion;
5. a political understanding of the body in relation to governance, with special reference to what we might term corporeal citizen-ship, namely sexual regulation and surveillance of bodies by state

legislation on reproductive technology, abortion, adoption, and parenting.   (Turner, [1996] 2000: 487)

He then uses his sociology of the body to develop an embodied
understanding of citizenship as *personhood*, where each person is both
seen as, and is *aware of*, their own vulnerabilities. How he does this and
the implications of his theorizing will be considered in more depth in
Chapter 7. Ultimately, however, Turner (1993a/b) proposes, along with
some other key thinkers (Soysal, 1994, Delanty, 2000), that there are
now good grounds for suggesting that another discourse, that of
human rights with its foundation in understandings of the de-centred
and contextualized self, may provide the most sustained challenge to
the idea of citizenship, and may indeed mark the end of the concept
entirely. The extent to which Turner provides a convincing alternative
to the notion of citizenship will also be considered in Chapter 7.

3
Social Movements

Introduction

Setting aside the debate regarding the term 'post-modernity', whilst in no way denying its importance, most social theorists would agree that over the past century, society has undergone a wide variety of changes that, when considered cumulatively, bring into some doubt the idea that we inhabit a 'modern' society. For example, 'struggle' and unrest are no longer focused within a homogenous 'working class'. Instead, divisions within the socio-economic groupings and the blurring of boundaries between groups have become widely understood, resulting in a questioning of the whole notion of 'class'. What has come to be known as late/r modernity is now characterized by a variety of forms of unrest that can alternatively be seen as either resulting from the breakdown of 'class' as the major social cleavage, or as further hastening the decline of class-based 'politics'. Issues relating to gender, sexuality, 'race', dis/ability, ecologism, and a wide variety of other belief- and value-based systems have now come to the fore. The proliferation of such social groupings at first glance appears to make the idea that we live in a 'movement society' increasingly plausible. The term must be used with caution, however, since it is unclear whether any agreement has been reached regarding whether or not all movements within a 'movement society' are based upon this proliferation of unrest, or what are the central factors necessary to transform unrest into a 'movement'.

Broadly speaking there have been two major 'schools' of social movement theorizing, roughly equating to an American and a European tradition (see Figure 3.1). The 1960s, however, proved to be a 'watershed' with regard to theorizing in this field. At that time, the older theories from both traditions were considered to be in need of revision, particu-

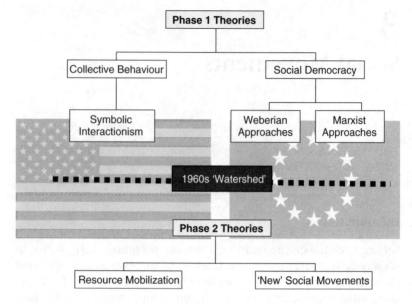

Figure 3.1   Social movement theories

larly in the light of a proliferation of social movements that no longer appeared to be dominantly concerned with structural inequality. The theories that developed before the late 1960s are termed here the 'First Phase Theories' and those that came after, the 'Second Phase Theories'. This chapter will begin by considering the First Phase Theories. The first phase of the American tradition centred on the *Collective Behaviour* approach to social movements, and, it is argued here, is best exemplified in the work of Herbert Blumer. For this reason, the chapter begins with an examination of Blumer's contribution to social movement theorizing. This is not to say, however, that the collective actor approach was the only first phase American theory. It would be wrong to overlook completely the structural-functionalist perspective of Parson's, for example. This approach has been heavily criticized, however, for regarding collective movements as irrational actors, and collective action as being solely the product of malfunctions of the social system. This approach, other than being the subject of much later criticism, particularly by Oberschall (1973), has not subsequently developed into a major strand of social movement theorizing and for this reason is not considered within this chapter.[1]

The 'First Phase Theories' in the European tradition are less clearly associated with particular theorists. Instead, European social movement theory has taken many forms, but can, nevertheless, be broadly termed a *Social Democratic* tradition and can be sub-divided into Weberian and Marxist approaches. These approaches will be discussed briefly before a more detailed consideration of what is meant by the notion of the '1960s watershed' and its effects upon subsequent theorizing.

In the second section of this chapter, the focus will then be upon the 'Second Phase Theories'. In the American tradition, post-1960s theorizing has been dominated by the *Resource Mobilization* theories, and included here as part of this category, the *Political Process* theories. Within this American tradition, the works of Oberschall, Tilly and Tarrow are particularly central, so these theorists will be considered in some depth. In post-1960s Europe a number of related approaches emerged based around notions of *identity, defence of the lifeworld, values and culture*. These approaches are rather loosely termed here as the 'New' Social Movement theories. These theories are most clearly articulated in the work of Touraine, Habermas and Melucci and their theories will be considered in turn within the chapter.

Phase 1 theories

Collective Behaviour: the American tradition

Blumer – symbolic interactionism

The *Collective Behaviour* explanation for social movements originates within the Chicago School and is probably best exemplified in the work of Herbert Blumer. Blumer was interested in the symbolic production and construction of identity and he saw social movements as being about producing new norms and solidarities. Social movements, according to his theory, are strongly linked with the value systems of a society and as such, are an integral part of any 'normal' society. That is not to say that social movements are not about change, but rather that their role as catalysts for change is essential to the inherent transformational quality of a 'normal' society.

Most social movement theorists would probably agree with Blumer that:

> Social movements can be viewed as collective enterprises to establish a new order of life. They have their inception in a condition of unrest, and derive their motive power on one hand from dissatisfaction with the current form of life, and on the other hand from wishes and hopes for a new scheme or system of living.   (Blumer, [1951] 1995: 60)

It is, however, the manner in which Blumer proceeded to theorize the 'careers' of social movements and produce a typology of different types of movement, that signals his particular approach to this field. In many respects, what Blumer provides is a 'joined up' approach that seeks to explain both the 'how' and the 'why' of social movements.

Implicit in Blumer's work is a focus upon the individual actor and issues of identity. Blumer was clearly concerned with social movements as examples of collectivities, the identities of which are simultaneously structured by individual members, and yet also structure the lives and identities of those members. He identified three major types of social movement, and these he termed the *'general social movement'*, the *'specific social movement'* and the *'expressive social movement'*. To begin with the last, the distinguishing feature of expressive movements is that they do not seek to achieve structural objectives. Expressive movements are not about social change. The tension and unrest out of which these movements emerge is not focused upon a particular objective, but rather takes the form of some kind of expressive behaviour. Nevertheless, these movements are not without effect, for some of this expressive behaviour may have *'profound effects on the personalities of individuals and on the character of the social order'* (Blumer, [1951] 1995: 77).

Blumer identifies religious movements and 'fashion' as two examples of expressive movements, with fashion probably being the most 'expressive' in nature and thus most clearly distinguished from a specific social movement. In particular, Blumer stated that fashion differs from other movements in that it does not develop into a 'society'. This is an important point because it establishes Blumer's ([1951] 1995: 76) over-arching view of general and specific social movements, that they are *'societies in miniature'*. Thus, fashion does not have a social organization, or develop a form of 'we-consciousness', instead it provides the means for expressing dispositions and tastes and in crystallizing these tastes, fashion constructs a common subjective life. This common subjective life is what Blumer describes as a 'Zeitgeist', and is a part of the development of a new social order.

In contrast, according to Blumer, general and specific social movements are *fundamentally* about social change, although they differ in the extent to which they are organized about their goals. General social movements are constituted by gradual changes in the values that people possess. Blumer terms these changes 'cultural drifts' and suggests that in particular, they take the form of changes in the way that people conceptualize themselves. Where there has previously been acceptance of the *status quo* and inertia, people begin to perceive infringements to their rights and privileges and they develop new opinions with regard to what they consider their entitlements to be. These new opinions are largely based upon individuals' hopes and dreams and the development of such ideas effects the way in which people look upon the reality of their own lives. As people come to form new conceptions of themselves, so they increasingly find a disjuncture between how they see their 'true selves' and the actual positions in which they find themselves. For Blumer this change in sense of 'self' explains how people come to experience dissatisfaction where before there was none.

The chief characteristic of general social movements is, therefore, *vagueness*, for *'these new images of themselves, which people begin to develop in response to cultural drifts, are vague and indefinite; and correspondingly, the behaviour in response to such images is uncertain and without definite aim'*. (Blumer, [1951] 1995: 61) As a result, Blumer considers the efforts of such movements to be 'groping' and as moving only slowly towards their goals. Further, according to Blumer, these social movements, of which he identified the women's movements as an example, are structurally disorganized with no clear leadership or membership and consist of unconnected individuals engaging in the struggle in a wide variety of loci.

According to Blumer, all social movements begin as general social movements, but whilst some remain uncoordinated, others develop into *specific social movements*. A social movement can be considered a 'specific social movement' once it possesses a well-defined objective or goal, has organization and structure and has a recognized leadership and membership. Again, emphasizing the importance of theorizing the individual when considering social movements, Blumer states that the membership of specific social movements is characterized by the development of what he terms 'we-consciousness', in which the individual senses that he/she is no longer struggling alone. This has clear implications for notions of shared identity and solidarity.

Although stating that specific social movements are distinguished from general social movements by higher levels of co-ordination, Blumer sees a 'career path' or continuum along which these movements will pass over time, becoming increasingly organized and solidified over the lifetime of the movement. Several key processes are seen to occur during this development process and Blumer identifies the role of *agitation*, the development of *esprit de corps*, and the degree of *morale* within the movement. The role of *agitation* is most important during the early stages of a specific social movement, although Blumer states that it may persist in a minor form during later stages of development. Agitation results in the awakening of people and creation of new impulses and ideas that make for restlessness and dissatisfaction. It cannot work however, where there are insufficient pre-existing grounds for disquiet but instead relies upon the pre-existence of some sort of injustice, discrimination or abuse, and seeks to encourage people to challenge the 'taken-for-granted'. Alternatively, agitation works well where people are already discontented or restless but where they are either too timid or do not know what to do. It gives people courage and the sense that they possess the means to change things.

Esprit de corps, as defined by Blumer, is probably the most important aspect of specific social movements since it determines who is an *insider* and who is an *outsider*. Further, according to Blumer, 'in-group/ out-group relations' are never neutral, and it is an essential part of the development of the social movement that the *outsiders* are demonized as enemies. *Esprit de corps* is also developed through such things as informal fellowship, in which individuals within the movements get to know one another and, through common sympathy and a sense of intimacy, the individual gains a sense of status and social acceptance. This 'fellowship' is a particularly uniting factor since, according to Blumer, it is often the case that individuals who become members of social movements have experienced prior loneliness and alienation. Involvement in ceremonial behaviour such as rallies, parades and demonstrations further enhance individuals' sense of vast support, and parading in numbers gives individuals a sense that both they and their views are important.

Blumer claims, however, that a specific social movement cannot survive on *esprit de corps* alone. Morale is also central to the maintenance of solidarity, especially in the face of adversity. To survive over time, the members of specific social movements must be sure of the rectitude of their aims and that the achievement of their goals would result in a near utopian state of affairs. Further, members must have faith that the movement will eventually achieve its goals. This faith is essential if momentum is to be maintained even through the hardest of struggles and is shored up by the development of 'sacred' texts, by having leaders who are viewed as 'saint-like' and by developing myths surrounding such things as the inhumanity of one's opponents.

Finally, ideology plays a part in maintaining morale, and is particularly important when a movement faces clear opposition from outsiders for it provides, amongst other things, a clear statement of the objectives of the movement, a critique of the *status quo* against which the movement is struggling, and a body of 'defence doctrine' that

justifies the actions of the movement. According to Blumer this ideology takes two forms, academic and populist. Populist ideology within
a movement makes the more academic forms of the ideology more
readily comprehensible. The relationship, therefore, between the
'academic' and 'non-academic' members of a movement is key to
the success of a specific social movement:

> To be effective (...) the ideology must carry respectability and pres-
> tige – a character that is provided primarily by the intelligentsia of
> the movement. More important than this, however, is the need of
> the ideology to answer to the distress, wishes, and hopes of the
> people. Unless it has this popular appeal, it will be of no value to
> the movement.   (Blumer, [1951] 1995: 73)

This issue will be considered again in relation to the findings of the
research upon which this book is based in Chapters 5 and 6.

For Blumer ([1951] 1995: 73), the manner in which all of these
aspects of a specific social movement come together to facilitate the
process of gaining supporters, keeping hold of supporters and reaching
the objectives of the movement, depends upon the particulars of the
situation and the nature of the movement: *'For, tactics are always
dependent on the nature of the situation in which the movement is operating
and always with reference to the cultural background of the movement'*.

The value of Blumer's theorizing, quite apart from the breadth of
explanation he provides, is, therefore, the way in which he outlines a
new way of theorizing social movements as a form of collective behaviour. In emphasizing the potential for social creativity to be found
within such behaviour, Blumer provided one of the first 'positive' theories of social movements. Blumer's contribution is also vital in that, in
stressing that social movements are part of the value-systems of a society, he is therefore highlighting the *context-specific* nature of social
movements, an issue that is still key to social movement theorizing.
Whilst the dominant importance of Blumer's theories declined after
the late 1960s, some aspects of his work have thus, nevertheless,
remained influential.

Social Democratic approaches: the European tradition

At the same time as the *Collective Behaviour* approach was being developed in the United States, other approaches were emerging in Europe.
Of key importance in explaining the differences between the European
and American traditions is the fact that European societies have been
more 'traditional' and class-based than the society of the United

States. In addition, according to Eyerman and Jameson (1991), the European, *Social Democratic* tradition was more philosophically informed than the *Collective Behaviour* approach, with the two major and competing theoretical interpretations arising from the work of Weber and Marx respectively.

For Marx, society was comprised from a *'moving balance of antithetical forces that generate social change by their tension and struggle'*. (Coser, 1971: 43) Thus, social struggle was at the heart of social progress. The main actors in this social struggle, according to Marx, were the economic classes whose interests conflict. This 'political' conflict between the classes becomes more acute as more and more changes occur to their relative positions during the process of economic development, and as increasing consciousness of their interests emerges within each class. Most importantly, according to Marx, the result of these contradictions and tensions within capitalism is the development of a class-consciousness within the *oppressed classes* who, by banding together in collective action, will seek to overthrow the dominant class.

Much subsequent Marxist theorizing on social movements within this first phase European tradition of theorizing has echoed Marx's views on collective action and has tended to view social movements with some anticipation. Such approaches have considered social movements to be signs of a forthcoming collapse of the existing capitalist order within society. For many Marxists, then, social movements possess the potential for social change, and the image of the collective actor is that of the *'self-activating class'* rather than the faceless mass (Eyerman and Jameson, 1991: 16). The theories within this branch of Marxism have tended, therefore, to focus upon what these movements represent, and what potential they may have for creating social change. It should be stated, however, that this somewhat 'Leninist' approach has not been the only line of thought within this tradition. Some Marxist approaches have attempted to retain a critical distance from the Leninist model. Even so, they still tend to emphasize the importance of politics and to reduce social movements to their political expression (Melucci, 1996). In short, all Marxist accounts have tended to be concerned less with understanding the *variety* of reasons why social movements emerge, or *how* they take shape.

In contrast to Marx's hopeful and positive views on social movements, Weber viewed such things as crowds and mass movements with some concern, preferring to see them as necessary but transitory factors in social transformation. Weber's classification of social stratification was rather more complex than that of Marx and suggested a more pluralist basis for social conflict (Coser, 1971). Weber rejected Marx's vision of a society polarized into the 'haves' and the 'have-nots' and in so doing provided a more complex analysis of power in society. Although Weber did agree with Marx that economic power is the predominant form of power in many modern societies, he saw power existing on other bases. One example Weber provided is the power that exists within bureaucracies, but more crucially for theorizing on social movements, Weber also perceived power to reside in the potential of an individual, or a group of individuals to achieve their goals through joint action, even against the opposition of others.

This aspect of Weber's work on social movements is somewhat misleading, however, for it suggests a more positive view of social movements than Weber perhaps intended. This point is addressed in the work of Michels (1959), Weber's friend and confidant. Michels defined the life-cycle of social movements as a process in which charismatic leadership becomes routinized and bureaucratic institutions are established. He perceived this maturation of social movements in which previously dynamic social forces become routinized into stagnant, top-heavy institutions, to be a necessary part of the life-cycle of social movements in modern society.

This idea, that modern societies are characterized by an institutionalization of mass movements, is something that in many respects united the first phase European approaches to social movements. Theorists from the Marxist and Weberian perspectives agreed that the first half of the 20th century had been characterized by social democracy, exemplified by the development of the welfare state, achieving a central role in society and social movements moving to the very core of society. This notion of the institutionalization of 'movement' was to be challenged greatly during the 1960s however, the events of this period instigating a radical re-think of social movement theory.

The 1960s 'watershed'

On 28 August 1963, between 200,000 and 500,000 people marched on Washington D.C. in what has been dubbed the 'March on Washington for Jobs and Freedom'. This protest culminated in the now famous '*I have a dream*' address by Martin Luther King Jr. (Giugni, 1999). This famous mass mobilization was one of many during the period and these widespread protests raised serious questions for social movement theorists. Della Porta and Diani (1999: 2) identify the issues raised as follows:

(...) questions of a practical nature, relating to the evaluation of emerging forms of social and political participation, and the response to them. (...) Furthermore, actors engaged in the new conflicts (youth, women, new professional groups and so on) could only partly be characterized in terms of principal political cleavages of the industrial societies. It was even less appropriate to view these actors in terms of class conflicts, which certainly constituted the principal component of these cleavages.

Initially, theorists attempted to explain the 1960s movements by relying upon earlier approaches, such as the collective behaviour theories, or the social democratic ideas. The result of such theorizing was to continue to view social movements as being the products of such things as 'alienation', the actions of social deviants or misfits, 'relative deprivation', or status inconsistencies. In short, as Stryker *et al* (2000: 2) have commented:

(...) social movements were viewed largely as the products of unbridled affect, of non-rational and irrational wellsprings of action. Social movements were taken to be anything but well-considered responses to legitimate concerns about real but oppositional interests.

Since many social movement theorists were, and continue to be, active participants within social movements, it was not entirely surprising therefore, that there was considerable opposition to this view of social movement activity as being 'irrational'. In consequence, out of this opposition to the existing theories emerged what are termed here the 'Second Phase Theories', namely, in the United States, the *Resource Mobilization* and the closely related *Political Protest* models, and in Europe the 'New' Social Movement theories. A consideration of these 'Second Phase Theories' forms the next section of this chapter.

Phase 2 theories

Resource Mobilization and Political Process: the changing face of the American tradition

As previously stated, until the late 1960s much of the American tradition of social movement theorizing had drawn heavily upon Blumer's work. From the 1970s onwards, however, this social psychological approach to theorizing social movements was heavily criticized. A major critique of the *Collective Behaviour* approach came *via Resource Mobilization* theory and the work of the key proponent of this approach, Oberschall. Equally important was the *Political Process* model of Tarrow and the critique of the *Collective Behaviour* approach put forward by Tilly, whose theories appear to fall somewhere in between the *Resource Mobilization* and the *Political Process* models.

In many respects, it is very difficult to define the distinguishing features of these two approaches, so akin are they to each other. Both theories see social movements as being about well-organized, purposeful, rational action. In so emphasizing organizational and political factors, social psychological variables are de-emphasized within both models. In addition, according to both theories, it is unnecessary to focus the theoretical explanations of social movements upon the structural tensions or conflicts that have prompted the protest. The focus of this social movement theorizing is instead, therefore, more the 'how' and 'when' of social movements rather than the 'why'.

Oberschall

Oberschall drew upon the concept of 'resource management' which had been introduced by Charles Tilly in his early work. Tilly (1978) had provided a new basis for the analysis of mobilization, countermobilization, the struggle for power and the manner in which individual resources could be utilized for achieving collective group goals through the process of conflict. Although Tilly, as will be discussed subsequently, went on to modify his own theories to the extent that they no longer belong entirely to the *Resource Mobilization* tradition, his early work did provide an important starting point for the development of this approach by Oberschall.

For Oberschall (1973: 28), social conflict arises out of the dynamic relationship between mobilization and social control:

> Mobilization refers to the processes by which a discontented group assembles and invests resources for the pursuit of group goals. Social control refers to the same processes, but from the point of view of the incumbents or the group that is being challenged.

Further, social structures, according to Oberschall, can be analysed according to how resources are managed and allocated in the process of pursuing a group goal. For example, Oberschall cites the experiences of the Black Power Movement and other such civil rights movements as examples of the problem that negatively-privileged groups face when trying to mobilize their meagre resources for the pursuit of their group goals. He then theorizes the extent to which external support can make up the resource deficits of such movements. Oberschall (1973: 29) also provides a useful analysis of the Hungarian Revolution of 1956, and in so doing demonstrates how a *'shared culture, national sentiments, and historical tradition can be rapidly converted into a resource base for conflict, even in the face of an authoritarian regime'*.

In other words, Oberschall provides us with a clearer understanding of what kind of things can be utilized as 'resources' by a movement. Finally, Oberschall states that participation, leadership and ideology within a movement can all be analysed according to cost-benefits and resource allocation. His approach does, therefore, tend to stress the instrumental bases for the various actions, interactions and relationships that occur within social movements. In this respect, and in the manner in which Oberschall makes use of such notions as risk/reward ratios, the influence of economics upon his theorizing is clear. Indeed, Oberschall himself states that injecting some economics into theorizing upon social movements was his intention.

Overall, however, the most important aspect of Oberschall's development of *Resource Mobilization* theory is, as Melucci (1996: 291) has commented, the idea that: *'In order for a protest movement to form, common sentiments of oppression or an identification of a common enemy will not suffice; there must also be a minimal organizational base and leadership'*. It is this notion of the necessity of pre-existing networks of social ties that provided the starting point for the theorizing of Tilly.

Tilly

For Tilly (1993: 4), social movements should not be theorized or spoken about as 'groups': *'thence assigning (them) a continuous life resembling the natural history of an organism'*. In other words, Tilly rejects Blumer's notion of social movements as having 'career paths'. Social movements, Tilly argues, can be distinguished from organizations proper, belief-systems and even individuals by the manner in which they *do not* possess self-reproducing 'natural histories' according to which they form, flourish, undergo change and eventually disappear. Instead, Tilly (1993: 6) proposes that social movements are best viewed as resembling:

> (...) dragons living continuously somewhere in the social underground, but emerging recurrently from their labyrinths to stomp around roaring.

In other words, social movements do not arise from the ether in some mysterious manner. Instead, according to Tilly, they depend upon pre-existing groups and networks such as voluntary associations, fronts, federations and others. Echoing the *Resource Mobilization* model, Tilly sees these networks as resources that can be mobilized by key players in a movement. Although denying social movements a life-cycle similar to that of an organism, Tilly (1993) does state that the actions of these key players or 'political entrepreneurs' brings coherency to strategic interaction. In particular, Tilly highlights the role of 'social movement specialists' in co-ordinating collective action, consistently publicizing the struggle engaged upon and influencing the routine behaviour of supporters, rivals and those observing the movement.

Tilly, although echoing much of the *Resource Mobilization* model in the manner in which it rejects social psychological explanations for social movements, does take from the *Collective Behaviour* model of social movements a belief in the context-specific nature of such movements. Further, echoes of the *Collective Behaviour* approach, in particular Blumer's notion of *esprit de corps* and *morale*, can especially be seen in the work of Tilly (1993, 1999) when he identifies the manner in which solidarity is reinforced within movements by such things as slogans, banners and other '*identifying devices*' (Tilly, 1993: 12). It is at this point, however, that the two models begin to diverge, for Tilly considers such techniques to be 'auxiliary activities', being of only secondary importance to the factors within his quite programmatic notion of mobilization.

Tilly's (1999: 261) approach to theorizing social movements is best exemplified in his notion that social movements function according to the following multiple:

Numbers × Commitment × Unity × Worthiness.

For a social movement to succeed as a political force, it must be able to show evidence of each element. Providing that none of the four elements falls to zero, at which point the movement would lose its standing as a political force, a deficiency in one area can be compensated for in another. As an example of this 'scorecard' schema, Tilly cites terrorism, and in particular ostentatious self-destruction, as being a characteristic strategy of small sections of divided movements. In this example, the small section of the movement would be demonstrating high levels of *commitment* and *worthiness*, and thus compensating for a deficiency in *numbers*.

Further, according to Tilly, additional coherency is given to a movement when it interacts with outsiders, particularly those in powerful positions. A series of strategic interactions will become viewed as a coherent social movement when those in power, and other third parties, react to this series of struggles by treating it as *'successive manifestations of the same phenomenon'* (Tilly, 1993: 6). The relationship between those in power and social movements is a complex one, however, for whilst it is often the case that the powerful are the object of claims made by social movements – and possess therefore, an inherent desire to undermine social movements – they may also at times become activists, at least to a degree, if it proves politically advantageous.

Tilly (1993) concludes, therefore, that social movements will vary according to four main factors: the nature of the claims being made; the prevailing political opportunity structure; the shared understandings of the participants; and the social structure from which members are drawn. It is Tilly's second point regarding the effects that the nature of the polity can have upon the development of social movements that is also key to Tarrow's theorizing.

Tarrow

In general, Tarrow's aim was to understand which characteristics of the political system influence the growth of less institutionalized political actors, in the course of what he termed 'protest cycles' (Tarrow, 1989). Della Porta and Diani (1999: 10) have commented that:

> The 'political process' approach succeeded in shifting attention towards interactions between new and traditional actors, and between less conventional forms of action and institutionalized systems of interest representation. In this way, it is no longer possible to define movements in a prejudicial sense as phenomena which are, of necessity, marginal and anti-institutional, expressions of disfunctions of the system.

Tarrow views social movements as part of the 'normal' functioning of the political system and yet stresses the context-specific nature of social movements. In both these respects, therefore, Tarrow also echoes the ideas of Blumer and the *Collective Behaviour* approach.

According to Tarrow, the most important context is the 'political opportunity structure' in which a movement exists. His central argument is that individuals join social movements in response to political opportunities that have arisen and then, through the process of collective action, they go on to create further political opportunities.

In perceiving social movements as being firmly linked with the polity in this way, Tarrow (1994: 24) is arguing that as far as the outcomes of the actions of social movements are concerned, although movements nearly always perceive themselves as being external to the key institutions, nevertheless collective action: '*inserts them into complex policy networks, and, thus, within the reach of the state*'.

The second central concept in Tarrow's theorizing is the notion of 'contention by convention'. According to Tarrow, the theory of collective action/behaviour had become somewhat preoccupied with the problem of how individual actors become mobilized to achieve group goals. For Tarrow, this traditional focus is misplaced, for there is nothing particularly problematic about collective action *per se*. Instead, the problem needing analysis is the manner in which collective action is sustained:

> Movements do have a collective action problem, but it is social: coordinating unorganized, autonomous and dispersed populations into common and sustained action.   (Tarrow, 1994: 9)

Social movements, he argues, partly solve this problem by responding to political opportunities using established forms of collective action: *contention by convention*. In this respect, Tarrow (1994: 19) draws upon the work of Tilly:

> Tilly observes that people cannot employ routines of collective action of which they are ignorant; each society has a stock of familiar forms of action that are known by both potential challengers and their opponents – and which become habitual aspects of their interaction.

According to Tarrow, however, although social movements do draw upon these established forms of collective action, the question of how this action is co-ordinated and sustained remains. For Tarrow, *mobilizing structures* are necessary for activating and sustaining collective action. Existing institutions often represent these mobilizing structures. Tarrow cites the work of Aldon Morris (1993), in which Morris demonstrated that the origins of the Civil Rights Movement in America are interwoven with the role of the Black Churches. Tarrow also makes links with the work of Melucci, who highlights the role of movement networks in creating the collective identity of movements in Italy. Tarrow's work, therefore, represents an important link between the American and European traditions.

'New' social movements: the changing face of the European tradition

Although much literature on 'new' social movements exists, there are three major proponents of this approach to social movement theorizing: Touraine, Habermas, and Melucci. In many respects the theories of Habermas and Touraine are very similar. They remain, however, quite independently influential. Melucci's work draws heavily upon the work of both Touraine and Habermas, although he is more critical of Touraine. For the purpose of comparison, therefore, these theorists will be considered in the order, Habermas, Touraine, Melucci.

Habermas: social movements at the seam between the 'lifeworld' and the 'system'

Definitions of 'new' social movements see these movements acting within a broadly defined socio-cultural sphere (Pakulski, 1997). 'New' social movements in comparison with older movements are viewed as being concerned with redefining culture and lifestyle rather than structural reforms (Martell, 1994). In defining social movements thus, 'new' social movement theorists clearly echo the work of Habermas (1981: 33) when he says that:

> (...) the new conflicts are not sparked by problems of distribution, but concern the grammar of forms of life.

For Habermas there is a paradox at the centre of modernity and this paradox concerns the nature of the relationship between what he terms the 'lifeworld' and the 'system'. Habermas' conclusion to *The Theory of Communicative Action* (1987) is bleak, for he sees the 'lifeworld' as being threatened by the 'system', with reasoning that is only appropriate to the formally organized domains of action taking over those functions of social life that should belong to communicative action. This is what Habermas means by the 'colonization of the lifeworld' and it is this understanding that makes him question the notion that modernity has made society more just.

This is not to say, however, that Habermas has given up entirely on the notion of modernity as a 'good thing'. In fact, Habermas sees the role of the 'new' social movements as being an essential mechanism for preventing and working against the encroachment of the 'lifeworld' by the 'system'. Whilst the 'colonization of the lifeworld' makes workers into *consumers* and citizens into *clients*, thereby minimizing the opportunities for overcoming modernity's injustices, the 'new' social movements seek to break and restructure these redefinitions (Habermas, 1981, McAfee, 2000). Further, Habermas (1981: 36) sees the 'new' social movements as being motivated by the unease members experience as a result of the *'culturally impoverished and unilaterally rationalized praxis of everyday life'*. Resistance, he claims, takes the form of placing a high value on the 'particular' and is intended to encourage the *'revitalization of buried possibilities for expression and communication'*. (Habermas, 1981: 36)

Habermas (1981: 36) is, therefore, painting a picture of the 'new' social movements as existing at the *'seam between system and lifeworld'* and his call is for nothing less than the re-kindling of the promise of democracy and in so doing to ensure that the 'system' be made less autonomous and more accountable to the 'lifeworld'. In this respect, Habermas' work can be seen to provide an important precursor of theories of 'engagement', such as that proposed by Ellison (2000), which seek to forge a link between sociological understandings of social movements and sociological understandings of citizenship. According to Delanty (2000), it is precisely this view of social movements, as existing within the 'meso-level' of society, between the micro- and the macro-levels, that is key to understanding contemporary citizenship and democratic transformation. Roche (1995: 88) echoes this when he says that:

> (...) the new sociology of citizenship could be said to have much in common with the sociology of citizenship movements.

Roche's use of the term 'citizenship movements' is interesting because it suggests that he also perceives that the essential characteristic of contemporary social movements is that 'citizenship' is their project – it is what they are truly *about*. This link between citizenship and social movement theorizing is considered in more depth within Chapter 6 of this book.

Clearly, therefore, Habermas' theories have been influential. It must be noted, however, that whereas many 'new' social movement theorists continue to draw heavily upon Habermas' early work, in which the role of such movements is seen as being to prevent the colonization of the lifeworld by the system, Habermas himself has moved somewhat away from his earlier theorizing. In comparison to the ideas set out in his work *The Theory of Communicative Action* (1987), Habermas (1996) has more recently viewed the role of social movements rather differently and he now considers law to be central to radical politics and views social movements as embracing the state domain to a degree, whilst maintaining a firm link to civil society. In other words, Habermas considers it possible for social movements to exist at both the macro- and the meso-level. In some respects, however, it is the argument here that this is not too great a departure from his earlier theorizing, it merely demonstrates the difficulties associated with attempting to answer the questions of 'why', 'how' and 'when/where' of social movements.

Touraine

As previously stated, there are many similarities between Habermas' and Touraine's approach to social movement theorizing. One of the key similarities is that Touraine also considers 'new' social movements to be the result of the general crisis of modernity. Two major problems face modernity, he claims; the first involves issues of social order and the second is concerned with issues of instrumental action. Touraine raises the question of how social order is possible within societies that are entirely defined by their capacity to *change*. Capitalism, for example, is characterized by its capacity to destroy old forms of production in order to make way for newer forms. For Touraine, the result of this process is a society that is characterized by anomie, uprootedness and a tendency to subordinate all aspects of individual and collective life to economic interest. According to Touraine, anything that cannot be expressed in monetary terms is destroyed by this process of modernity.

Touraine also states that the so-called triumph of instrumental action has failed to lead to a balance between individual interests. Modernity has been characterized by the subordination of the individual to the impersonal laws of rationality, which has in turn, increased the power of the elites. This power, according to Touraine (1987a: 208) *'in a highly mobilized or modern society'* is *'everywhere...'*. Here the echoes of Foucault's (1979) work on power are clear, for Touraine's theorizing is very similar to Foucault's notion of the diffusion of power through systems of normalization, cultural and social control.

According to Touraine, this 'crisis of modernity' has inspired two particular types of social movement. The first are the neo-communitarian movements, which seek to defend cultural identity. The second are the anti-modernist movements, which seek to resist mass production and to defend personal aesthetic or moral experience. The key point, however, according to Touraine, is that neither type of movement calls for the triumph of particularist over universalist values, or vice versa. Instead, the focus of the 'new' social movements is on the production or defence of the *subject*, be it the individual or collective:

> We do not defend minorities' rights because they fulfil a specific function or try to increase the level of social integration; we defend directly the right of a given group to assert its own identity, while fifty years ago we would have been more universalistic, more integrationist, fighting against obstacles to the assimilation of minorities (...)   (Touraine, 1987a: 211)

Further, in his work entitled *An Introduction to the Study of Social Movements* (1985), Touraine makes it clear that he considers social movements to be only one form of social conflict, but that they are defined precisely by their preoccupation with making claims for the recognition of the other as *subject*. For Touraine (1985: 760), therefore, *'the concept "social movements" only refer(s) to conflicts around the social control of the main cultural patterns'*.

Having established what he regards these new forms of conflict to be *about*, Touraine then goes on to develop a somewhat complex schema for both defining 'new' social movements in a given situation and, to a certain extent, explaining *how* they function. For Touraine (1985), social movements are defined by the relationship between conflicting actors and the stakes of their conflict. Thus the action of social movements can be seen to involve three components: firstly, the identity of the actor (*i*), secondly, the definition of the opponent (*o*), and thirdly, the stakes or cultural totality which define the field of conflict (*t*) (Touraine, 1985. See also Prioetto, 1995). A social movement is thus defined as the relationship *i-o-t*. This represents a quite complex vision of social action since it depends upon sustaining relations of creative tension between all of the three fundamental components (Prioetto, 1995).

All three of these factors – *i-o-t* – are bound together in the same social world and express the central conflict of a particular type of society. It is in this respect that Touraine's theorizing on social movements is most ambitious, for he places his theorizing on social conflict right at the heart of his general social theory. Using the concept of *historicity*, which is defined as the interweaving of a system of knowledge, a type of accumulation and a cultural model (Della Porta and Diani, 1999), Touraine identifies four types of society: agrarian, mercantile, industrial and 'programmed'. Touraine prefers the concept 'programmed' society to the term 'post-industrial society', but in many respects, the two terms mean the same thing. For Touraine (1987b: 127), a 'programmed' society is characterized by the *'production of symbolic goods which model or transform our representation of human nature and the external world'*. The basis for power in such a society therefore, becomes the control of information and these cultural resources and, echoing Habermas' notion of the colonization of the lifeworld and the system, Touraine then argues that:

> Mobilizations by social movements address (...) the defence of the autonomy of civil society from the attempts of public and private technocratic groups to extend their control over ever-widening areas of social life.   (Della Porta and Diani, 1999: 46)

Touraine's theorizing has thus been concerned with social movements as being not just the result of, but also key to, the transformations in modernity. Whilst his theories have been highly influential they have not, however, gone un-criticized.

Melucci

Melucci, whilst drawing considerably upon Touraine's work, also provides a clearly articulated critique of Touraine's notion of 'conflict' and 'identity'. For Melucci (1996), Touraine failed adequately to distance his theorizing from earlier definitions that portrayed social conflict in an overly deterministic manner. The problem for Melucci (1996: 45) is how to *'explain conflict in terms of social relations without turning it into a primal dimension'*. Melucci also criticizes Touraine for failing adequately to deconstruct the notion of identity. For Touraine, identity is taken as a given, whereas Melucci views identity rather differently, preferring the term 'potential for individualization'. He views this 'potential for individualization' as a process upon which action is entirely dependent. This critique of Touraine is central to the development of Melucci's own theorizing in his field, for he begins by reconsidering the basis of social conflict and then goes on to establish *how* collective action occurs.

Melucci (1985, 1989, 1994) begins his theorizing by drawing upon the work of Habermas and the notion of the colonization of the lifeworld, claiming that the role of the 'new' social movements is to oppose the excessive intrusion of the state and the market into the realm of the individual and to protect each individual's identity from the manipulation and control of the system. In other words, for Melucci, the 'new' social movements are about reacting against the colonization of the lifeworld by the system. Indeed, Melucci (1989: 38) has commented that: *'among my criteria for defining a social movement is the extent to which its actions challenge or break the limits of a system of social relations'*.

For Melucci, the idea of the 'colonization of the lifeworld' is intrinsically linked to the notion of 'complex societies'. In this respect he echoes the work of Foucault (1970, 1979, 1980a, 1980b), for both authors perceive complex societies as being characterized by a homologizing of behaviour patterns, brought about by the manipulation of the information and cultural codes which form the basis of communication and consensus. For Melucci the present is characterized by society's capacity for intervening in the production of meaning. Areas that have previously escaped control and regulation are no longer free from interference by the system. Melucci (1989: 45) suggests that these areas may include '*self-definition, emotional relationships, sexuality and "biological" needs*'. At the same time, however, Melucci states that there is a parallel demand from the lifeworld for some control to be measured over the conditions of personal existence.

In firmly linking notions of the lifeworld and the system to theorizing on social movements, both Habermas and Melucci are placing considerations of social movements at the heart of social theorizing, for their theories have clear implications for the agency/structure debate. In the work of Melucci, this is most clearly demonstrated by his theorizing on the notion of 'identity'. As previously stated, Melucci suggests that the concept of 'identity' is increasingly redundant and that a consideration of the 'potential for individualization' is of greater value. He defines this 'potential for individualization' as involving on the one hand the possibilities for an individual to have control over the conditions of his/her action, and on the other hand the expropriation of these '*self-reflexive and self-productive resources by society itself*'. (Melucci, 1989: 48) For Melucci, social movements are *about* challenging the powers that seek to control these social resources.

In seeking to redress this balance between the lifeworld and the system, agency and structure, social movements, Melucci (1985: 810) claims, are therefore striking at the very heart of society's accepted 'truths':

> (...) movements question society on something 'else': who decides on codes, who establishes rules of normality, what is the space for difference, how can one be recognized not for being included but for being accepted as different, not for increasing the amount of exchanges but for affirming another kind of exchange?

It is the argument here, however, that what is sometimes less clear within Melucci's work, and indeed the work of many of the 'new' social movement theorists, is the extent to which he acknowledges that the redistribution of material resources may still be a *central* aim for many social movements. In a later work, Melucci (1989: 56) does not appear to be rejecting completely the idea that social movements are still about addressing structural inequalities, but he does make it clear that he sees this as only *one aspect* of the aims of social movements, for they are about: '*(...) more than (...) the demand for equality*'.

Having established what social movements are *about*, however, Melucci is more concerned with 'how/where' collective action occurs. He claims that a form of 'political reductionism' has characterized the views of researchers in this field and he cites the work of Tilly and Tarrow as examples of this. According to Melucci, Tilly and Tarrow's quantitative studies of social movements have considered collective events as discrete units of analysis. This research, according to Melucci, has produced some useful data concerning the *product* of diverse relationships and the goals of action. This he claims, however, is a *constructivist* view of social movements, focusing as it does upon the outcomes of collective action. For Melucci (1989: 45), this emphasis upon the effects of action can become unhelpful if it ignores the '*creation of cultural models and symbolic challenges inherent in the "new movements"*'.

In seeking to explain the 'how/where' of collective action, Melucci considers social movements to be positioned outside the established boundaries of political systems, in what he terms 'social spaces' (1989, 1993, 1996). These social spaces exist as a result of forms of behaviour that do not 'fit in' with the system, for example, conflict, deviance and 'cultural experimentation' (Melucci, 1989). According to Melucci (1993), on the one hand these social spaces prevent social movements from becoming institutionalized and on the other, they ensure that society is able institutionally to process the issues and conflicts arising from the goals and meanings of the social action undertaken by social movements.

Although focusing upon the this aspect of social movements, nevertheless in viewing the area in which social movements operate as a new and valuable '*"sector" or "subsystem" of the social*', Melucci (1996: 3) stresses the important role/effect of social movements in preventing the system from closing in upon itself. Similarly, in an earlier work Melucci (1985) stresses the transformative nature/purpose of 'new' social movements, for he sees them as forcing the ruling groups to innovate and to include in the decision-making process groups that have previously been excluded.

Melucci (1993: 190) also makes an interesting link with notions of power, when he states that social movements: *'expose the shadowy zones of invisible power and silence which a system and its dominant interests inevitably tend to create'*. This is an idea that has been developed further by a number of authors, a key example being in the work of Foweraker (1995) who, in addition, makes an important link to citizenship theorizing in that he envisages social movement activity as being *about* citizenship, which in turn is *about* challenging these systems of power in defence of group rights. The issue of the connection between citizenship theorizing and social movement theorizing will be considered in more depth within Chapter 6.

Conclusion: the future for social movement theorizing?

From this discussion, it would seem that whilst there are many differences between the various approaches to theorizing social movements, there are also continuities. Two major questions, however, remain and it is the argument here that these represent the fundamental issues yet to be resolved within social movement theorizing. Firstly, it would appear that it is now time to re-look at the social movements of the 1960s and ask again, what was so fundamentally different about these movements in comparison to those that came before? One of the most apparent 'differences' between many of the social movements that existed pre-1960s and those that came after the '1960s watershed' is the fact that from the 1960s onwards social movement activity has been seen to be more 'successful'. Whilst early movements, for example the Chartists and the Jarrow Hunger marches, were perhaps largely unsuccessful, there is now a sense that movements such as the Feminist Movement, the Black Power Movement and 'single issue' movements such as the Greenham Common protests, have really 'changed the world'. The important question, therefore, is whether social movements themselves have changed or whether the protest environment in which they take place has altered, thereby affecting the ability of protest to bring about change?

From the literature it is clear that theories that emphasize the 'newness' of the 'new' social movements rest upon notions of the crisis of modernity and the dawn of post-modernity. These are contested concepts, however, and care should be employed when using them as the basis for theorizing. Without a doubt, during the past 40 years society has undergone radical transformation, but there appears to be little consensus surrounding the key aspects of this change. Whilst

Melucci (1996) is clearly one of the theorists responsible for introduc-
ing the concept of the *'new' social movements* into sociological debate,
he is, however, concerned about the arid debate that he considers has
ensued between supporters and critics of 'newness'. For this reason he
is anxious that in debating the validity of the term 'new' social movement, theorists in this field do not lose track of the fact that contemporary social movements are signalling that radical transformations are
occurring to the reality in which we live. The challenge then for theorists in this field is to rise above this sterile debate about 'old' and 'new'
social movements and to consider them afresh in the context in which
they now exist. Establishing a convincing method for examining social
movements in this way, is essential.

One way forward, it is proposed here, may be to forge stronger links
between citizenship and social movement theorizing. This may prove
to be effective because understanding the way in which citizenship has
changed over time is key to understanding the social and political
environment in which social movements act. Understanding the
nature of contested citizenship is also likely to be key to understanding
social movements. For example, if 'cultural citizenship' is the basis of
social movement activity, then the second phase European theories of
social movements, with their focus upon such things as values, culture
and identity, may well provide the key to understanding conflict
today. Touraine (1985) is clear that citizenship as 'identity' has become
central to social movements but is equally certain that without the full
recognition of the other as subject, calls for the acceptance of difference, specificity and identity can lead to ghettoization and intolerance.
Further, he fears that whilst this now 'anxious' search for identity may
result in new definitions of social 'norms', there is also a risk of an individualism that excludes successful collective action.

If, however, there is evidence to suggest that more structural inequalities may also be a central part of this process of engagement, then it
may be necessary to return to some of the older explanations for social
movements. The possibility that this may be the case raises a further
challenge for any future theorizing on social movements, for if we can
no longer completely disregard the earlier 'First Phase Theories' as
explanations for *why* social movements exist and what they are *about*,
perhaps we need not see these two phases of theorizing as incommens-
urable in other respects.

Cohen (1985) may have offered a starting point for tackling this
challenge when she proposed a more critical consideration of the relationship between collective action and identity as the basis for future

theorizing on social movements. Thus, in her model, social movements are viewed as having a fragile composition, often being fragmented and composed of individuals with diverse opinions and interests:

> (...) the striking feature of the contemporary (...) situation of movements is heterogeneity. The old patterns of collective action certainly continue to exist. In some movements, they may even be statistically preponderant. It would thus be futile to speak of the new identity of the movements. Since all movements are complex phenomena, however, heterogeneity itself cannot be the unique aspect of contemporary contestations. Instead, it is the thesis here that some identities, implying specific forms of organization and struggle within the contemporary movements, are new (...), and that there are good reasons to consider these to be of major significance. (Cohen, 1985: 665)

Cohen thus acknowledges the continuing importance of older forms of 'struggle' whilst acknowledging, to an extent, the validity of the claims of the 'new' social movement theorists that 'new' forms of 'struggle' are also taking place. Acknowledging diversity of *aim* and *action* within one movement in this way may well be the starting point for a more convincing theory of contemporary social movements.

The idea that social movements may possess diversity of aim and action according to the social and political environment in which they exist is an idea that also forms the basis of Ellison's (2000) work on 'defensive and pro-active engagement'. In many respects his ideas echo Cohen's, but he has advanced further in theorizing the link between these processes of engagement and citizenship theorizing. His work is therefore, of central importance to the argument within this book and as previously mentioned in Chapter 2, will be considered in more depth within Chapter 6.

4

Issues in Disability

Introduction: a brief history of theorizing on disability

Prior to the 1970s, to have an impairment was regarded as a 'personal tragedy' and this thinking existed not only within the wider public sphere but was also a major influence upon service providers and policy-makers. As Barnes *et al* (1999: 10) have commented, these prejudices and stereotypes had profound and unfortunate effects upon the lives of disabled people:

> It seemed to dictate a life as a passive 'victim' characterized by social exclusion and disadvantage, and by dependency on assistance from family and friends and a 'safety net' of state welfare benefits and services.

Curiously however, despite social science's history of exposing social inequalities, the position of disabled people in society had generated little research and had prompted almost no theoretical interest. Further, during the 1970s, strong objections began to emerge against the small amount of research and theorizing that had taken place during the 1960s, most notably in the work of Parsons on the sick-role and Goffman on stigma.

Parsons and Goffman

For Parsons (1951), for a society to function properly all of its members must play their appropriate roles. Health is viewed as the 'normal' state and is linked to optimum capacity. In contrast, illness is regarded as being akin to a form of social deviance since it is a disruptive and 'abnormal' state. Since illness along with deviance of all types is viewed as a threat to the smooth functioning of the system, it must be managed and controlled. The first part of this management of illness, Parson's termed the 'sick role' which he perceived to be a form of sanctioned social deviance, controlled and managed by the medical profession. For Parsons, power imbalances between doctor and patient are necessary to serve the interests of society and such relationships are entirely benign.

As previously stated, however, Parsons' work and his notion of the sick-role have been heavily criticized. Firstly, it has been argued that the sick-role is an 'ideal type' that, whilst being of some benefit when seeking to understand acute illness, does not relate as successfully to the experience of long-term or permanent impairments/conditions. Secondly, this sick-role theorizing has been criticized for failing to take a more critical stance towards the role of doctors and other therapeutic professionals. The sick-role model tends to assume that the role of these health care professionals is to seek to 'normalize' the disabling consequences of a particular illness in a manner that clearly reflects the psychological notion of 'adaptation'. As Albrecht (1992: 74) has commented, this *idealised process seems too facile*. Many disabled people have rejected this perceived role of the health care professional, claiming that it has led to them being treated as objects and manipulated against their wishes into abnormal lifestyles. Further, Oliver (1996) has proposed that such thinking is the result of the 'psychological imagination' and rests upon assumptions made by non-disabled people about what it is like to have an impairment.

This notion of illness as a form of social deviance is also to be found in the work of Goffman, although he elaborated the idea rather differently. In *Stigma: notes on the management of spoiled identities*, Goffman (1968) broadly defined the term as 'abominations of the body' and went on to list as examples such things as physical deformities, differences according to 'race' or religion and faults of character. In each case, the notion of the 'normal human being' becomes a normative system for grading those who are perceived to have a 'stigma' and for categorizing them as being 'not quite human'. Goffman then went on to consider how people seek to manage their 'spoiled identities', for example how people with an acquired disability manage their re-identification, or how those with a more visible 'stigma', *the discredited*, differ from those with a less visible 'stigma', *the discreditable*.

The current consensus within Disability Studies appears to be that in moving theory on from Parsons in this way, Goffman's work must be considered of considerable value. Equally, however, it is clear that

Goffman's work has left Disability Studies with a number of important questions which are yet to be resolved adequately, such as: 'To what extent can disabled people resist the process of becoming stigmatized?', 'To what extent can individuals create their own identities?' and 'When both intellectual and physical differences are equally visible, why do such differences possess such contrasting meanings?' (Barnes *et al*, 1999)

Critics of Goffman, however, have highlighted the following: on the one hand Scambler and Hopkins (1986) have proposed that there is evidence to suggest that the 'felt' stigma or anxiety of disabled people may, sometimes, be greater than the actual discrimination experienced. On the other hand, Gussow and Tracy (1968) and Ablon (1981) have argued that theories that focus upon such things as anxiety may be providing an inaccurate 'doom and gloom' account of stigmatized identities. Indeed, Booth and Booth (1994) provide evidence to suggest that negative labels and being treated as 'sub-human' can sometimes be rebuffed. In the light of such complexity, Goffman's account must be viewed cautiously.

Medical Sociology versus Disability Studies

After Parsons and Goffman, two fresh approaches to the sociological understanding of illness/disability emerged partly, at times, as a result of further development of their ideas, but also resulting from criticisms of their work as previously stated. The first approach is that of Medical Sociology. This approach has sought to develop an interpretative account of illness that moves away from definitions of impairment that have been established by the medical professionals, and focuses instead upon exploring the symbolic and material interactions between disabled people and wider society. Research in this area began by considering such things as the interactional difficulties experienced by people with chronic illness (Strauss and Glaser, 1975). The focus of Medical Sociology then moved to a consideration of matters such as the range of financial, medical-care based and employment barriers facing people with chronic illness. From such research emerged the notion of the 'handicapping' environment.

More recently, the emphasis in Medical Sociology has been upon the active way in which disabled or chronically ill individuals adapt and make use of various coping strategies in order to gain control over their lives. Key to this research have been the terms *coping* and *competence*. Medical Sociology has highlighted the manner in which disabled people strive to retain a sense of their own competence. Such research has also been concerned with the ways in which both lay and professional attitudes towards disabled people can radically constrain disabled people's abilities to make use of a number of central coping strategies.

For Jenkins (1998), a contextualized understanding of personhood is central to understanding the notion of competency since the competence of an individual is always, to some extent, determined by his/her performance with regard to an arbitrary and culturally determined selection of aptitudes. This is not to say, however, that Jenkins is denying the reality that (in)competence can, and does, reside at least in part in the physiology of embodied persons. Indeed, one of the strong points of Jenkins' approach is that he does not ignore such things as the effects of impairments. He does, however, stress that we need a *social* framework in which to understand these issues.

Writing from a Bioethics perspective, Silver (2002) has made a useful link between theorizing such as Jenkins' on competence and how understandings gained through such analyses can be used to further the rights of individuals in relation to autonomy. For Silver, competency rests upon the notion of autonomy. Thus, to be competent one must be autonomous. A problem then arises, for traditional approaches to autonomy tend to focus upon its instrumental rather than intrinsic properties. According to Silver, medical professionals have tended to focus upon the instrumental properties of autonomy alone, thus avoiding the potential moral problems that can emerge when a person's intrinsic autonomy clashes with what the medical professional considers to be their 'best interests'. Silver (2002: 462) proposes that instead of focusing on the instrumental properties of autonomy in this way '(...) *the standard of competency we ought to employ is as follows: is the person making her own decisions, is she shaping, however well or badly, her own life. If she is, she is competent, because she can be autonomous'*.

In other words, Silver states, we need to reject the notion of 'relative competence'. This notion of 'relative competence' is clearly akin to Jenkins' notion of the arbitrary and culturally determined nature of competence. Silver (2002: 464) takes this critique of relative competence one step forward, however, by commenting that:

> I would argue that no amount of these relative incompetencies should amount to rendering a person incompetent in the sense that we are discussing: incompetent to make decisions that normally everyone has a right to make. That sort of competency should not depend on your ability to make a decision well, but on your ability to make it at all.

What is new and thought provoking about Silver's approach therefore, is the way in which he links the issue of competency with autonomy and ultimately with human rights discourses.

Currently, however, some new and even more contentious strands of theorizing are emerging from within Medical Sociology. The phenomenological approach, as has been usefully described by Hughes and Paterson (1997), is viewed by many within the field of disability as striking at the very heart of the Social Model of Disability – the model which dominates Disability Studies. This phenomenological approach to disability reflects a wider trend within Sociology over the past ten years that has seen the 'body' rediscovered and 'bodiliness' positioned, increasingly, centre-stage. The phenomenological approach to disability considers there to be an important link between this 'sociology of the body' and theorizing on disability, and calls for an 'embodied' notion of disability. Drawing upon the work of both Bryan Turner (1984, 1992, 2000) and Terence Turner (1994), this approach proposes that the Cartesian compartmentalism that had led to the separation of impairment and disability, be abandoned in favour of a *'realignment between body, self and society'* (Bendelow and Williams, 1995: 156).

In this respect, this trend in Medical Sociology was somewhat overdue, for, some 30 years previously, Merleu-Ponty (1962) commented that social action is not only intersubjective, but also intercorporeal. Further, within the field of disability itself, writers such as Jenny Morris (1991) had complained that the Social Model of Disability denies the existence of pain and affliction, experiences that are truly 'embodied'. Nevertheless, this phenomenological approach to disability remains as yet little more than an important strand within Medical Sociology, and is strongly opposed by many within Disability Studies.[1] The basis for the opposition to this approach is, in many respects, understandable, for as will be discussed in the following section, many disabled people consider references to 'bodiliness' to be inextricably linked to the idea of 'suffering', which is, in turn, linked to the personal tragedy model of disability. This model has been widely accepted as being disempowering and victim blaming.[2] The challenge for theorists who favour the phenomenological approach to disability is, therefore, to overcome such fears and to persuade people that:

> A phenomenological approach to suffering in which the reversibility of impairment and disability made it possible to think of suffering as a concept which reflected the mutual engagement of pain and oppression may be a way of reflecting the fact that disabled

people do suffer. However, at the same time, by foregrounding the concept of oppression, suffering is removed from its connotative association with a charitable response to tragedy. To recast suffering as a dialectical concept on the threshold between pain and oppression not only politicises the medical, but exposes the disablist basis of the charitable response.   (Hughes and Paterson, 1997: 336)

It will be interesting to see whether such an important new development will bring about the end of the historical division between Medical Sociology and Disability Studies. Certainly, there is already evidence that several writers from Disability Studies are now breaking away from key orthodoxies of the field and some interesting connections between their work and the phenomenological approach to disability will be discussed later in this chapter. The major issue that continues to divide Medical Sociology from Disability Studies is, however, the extent to which each approach acknowledges that the material world also disadvantages disabled people. Whilst many medical sociologists consider Disability Studies to have provided an over-socialized image of disability that does not move beyond 'outdated' Marxist accounts (Bury, 1997), writers within Disability Studies have criticized Medical Sociology for failing to engage with the material world and the manner in which material difficulties disadvantage many disabled people.

For Disability Studies, the central focus of research in this field must be upon the barriers and constraints placed upon the lives of disabled people by a 'disabling' society. The central inspiration of this approach has been the 'Social Model of Disability', the origins of which lie firmly within the campaigns by disabled people against discrimination and material disadvantages during the late 1960s and into the 1970s. Probably the first step was taken by Hunt *et al* (1966) who highlighted the way in which powerful groups within society categorize disabled people as 'abnormal' and in so doing perpetuate the notion of disability as both a personal tragedy and as something to be greatly 'feared'. Further, Hunt's edited collection exposed the ways in which disabled people are perceived as being economically useless. Hunt himself then went on to become a key figure within the wider disability movement, since he was central to the formation of the Union of the Physically Impaired Against Segregation UPIAS, an organization that was run *by* and *for* disabled people and which maintained a very critical stance towards those organizations that were run *for* disabled people.

In 1976, UPIAS published *Fundamental Principles of Disability* in which the organization made it clear that it is 'society' (*sic*) that disables people with impairments. Whilst it would not be true to say that this publication denies the reality of impairment, nevertheless, the focus is upon the manner in which 'society' increases the dependency of disabled people and prevents them from participating equally within the economic and social sphere. This notion of disability as a form of social oppression then became the dominant theme within Disability Studies and is clearly the precursor of the later more materialist accounts of disability provided by Abberley, Finkelstein and Oliver, amongst others.

For Abberley (1993), work on disability can be compared usefully to research undertaken on the subjects of sexism and racism. This focus upon the notion of social oppression led Abberley to conclude that it is social relations that create the material disadvantages that, in addition to impairment, generate disability. What is, arguably, less well developed in Abberley's work is a picture of *who* is supposed to be benefiting from the oppression of disabled people. He appears to be edging towards a Marxist account of disability, referring as he does to 'capitalism' as being the victor when it comes to the social oppression of disabled people, but he takes this little further.

Finkelstein, on the other hand, provides a much more developed materialist account of disability. For Finkelstein (1980), disability can be viewed as a social problem that is directly linked to changes in the mode of production. His theory rests upon the idea that changes in technology are key to understanding changing attitudes towards disability. Thus, it was only with the advent of industrial capitalism that disabled people became excluded from the workplace. New technology meant that disabled people could not 'keep up' and this became the basis for segregation.

This idea is clearly echoed in the work of Oliver (1990), although he is considered to have advanced the concept somewhat to produce the most highly developed materialist account of disability. For Oliver:

> (...) definitions of disability, as of other perceived social problems, are related both to economic and social structures and to the central values of particular modes of production. He explains the emergence of the individualistic and medicalised approach to disability in terms of the functional needs of capital, especially the need for a workforce that is physically and intellectually able to conform to the demands of industrialization. But it is not simply the mode of

production which precipitated the development of personal tragedy theories of disability, but also the 'mode of thought' and the relationship between the two.   (Barnes *et al*, 1999: 84)

By this, Oliver is suggesting that it was not simply the mode of production that altered during the process of industrialization, but also that there was an important shift in ideology. He proposes that the first ideological shift – towards individualism – was brought about by the growth of the free market economy and the spread of wage labour. The second ideological shift he considers to be the medicalization of the mechanisms of social control, which led to the development of the concept of 'able-bodiedness' – a standard against which 'normality' can be judged.

The strength of this Social Model of Disability has been, therefore, to give *'disabled people the confidence to campaign for rights in a way that was uncompromisingly based on social oppression'*. (Campbell, 2002: 473) Further, in maintaining a clear focus upon the manner in which disability is socially produced, this model has moved away from biomedical models and towards an understanding of disability in terms of current debates on citizenship/social exclusion. So powerful has been the perceived emancipatory capacity of this model, however, that criticizing the approach is something that has been viewed as being highly contentious.

Nevertheless, there are some important criticisms of the Social Model that do need to be addressed. Oliver's account, for example, has been criticized for failing to consider adequately the very different experiences of disabled people and for ignoring the role of impairment in the disabling process. Pinder (1997) highlights what is the central problem in this field, namely that the Social Model of Disability is not just an academic model, but has been the central feature of disability politics since the 1970s. For Pinder (1997: 304) the central tension is *'between the search for clear-cut, univocal messages crucial for the success of any political movement, and the necessarily more complex and subtle reality of peoples' lived experience'*.

Shakespeare and Watson (1997) admit that there has been a great reluctance on the part of key writers in Disability Studies to address the issues of impairment, for example, because it is seen to weaken the Social Model. They state that: *'Debates are necessary, and recognising difference within the disabled community is overdue'*. (Shakespeare and Watson, 1997: 299) Furthermore, they comment that the tendency within the disability movement to silence dissent in favour of *'marching to the beat of a single drum'* (Shakespeare and Watson, 1997: 299) should be resisted.

Of course, the earliest critiques of mainstream Disability Studies arose during the early 1990s when Feminist writers such as Jenny Morris (1991) highlighted the fact that accounts of disability tended to be male dominated and constructed. Morris, along with a number of others, has written convincingly about the 'double disadvantage' faced by disabled women that results in them being placed in a worse position, economically, socially and psychologically, than either disabled men, or non-disabled women. This critique was later extended in relation to Disability Studies' failure to adequately theorize the position of Black disabled people and other minority groups such as gay and lesbian disabled people.

Such issues have become the 'hot topics' in Disability Studies and have been key to current debates within the field surrounding the issue of impairment and the body. Such debates are also taking place within Medical Sociology, as previously discussed. The work of authors such as Begum (1992) and Haraway (1991) have been particularly influential. Begum's notion of the 'dominant body ideal' and how this leads to the construction of defective bodies, and Haraway's (1991: 10) related idea that *'(n)either our personal bodies nor our social bodies may be seen as natural.'*, have greatly supported the argument made by feminist writers on disability that the experience of impairment must be included in any analysis of disability. There is, therefore, a growing awareness within Disability Studies that the 'traditional' Social Model provides a picture of the body as having no history, and of impairment as being entirely opposite to disability because it is not socially constructed. As Hughes and Paterson (1997: 329) have commented, this dominant model must be questioned for it:

> (...) also posits a body devoid of meaning, a dysfunctional, anatomical, corporeal man obdurate in its resistance to signification and phenomenologically dead, without intentionality or agency.

There are, therefore, two key challenges facing Disability Studies today, the first being the need to theorize the 'body' adequately from a disability perspective. The second challenge is overcoming the resistance to such theoretical developments by key figures within the field. Both Oliver (1995, 1996) and Finkelstein (1996) have argued forcefully against the idea that understanding the 'body' is key to understanding *disability*. For them, considering the body and impairment 'fudges' the critical issue of causality and the source of disability. That is not to say however, that either theorist entirely ignores the issue of impairment.

Oliver (1996), for example, calls for a Social Model of impairment to stand alongside the Social Model of disability. His argument is that whilst non-interchangeable, these two models might together produce a social *theory* of disability. Ultimately, however, whilst his argument may seem appealing, it is proposed here that it perpetuates the distinction between impairment and disability.

In addition to Oliver and Finkelstein's theoretical opposition to placing the 'body' at the heart of theorizing on disability, other writers have claimed that such an approach reduces the opportunity for political and cultural praxis by disabled people. Barnes (1999: 580) has commented that the new trend in theorizing, which he believes arises from the liberal arts and cultural studies, *'seems to be written by a particular sort of academic luvvie who write mainly for themselves and other academics rather than for a wider audience: consequently, it is replete with obscure and esoteric jargon, virtually inaccessible to all but the most dedicated of readers and, most importantly, politically benign and pragmatically irrelevant'*.

In the light of such resistance to the idea of an embodied notion of disability from within Disability Studies it is unclear, therefore, whether significant advancements in this theorizing will occur from within this field, or whether such ideas will find more fertile ground within Medical Sociology. What is clear, is that in both Medical Sociology and Disability Studies there is a significant and growing minority of authors who are keen to move beyond materialist accounts and to acknowledge the value that contributions by a range of theorists in the fields of semiotics, critical theory, post-structuralism, feminism and phenomenology can make to understandings of disability. Some of these issues will be considered in more depth as they relate to the findings of the research upon which this book is based, in Chapters 6 and 7.

Experiencing disability

Whilst the aim of the first part of this chapter was to provide an overview of the main theories of disability, the aim of this next section is to consider the empirical evidence to support the widely accepted notion that disabled people occupy a position in UK society that is characterized by discrimination and disadvantage. The body of research that has been carried out on the lives of disabled people is large and encompasses most, if not all, areas of experience. Given the extent of this research, it would be impossible within the confines of this chapter, or book, to consider all of these issues adequately. For this reason, two key areas have been chosen, and it is hoped that these will, when considered together, provide the reader with an overview of the current position of disabled people within UK society. These two areas are: equal opportunities: and the 'coming out' of disability.

Before considering the first of these areas, however, it must be stated that care must be taken when using the term 'reality' when describing the lives of disabled people, for there is a risk that in describing a collective reality for all disabled people, the wide variety of experiences of disability are reduced to some sort of common denominator (Corker, 1999). With this risk in mind, an effort has been made to avoid universalizing the experience of disability and wherever is appropriate, to mention differences.

Equal opportunities

The issues relating to equal opportunities for disabled people are wide ranging and the injustices facing disabled people in relation to educational and employment opportunities, income inequalities, access to transport and the built environment, and opportunities for independent living and 'family life' – to name but a few important issues – have been well documented. Within the confines of this book it is not be possible, therefore, to consider each of these issues and for this reason I have chosen to focus on the position of disabled people in relation to the following: educational opportunities; employment and income. These issues have been chosen not least because, as is discussed in greater depth within Chapter 6, a consideration of the position of disabled people in relation to education, income and employment allows us to assess the extent to which disabled people are a part of a meritocratic system – this system being key to one of the most influential models of citizenship, the social-liberal account.

Education

It is widely accepted that historically, children with perceived impairments have been socialized in such a way as to foster low self-expectations of success in education or in work:

> Besides perpetuating the age old myths and ignorance surrounding both impairment and disability, the special school system consistently fails to provide disabled school leavers with the skills and confidence necessary for adulthood in a world increasingly geared towards the needs of a mythical non-disabled majority.   (Barnes, 1997: introduction)

Groups of disabled people calling themselves 'survivors of the special school system' have united to argue forcibly for the complete abolition of the special school system and their calls have not gone entirely unheeded. The current drive towards 'mainstreaming' is precisely because of a growing acceptance by government and educationalists that the special school system disadvantaged/s disabled children.

In terms of evidence to support these claims, it is clear that the educational attainments of young people who have gone through special needs education are indeed considerably less than for the average student in mainstream education. As a consequence, disabled children leave school with fewer qualifications and skills than their non-disabled peers. For example, Thomas (1997) found that just 4 per cent of pupils in special needs schools attain grades A–C at GCSE. These findings have been explained in a number of ways: partly, it is suggested, it is due to the fact that children who have been labelled as having 'Special Educational Needs' (SENs) experience a much narrower curriculum than their non-disabled peers. It is also thought to be because special need schools enter less than a third of pupils for GCSE's. Finally, whilst it might be tempting to argue that lower attainment is due to a lesser ability on the part of pupils, there is also evidence that the low expectations of teachers constrain the performance of disabled children.

Interestingly, despite such evidence, there have been arguments in favour of special needs education. These arguments have come not least from many parents of disabled children and some disabled young people. Deaf people, in particular, and their organizations have consistently argued in favour of schools for the Deaf. They argue that Deaf children require regular contact with their Deaf peer groups and Deaf adults as role models, in order to combat oppression and to develop a strong and positive self-identity. According to such Deaf organizations, forcing Deaf children into mainstream education denies them access to the Deaf community and Deaf culture. Arguing from a different standpoint, many other parents and disabled children have stated that they consider special needs education to be preferable to mainstreaming on the basis that only special schools and the teachers in such establishments have the necessary facilities and training required for educating disabled children. Such groups have also argued that too often only 'lip service' is paid to the integration of disabled children into mainstream schooling, with the result that such children find themselves educationally and socially isolated.

As previously stated, however, 'inclusive education' is now the favoured approach to educating children with special educational needs. The moves towards mainstreaming began as far back as 1978 with the publication of the Warnock Report. This report was a direct response to early criticism that was directed against the special school system and was important in that it argued for special needs provision within mainstream schooling. The 1981 Education Act and subsequent legislation clearly built upon the Warnock Report, but according to many critics, was imperfect in certain key respects. Firstly, pupils with severe learning disabilities remained apart from mainstream schooling; hearing and visually impaired children were largely excluded from the new initiative; and finally, the increased costs involved in providing mainstream schooling for children who had been labelled as having SENs resulted in a tendency on the part of Local Education Authorities (LEAs) to avoid statementing too many children, allowing some children genuinely in need of support to 'slip through the net'. The later 1993 and 1996 Education Acts did seek to address some of these issues and to promote more clearly the idea of an inclusive policy, but doubts have continued surrounding the extent to which all the issues have been resolved.

Some critics have suggested that such problems demonstrated that the government, despite appearances, was not really giving sufficient support to mainstream schooling for disabled people. It is certainly the case that education as an issue was omitted from the Disability Discrimination Act 1995. Critics of the government's actions at that time suggested that whilst it may have been true that key policy-makers shared with many parents of disabled children a concern that mainstream schooling may disadvantage some disabled children, it was also the case that there were concerns surrounding the effects that integration may have upon mainstream schools, particularly in the light of the increased importance of performance indicators and league tables of educational attainment.

Since 1995, however, some major advances have taken place in terms of 'mainstreaming'. In 1998, the Labour Government announced an increase in resources for inclusive education as part of its Action Programme for Special Educational Needs. There are now greatly increased funds available to support inclusive education. In 2001 the government also introduced the Special Educational Needs and Disability Discrimination (Amendment) Act, which set out the responsibilities of Primary, Secondary, Further and Higher Education institutions to engage in non-discriminatory practices in terms of disabled students and to further the inclusion of disabled people into non-segregated educational settings. This act also made clear the responsibility of the teacher-training agency to ensure that an awareness of the needs of disabled children is an integral part of teacher training.

Despite this legislation, however, whilst the national percentage of 5–15 year olds in special schools across England fell between 1997–2001, worrying variations remain in the approach taken to placing disabled students according to the Local Education Authority responsible (Norwich, 2002). Thus, although major improvements have occurred in terms of mainstreaming in some regions, disabled children in other areas remain disadvantaged. Additionally, although a report written by PricewaterhouseCoopers, on behalf of both the UK charity for people with cerebral palsy – Scope – and the UK National Union of Teachers (NUT), states that many schools believe that children with special educational needs (SEN) are benefiting from being a part of a mainstream school,[3] there is as yet little hard evidence to support this belief. Despite the introduction by the UK government of a 'value-added measure' in both secondary and primary school tables in England[4] – a measure that is intended to show the progress of students between key stages 1 and 2 and between key stage 3 and GCSE/GNVQ examinations – there is still insufficiently detailed information on the particular progress of children with SEN.

This is also one of the key findings of a recent report from the UK Office for Standards in Education (OFSTED) (2004) on inclusive education that, in addition, points to a range of weaknesses in the way that the current framework for inclusion is being put into practice. These weaknesses include: continuing low or insufficiently well-defined expectations of achievement for children with SEN; 'inconsistent' quality of work to improve the literacy skills of these pupils; and SEN teaching generally being of *'varying quality, with a high proportion of lessons having shortcomings'*. (OFSTED, 2004: 5) Thus, whilst substantial improvements to the educational provision for disabled children and young adults have been made, particularly over the past few years, it would appear that there are still issues that need to be addressed.

Income and employment

Such problems in terms of education are reflected in the experiences of disabled people within the UK labour market. In the current political climate, characterized by a second term of a New Labour government that prides itself on being a champion of social justice, the employment figures for disabled people make uncomfortable reading. Currently, employment rates amongst disabled people in the UK remain low, at around 49 per cent, a figure that is significantly below the level of employment for non-disabled people (around 75 per cent).[5] Even after allowing for the fact that some disabled people cannot or do not wish to be employed, non-disabled people are still four times more likely to gain employment than disabled people. Maintaining employment after becoming disabled is another area where disabled people experience major disadvantages. Each year in the UK around 3 per cent of those in work become 'limited in daily activities', of whom approximately half also report disability within the following or subsequent year. Of these, one in six loses his/her employment in the first year after becoming disabled. Given that disabled people make up a large and growing percentage of the working-age population, between 12–16 per cent depending on the definitions used, this means that a significant number of individuals are being discriminated against.[6]

By means of explaining this situation, it is tempting to point to the smaller proportion of disabled people who have good educational qualifications and to argue that this makes many disabled people less attractive to potential employers. It is undeniable that this may often be one of the factors influencing rates of employment amongst disabled people. There are other factors, however. For example, it is well documented that many employers make negative assumptions about disabled people in terms of perceiving them as unreliable workers. The damaging impact of this assumption upon the job prospects of disabled people is well recognized. The young persons' careers advice service Connexions[7] has an area of its website dedicated to tackling such negative assumptions, as does Scope. Connexions is concerned, amongst other issues, with raising awareness amongst employers about the fact that, overall, disabled people take less sick-leave than non-disabled people.

Scope has also highlighted the fact that disabled people are no more likely to be generally ill than their non-disabled colleagues[8] and in 2003 this organization ran a major campaign about the issue of employment for disabled people entitled: '*Ready, Willing and Disabled*'. The slogan for this campaign stressed the fact that it is not only disabled people who lack qualifications who are disadvantaged within the labour market, but also those who have qualifications which should put them on an equal footing with many non-disabled people.

The basis of this campaign was a survey into the attitudes of employers to disabled people, and the results of this survey, as documented by Daone and Scott (2003), demonstrate the persistence of certain negative assumptions about disabled people as workers. The survey found that 19 per cent of employers said that the fact that they had never worked with a disabled person before, and so did not know what to expect, would prevent them from employing a disabled person. A further 11 per cent of employers said that they would not employ a disabled person because their clients or customers would not want to be served by a disabled person.

There have been many attempts to explain this persistent discrimination faced by disabled people in the labour market. The dominant approach within Disability Studies, however, has been to employ a materialist framework when seeking to understand this problem. Wolfensberger (1989) suggested that the social construction of disability and dependence is a covert function of the 'human service industries'. According to his argument, whilst the stated purpose of institutions such as the education system and the health care system are to rehabilitate people back into the community, their hidden agenda is to create and sustain large numbers of dependent and devalued people in order to secure employment for others. In other words, the social construction of disability functions to keep disabled people out of the labour market and thus reduce competition for jobs.

Earlier British authors such as those who contributed to Hunt's (1966) edited collection similarly proposed that disability should be viewed as a social construction of capitalism. Disabled people, according to Hunt *et al*, become the 'unfortunates' who cannot benefit from capitalism and are perceived as 'useless' because they cannot work. As a consequence, disabled people are marked out as a minority group and placed in a similar position to other oppressed groups such as Black people or homosexuals, because, like them, they are regarded as being 'different'. Hunt *et al* concluded that industrial capitalism increased prejudice against disabled people and that this prejudice in turn expresses itself in discrimination and oppression. This view was later echoed in the work of Abberley (1997) who highlighted the important role that work plays in the process of social *inclusion*. Abberley, however, arguably went on to develop a somewhat more nuanced approach than Hunt *et al*, writing that it would seem that historically, the rights of the human 'being' have come second to the universalizing of human 'doing'.

The importance of the work of theorists such as Hunt *et al* (1996) and Abberley (1997), has been to propose an understanding of the position of disabled people within the labour market in terms of both material considerations and cultural perceptions. Their views that the cultural perceptions of disability are not only the result of the material inequalities characteristic of industrial capitalism, but are also some of the central mechanisms by which such inequalities are maintained, is clearly supported in the work of Colin Barnes (1992a). Barnes (1992a: 1) provides extensive evidence for institutional discrimination, which he claims comprises a *'complex system of hostile environments and disabling barriers'*. He highlights, amongst others, such issues as:

Medical screening – despite some occupational health expert's scepticism regarding the value of such screening, such tests remain central to a large number of employers' recruitment procedures. The historical link between doctors and disabled people has perpetuated the widespread belief that impairment is the same as illness. Employers generally associate ill health with poor performance and excessive absenteeism. They are therefore wary of employing people with a history of illness, and by association, people with impairments.

'Vital abilities' – the majority of employers continue to describe most of the work in their establishments as unsuitable for disabled people to undertake, especially in relation to what they describe as the 'vital abilities' required to do the job. Since the need for many of these so-called 'vital abilities' would not stand objective analysis, this must be viewed as another example of the discriminatory attitudes of employers.

'Appearance' – Jones and Longstone (1990) discovered that 10 per cent of all vacancies displayed in Jobcentres stated that applicants were required to be of 'clean and tidy' or of 'generally good' appearance. Many disabled people are significantly disadvantaged in this regard either because they are unable to afford a 'smart' set of clothes suitable for an interview, or because for some disabled people their 'unconventional' body shape makes sourcing suitable clothing a problem. Such difficulties should be understood by employers and taken into account when considering a disabled applicant, but in reality the problem is exacerbated by the emphasis that many male employers place upon the physical attractiveness of prospective employees. Morris (1989) found that some employers in the service sector felt that the sight of a disabled woman disturbs some clients.

What would appear to be clear from Barnes' list, however, is that materialist accounts, whilst important, cannot entirely explain the position of disabled people in the labour market. When, for example, Barnes considers the impact that some disabled peoples' 'non-conventional body forms' may have on their job prospects, it is the argument here that his evidence points towards the power of *stigma*. It would seem likely, therefore, that whilst materialist 'dual market' theories may well provide a major explanation for the position of disabled people in the labour market, especially during times of high unemployment, other factors must also play a part in perpetuating discrimination against disabled people during times when the job market is more buoyant.

The barriers facing disabled people who wish to *enter* the labour market are not, however, the only employment problems facing disabled people. For disabled people who do work there is also the issue of underemployment and the particular problems associated with sheltered employment. All too often, the only type of work that is available to disabled people is poorly paid and requires only low skills. Such underemployment is undemanding and is both psychologically and financially unrewarding. People who have been labelled as having 'severe' impairments often experience this problem most acutely. For such individuals, it is frequently the case that the only work available is in sheltered employment, in organizations such as Remploy. These workers are some of the poorest wage earners in the country.

In the face of such problems, the British government has historically opted for a fairly minimalist and voluntaristic policy response. Of those initiatives that have existed, few have been rigorously enforced. For example, enshrined in the 1944 Disabled Persons (Employment) Act, was the requirement that all employers of 20 or more employees must employ a 3 per cent quota of disabled people. The failure of employers to support this quota has been largely ignored by successive governments. Indeed, there have only been ten prosecutions since the quota was introduced, the last case having been brought in 1975 and the maximum fine for employers remains unchanged from the level of £100 set in 1944 (Barnes *et al*, 1999). To make matters even worse, much against the wishes of disabled people, the quota scheme was entirely abandoned in 1994. In addition, new initiatives have often been criticized for being ill-conceived. The new policy initiative of the 1990s – the move away from sheltered employment and towards 'sheltered placements' in mainstream places of work for example – has been greatly criticized for exacerbating the problem of underemployment, doing little to combat employer discrimination and for failing to improve the chances for disabled people to move into 'proper' mainstream employment.

Further, the Disability Discrimination Act 1995, heralded by the government as one of the most advanced anti-discrimination legislation documents, is, arguably, flawed in relation to workplace discrimination. Whilst the Act does cover issues relating to recruitment, terms of employment, promotional opportunities, training and dismissal procedures, unlike the legislation pertaining to 'race' and sex discrimination, discrimination against disabled people is only illegal if it is 'unreasonable'. As Roulstone (2000: 440) has commented: '*The belief that the power of employers is substantially countervailed by the DDA has to be acknowledged as untenable*'.

Critics such as Roulstone (2000) have also suggested that even the most welcome new development, the New Deal for disabled people, is unlikely to deliver the enhanced employment opportunities envisaged, since the underlying power relations of employment remain largely unchallenged. Heenan (2002), however, has questioned Roulestone's critique of New Deal, suggesting that whilst it may not be a *perfect system*, there are nevertheless many positive aspects of the scheme. She demonstrates through empirical research with disabled respondents that there are many disabled people for whom the scheme has made a real difference to their lives. Thus, whilst the disadvantaged position of disabled people in terms of the labour market remains, small steps in the right direction are being made in relation to the lives of some disabled people.

One of the most profound and persistent implications of the continuing injustice faced by disabled people with regard to the labour market can be seen in relation to the average incomes of disabled people. Disabled people remain poor in relation to the general population. What is also clear is that the greater the severity of impairment, the lower the income (Burchardt, 2000). This situation persists despite the introduction of a number of specific benefits such as the Disability Living Allowance and other additional tiers of benefits that have been put in place with the aim of reaching further down the impairment severity scale. Whilst such policies have contributed to a substantial decrease in the numbers of disabled people in the bottom tenth of the income distribution, it nevertheless remains obvious that those with the most severe impairments remain significantly disadvantaged (Burchardt, 2000).

Positive developments have not, therefore, been sufficient to counter the wider trends towards income inequalities both among disabled people and in relation to disabled people's position in society as a whole. Indeed, the continuing disadvantage experienced by many disabled people in terms of income is part of a wider problem facing the UK. In terms of international comparison, the expansion of social security systems and/or safety nets in most countries has mitigated, to some extent, the observed trend of increasing income inequality over the past 20–30 years. When compared internationally, for example with other countries within the EU, Australia, Canada, Japan and the

United States, the UK, however, has seen a *below average* increase in growth of social security transfers as percentage of GDP (1979–around 1994), despite a continuing increase in income inequality. Other countries with a below average growth rate include: Australia, Germany, Ireland, Italy, Japan, the Netherlands, Switzerland and the United States. Countries with an above average rate of growth in social security transfers include: Canada, France, and the four Nordic countries (Caminada and Goudswaard, 2000).

In many respects these figures are not surprising given the fact that the Scandinavian welfare model, for example, acts within a market economy in which inequalities in income distribution and the concentration of wealth and power are allowed less free play than is the case in the UK and elsewhere. It is difficult, therefore, to avoid reaching the conclusion that despite having a more 'left-wing' government, UK social security policy continues to be influenced by a more conservative neo-liberalist ideology. Thus, despite the current government's increased targeting of social protection benefits to those in the most need,[9] including many disabled people, overall, income inequality continues to rise, further disadvantaging socially excluded groups of which disabled people are but one.

Verdict: inequalities of opportunity

What is clear from the discussion above is that systematic inequalities continue to exist between disabled and non-disabled people in both public spheres – education and the labour market. Further, when considered in its entirety, what the research discussed above clearly demonstrates is that moral issues surrounding what kinds of lives are valued within a society and are considered to be worthy of inclusion within the 'mainstream', continue to structure the lives of disabled people. In the final part of this chapter, the ways in which disabled people and groups have themselves been challenging these issues, through such things as the disability identity,[10] the disability movement and disability culture will be considered.

The 'coming out' of disability

The fact that disabled people are devalued and stigmatized by society has been well documented by a large number of authors (see Karpf 1988, Morris, 1991, Ross, 1997), but arguably, chief amongst these authors are Colin Barnes and Tom Shakespeare. Barnes (1992b) has provided one of the most powerful analyses of this process of stigmatization through his discussion of the disabling imagery used by the media. According to his argument, such images as they appear in films, in books, in the press and on television, form the *'bedrock on which the attitudes towards, assumptions about and expectations of disabled people are based'*. (Barnes, 1992b: 19) For Barnes (1992b), these disabling images include:

- The view of the disabled person as a 'curio'
- The view of the disabled person as a 'super cripple'
- The view of the disabled person as an object of ridicule
- The view of the disabled person as a burden
- The view of the disabled person as their own worst and only enemy
- The view of the disabled person as incapable of participating fully in community life
- The view of the disabled person as an object of violence
- The view of the disabled person as sinister and evil
- The view of the disabled person as sexually abnormal

Perhaps the most profound and frequently occurring disabling image, however, is that of the disabled person as pitiable and pathetic. For Barnes, this entirely negative view of disability is recurrent in all media depictions of disability and is key to perpetuating the myth that disability is always synonymous with suffering. According to his analysis, such a view of disabled people succeeds in focusing attention upon the medical aspects of impairment whilst diverting public attention away from the social factors that disable people. Further, such attitudes towards disabled people are revealed, Barnes claims, by the frequent use of patronizing and offensive language such as 'the plucky' and 'the brave', or the 'victim' or 'unfortunate' to describe disabled individuals.

Most interestingly and controversially, perhaps, Barnes also identifies one final disabling image, that of the disabled person as 'normal'. Whilst he admits that in some respects the appearance of such images in the media recently is an important step, he nevertheless identifies three risks associated with this imagery. Firstly, in emphasizing 'ability' not impairment, he suggests that such images essentially deny the reality of impairment and undermine the positive disability identity which many disabled people are seeking to celebrate. Secondly, there are limits, Barnes claims, to this notion of disabled people as 'normal', for after all, 'normal' people are rarely dependent upon the goodwill of others in order to survive. Thirdly, the focus of this new approach within the media tends to be about stressing the 'normality' of certain individuals with impairments, rather than questioning how society *disables*. Thus, for Barnes, even seemingly positive new developments in public attitudes towards disability can in fact be little more than a re-packaging of familiar attitudes.

Shakespeare echoes Barnes in his belief that disabled people remain devalued and stigmatized within society and in some of his most recent work he has been tackling the issues raised by advances in medicine and genetics. For Shakespeare (1998), the problem with the technology of the 'new genetics' is that it fails to consider impairment as part of the human condition. Instead, according to Shakespeare, such new technologies further disadvantage disabled people by perpetuating the idea that disability is a purely medical problem which can and should be dealt with in purely medical terms, so avoiding the issue of the social construction of disability. Further, as he also highlights, there are some major ethical dilemmas associated with seeking to eliminate disability, for the underlying logic to such an approach must be that a disabled person's life is not worth living. Whilst there are clear implications of this in terms of disabled people's rights to life, the other effect of such attitudes is further to disadvantage those individuals who acquire a disability in their lifetime.

> The drive to use genetic and obstetric techniques to remove disabled people from the population fails to consider the millions of people developing impairments as a result of accident or disease during the life-course. Resources would be better spent on creating an inclusive and barrier-free society, and promoting the civil rights and independent living of disabled people. Society should value disabled people, alongside all human life.   (Shakespeare, 1998: 679)

Given, therefore, that the dominant culture is replete with these disabling images and attitudes, the challenge for many disabled people has been how to develop counter images and values that are empowering and promote the idea that society should value people with impairments. The following discussion will focus upon two main areas: firstly, issues relating to disability identity politics; and secondly, issues relating to the thorny question of the extent to which disabled people can be considered to be a part of an alternative culture, distinct from 'mainstream' culture.

Disability identity politics

Peters (1996: 219) examined the current state of the politics of the disability identity and concluded that there is no 'positive' identity of disability:

People with disabilities have largely assimilated these tarnished images in society and the academy. Accepting the idea that we are the Other, we continue to search for ways that will garner our acceptance in 'mainstream' society – mostly through political strategies and legal mandates – while at the same time denying our personal and multiple identities.

Yet, only one year later, Gilson *et al* (1997: 16) wrote:

The transformation from tentative affirmation of disability identity to proclamation of disability pride reflects the increasing importance of self-determination. A confident, positive disability identity within a broad, inclusive disability community has emerged. The benefit to disabled people to determine and relate their own stories is increasingly evident.

Since then, there has been little agreement surrounding this issue of a positive disability identity.

Of those who share Gilson's view, Shakespeare (1993), Morris (1991) and Oliver (1990, 1997) are probably the best known authors. All three authors see the development of a politicized disability identity as having the potential to bring about radical improvements in the lives of disabled people. Such thinking has led both Shakespeare (1993) and Oliver and Zarb ([1989] 1997), to make the not unsurprising link with new social movement theorizing. Shakespeare, Oliver and Zarb's new theorizing on this point is, however, as yet only tentative. Oliver and Zarb ([1989] 1997: 207 [my emphasis]), for example, have concluded that: '*the disability movement can, indeed, be considered as part of a new social movement generally*'. The word 'generally' is important here, however, for although clearly hoping to persuade the reader that the disability movement is a new social movement, Oliver and Zarb do admit that it does not share one of the four major characteristics of a new social movement. In relation to the idea that new social movements are characterized by 'post-materialist' or 'post-acquisitive' values being given precedence over those concerned with income, material needs or social security, Oliver and Zarb ([1989] 1997: 206) state:

Whilst it is certainly true that the disability movement is concerned with issues relating to the quality of life of disabled people, it is also true that many disabled people still face material deprivation as well as social disadvantage and the movement is centrally concerned with this. It would be inaccurate to attempt to characterise the disability movement as stemming from a middle-class, disabled elite concerned only with their own quality of life (...)

In other words, the disability movement's concerns with some of the persistent social inequalities discussed earlier in this chapter, cannot be denied, and must bring into some doubt the notion that the disability movement is a new social movement. Indeed, Erevelles (1996: 523) makes it quite clear that these post-materialist/post-structural values and disability make an *'uneasy alliance'*. In response to the post-structural idea that privilege should be given to the 'space of the discoursive' in order to produce many empowering possibilities, Erevelles (1996: 524) points out that many disabled people have argued that these:

> (...) imaginative meaning systems within discoursive spaces do not in any way alleviate the real material limitations that they face on a daily basis – material conditions that have caused many of them to live lives of extreme poverty.

Setting aside this issue of whether the disability movement is a 'new' social movement, there does seem to be a large number of authors who share the view that fashioning a positive collective identity for disabled people is a major part of what the disability movement both *is* and *should* be about.

There is evidence, however, to suggest that the disability movement in the UK has not been entirely successful in developing this positive identity and group consciousness across the disabled population as a whole. One of the key stumbling blocks has been the division that exists between groups of individuals with different impairments. Whilst some authors have suggested that these divisions have been established largely arbitrarily by charities and traditional welfare organizations, others, for example Priestley (1995), have proposed that these differences are very real and cannot be ignored. For Priestley, the tendency on the part of many of the key players in the disability movement has been to emphasize commonality over difference. This, he warns is unwise for:

> (...) it is clear that all social movements based (necessarily) upon a commonality of interests run the risk of alienating individuals and groups with unique personal experiences. In the present context,

unique personal experiences of impairment may often be perceived
as more immediate and important than the commonality associated
with disablement as a form of social oppression.   (Priestley, 1995:
159)

In particular, Priestley draws attention to what he considers to be the
legitimate concerns of many disability groups with special interests
such as ethnicity, gender or sexuality, that their special interests may
be perceived to be 'optional extras' to the *common experience* of disability. Priestley's point is taken further by Vernon (1999) who argues that
so-called 'simultaneous oppression' or 'double jeopardy' has often been
alleged to be the unique experience of a *minority* of disabled people. In
fact, according to Vernon, the experience of simultaneous oppression
is key to understanding disability itself, since the majority of disabled
people are not a homogeneous mass of white, heterosexual, middle-
class, young men!

For Vernon, it is essential that the disability movement avoids
making the assumption that other forms of oppression, for example,
sexism, have already been 'taken care of' by other movements. She
points to the growing literature that shows that disabled people experience racism (Begum, 1992, 1994, Sharma and Love, 1991 and Stuart,
1992, 1993, 1994); sexism (Fine and Asch, 1988, Morris, 1989, 1991,
1996, Lloyd, 1992); heterosexism (Corbett, 1994, Hearn, 1988); ageism
(Zarb and Oliver, 1993, MacFarlane, 1994); and class inequality issues
(Priestley, 1995). She then highlights the manner in which different
forms of oppression can interact, for example, for many disabled people, their socio-economic or class position can have profound effects
upon their options as a disabled person with regard to lifestyle. To
make matters even worse, Vernon (1999: 395) claims that the possession of more than one 'stigmatized' identity can result in lack of
acceptance even *within* oppressed groups: *'Being black and disabled can
sometimes mean that you are neither fully accepted in the black community
nor in the disabled community'*.

This is a potential problem for all groups experiencing simultaneous
oppression and is, seemingly, yet to be considered adequately by the
disability movement. Indeed, Fawcett (2000), drawing upon the work
of Nancy Fraser (1995a), states that focusing on disability as 'difference' can in itself be used in a normative way to 'gloss-over' pervasive
differences between disabled people – for example between academic-
ally able physically disabled people and individuals with learning
disabilities.

Fiona Williams (1996), however, again from a feminist perspective, suggests that whilst the above is undoubtedly true, it may sometimes be expedient to engage in the temporary 'fixing' or 'freezing' of differences in order to achieve key political and strategic goals. The challenge for the disability movement, however, in its quest to 'freeze' divisions within the disabled population even temporarily for political purposes, is to find an agreed disability identity behind which people are prepared to unite. Warren (1999: 123) has commented:

> (...) while users may be united by shared experience of forced dependency and a common goal of empowerment, it cannot be assumed that individuals agree about the identity to adopt in order to fight for that goal or the path of the battle: for example, some people reject the term 'disabled' as a stigmatising label, others object to the degree of emphasis placed on physical access by the disability movement.

As will be discussed in Chapter 6, this absence of solidarity amongst disabled people presents a problem when seeking to understand the nature of the citizenship rights being claimed by disabled people.

A disability culture?[11]

The debate surrounding the existence of a disability culture reflects this uncertainty with regard to the disability identity. The debate is also made considerably more complex due to academic disagreements surrounding the whole notion of *what is meant by culture*. Perhaps the most useful definition of culture, however, is provided by Raymond Williams (1980, 1981). For Williams, culture has two main aspects: firstly, the known meanings and directions into which members of a culture are socialized and which represent the traditional aspect of a culture; secondly, the new observations and meanings, which are offered and tested by a group, and which represent the creative aspect of a culture. Thus, for Williams, the significance of cultural practices and representations, such as those in the media and other art-forms, is that they are often one of the key ways in which a culture is created and maintained, whilst always providing opportunity for change.

The key point here, however, is that whilst Williams does stress the importance of forms of representation, he does not equate 'culture' with the 'arts'. This is important when considering the disability culture, because it would be a mistake to equate the disability culture with the Disability Arts Movement. Undeniably, the Disability Arts Movement has played a very powerful role in communicating the distinctive history, skills, customs, experiences and concerns of disabled people, which many people consider to be a distinctive lifestyle. The key question, however, is whether this distinct lifestyle expressed by Disability Arts truly represents a distinct disability *culture*.

There would appear to be two approaches to theorizing disability culture, and there are some key problems with each. Firstly, there are those who consider disability culture to be about challenging the cultural representations of disability that exist within mainstream culture in order to achieve for disabled people the equal respect and value that is given to other members of society. Such a position with regard to disability culture clearly perceives that such cultural practices are not only about tackling stigma, but in so doing are also about increasing equality of opportunity and outcomes for disabled people.

Whilst not denying the importance of such cultural challenges to mainstream prejudice, the question of whether such cultural strategies represent true cultural difference is a thorny one. Chapters 5 and 6 will consider this issue in greater depth. It is important to note here, however, that questions surrounding who can legitimately claim to be a part of the disability culture are also of considerable importance. Gilson and Depoy (2000) have highlighted the way in which the question of who can be a part of the disability culture is a constant source of tension. They suggest that individuals within the disabled population may find themselves positioned against one another as political advantage is sought. Additionally, individuals who aim to become assimilated into the mainstream 'normal' world may not choose to identify themselves clearly with the disability culture, but there are also other groups, for example people with a learning disability, who may also find that their cultural membership is unclear. This is unlikely to provide the basis for a shared cultural context.

The second approach to disability culture is similarly problematic. For many of the authors in this field, Oliver and Morris being key examples, disability culture is about 'celebrating' disability as 'difference'. This notion of celebrating difference is very much connected with the idea of the positive 'disability identity', and as such is equally contested. Critics of this approach have suggested that it is problematic to speak of 'disability pride' and the 'celebration of difference' in relation to the lives of people whose impairments are painful, debilitating or even fatal.

Adding to this debate it is the argument here that whilst many people in this field would agree that the quality of life of many disabled people is gravely affected by social factors, medical factors cannot be ignored. In the light of this and the diversity of experience with regard to impairment, it would seem overly optimistic, if not insensitive, to talk about *celebrating* disability across the disabled population. The tendency on the part of a number of key theorists in this field to ignore the very real reasons why some disabled individuals may feel unable to celebrate their difference is one of the key problems facing disability theory today.

Perhaps much of the discussion above can be summarized by saying that one of the key problems facing those who consider there to be a disability culture is the extent to which they perceive this culture to be distinct and 'exclusive'. For many commentators, there is a growing risk that in the manner in which key figures are defining disability culture, a 'confining social identity' (Gilson and Depoy, 2000) is being created for disabled people. Whilst on a positive note establishing such clear cultural boundaries may create *belongingness*, the fear is that it may also create *symbolic incarceration*.

Conclusion

As the various sections of this chapter demonstrate, despite some major improvements in the lives of disabled people, systematic structural inequalities between disabled and non-disabled people remain, as do the persistent negative attitudes towards people with impairments. Such prejudicial attitudes may themselves be responsible for reinforcing many of these traditional patterns of inequality.

Despite this gloomy conclusion, there is some hope for the future with regard to the position of disabled people in society. Theoretical developments in Medical Sociology and Disability Studies, and the collective power of disabled people in challenging the dominant views on disability, have already brought about some important changes in the lives of disabled people. In the future it is to be hoped that such progress will continue, and that Disability will be recognized by disabled and non-disabled people alike as a civil rights issue. Whether or not we will ever witness the true 'coming out' of disabled people is questionable, however, for as has been discussed in the later sections of this chapter, the ways in which factors such as impairment, gender, ethnicity, and sexuality impact upon experiences of disability and the sense of identity of individual disabled people, and create divisions within the disabled population, significantly weakens the notion of a collective disability identity or culture.

5
The Views of Disabled People

The specific purpose of this chapter is to consider the key findings of the research upon which this book is based. To this end, the qualitative data[1] presented has been grouped according to four main categories or themes. These themes are as follows:

- Structural issues
- Disabling attitudes–enabling identities
- Disability culture
- The disability movement

Structural issues

'Structural issues' are defined here as those that relate to the *access to*, and the *nature and experience of* certain key resources, such as education, employment and the built environment. A distinction is drawn here between these issues and more subjectively defined issues of public attitudes towards disabled people (in the form of disablism) or the private identities of individual disabled people, although the manner in which all these can interrelate is important.

The initial point to make is that respondents clearly identified a number of structural issues that were affecting their quality of life and life chances. Further, in many cases when asked a variation upon the question: *'What, if any, barriers or problems are disabled people facing today?'*, there was a marked tendency on the part of respondents to identify structural issues only, or before any other issues.

Respondents summarized the key problems facing disabled people today as being the perpetuation of dependency and their exclusion from the 'ideals of citizenship'. They stressed the role of the state and/or society in relation to this problem:

Member of L1:   (...) I think that there is a kind of hypocrisy, that is, that the state is working towards making disabled people more dependent. As the state cuts back on provision, disabled people can become more dependent on others – which I don't think is the way it should be because it really burdens others. We are getting back to 'cap in hand'.

Member of C3:   It's also about the circumstances being created which allow you to be a good citizen.

AB: So you have to be enabled to be a good citizen in some way?

Member of C3:   Participation is a big element of it – isn't it? If you can't actually participate fully in society, how can you even be a good citizen really?

Respondents frequently highlighted issues relating to experiences of schooling and in the workplace and of the types of barriers faced by disabled people in these two spheres. Respondents who chose to comment upon segregated special needs education were unequivocally critical of this type of education provision for disabled children. The following comments clearly echo the critique of segregated education provided by many authors within Disability Studies and provide strong support for the view that this type of educational provision can greatly limit the educational achievement of disabled children:

Member of L1 (re. special needs education):
    I don't know whether they think that it is best to encourage you to aim low, so that you don't then get disappointed.

Member of C3:   Well, my first school was (...) a private school and I learnt more there up to the age of 11. Then I went to a special school and I'd found that children there were just being (...) they didn't know anything! They weren't being taught anything (...) the staff just thought well, you know, they've got disabilities, they can't do this, they can't do that, we'll just get them through a day – and that was it. I just hated it. I know that there are still places like that.

The logical assumption that might be drawn from these types of comments might, therefore, be that disabled people favour inclusive mainstream education. The following excerpt from one group interview, however, suggests that whilst in favour of mainstreaming, some disabled people are gravely concerned about the way in which lack of sufficient resources may be disadvantaging disabled children in mainstream schooling:

AB: How would you set about building a more inclusive society? How does one do it?

Member of L1: I think you start in school, in (...) all the schools – inclusive education.

AB: Rather than segregated?

Member of L1: Yes.

Worker at L1: Only if they give enough money. Without the money actually people suffer....

Member of L1: [*agrees with worker – ed.*] in the long run.

The issue of mainstream education for disabled children was not discussed in sufficient depth by other respondents in this research, however, and this makes it difficult to draw any overall conclusions about the views of disabled people surrounding mainstreaming. Taking all of the comments made by respondents about both segregated and mainstream schooling for disabled people into consideration, what can nevertheless be concluded from the findings of this research is that disabled people clearly believe that they still face major structural barriers within the sphere of education.

Some respondents also made important connections between these important barriers within education and subsequent barriers within the field of employment:

Member of C3: (...) disabled people are still not encouraged to apply for jobs and to try and move into employment. (...) I mean, we have an education system discouraging people in their future development.

What is clear from this last quotation is that the disabled people in this research supported the idea that the attitudes of those involved in the education of disabled people have tended to restrict the job prospects of young people. This particular quotation goes one step further than this, however, for the respondent here is equally definite in stating that the education system has been *actively discouraging* the future development of disabled people.

Other important comments on the issue of employment came from respondents who are members of group 'S2', a self-advocacy group for people with learning disabilities. In the first quotation one member expressed his feelings about his experience of trying to gain access to employment:

> Member of S2: It's like when you go for jobs isn't it (...)? You just tell 'em you've got summat wrong with you – then they don't want to know at the end of the day...they treat you like scum in jobs.

In the second quotation, another member of group 'S2' who had gained employment within a sheltered workshop highlights the vulnerability of many disabled people once they are within the field of employment:

> Member of S2: I'm fed up with it. [*sheltered workshop – ed.*] (...) Staff treat people like kids. There are two staff always picking on me – 'Comb you hair!'. It happens a lot [*there – ed.*]. I don't like it. They're picking on me. [*Distress – ed.*]

What these two comments demonstrate is that not only do major structural barriers still exist to the full employment of disabled people, but also problems associated with their treatment by employers. That these problems persist despite changes to legislation to try to enforce equality of opportunity is something that frustrates many disabled people, as is clear from the following quotation:

> Member of C3: (...) almost everything at the moment I would say had some sort of barrier-creating effect (...) I mean, why something for instance as [*changes to – ed.*] employment practices [*legislation – ed.*], why that hasn't had a significant effect in terms of increasing the employment of disabled people is quite hard to understand.

In addition to issues relating to education and employment the respondents in this research also highlighted other areas where they perceived major structural barriers. Many respondents commented upon the need for improvements to services in order to maintain their own independence and sense of personal well-being. Members of group 'S2' stated that seeking to improve service provision was one of the key functions of their organization:

> Member of S2:   I think [*S2 – ed.*] wants to make services better for people with learning difficulties – Social Services, Health Services, the Police Services.

Other members of group 'S2' expressed their desire to have more choice in relation to services that impacted upon them and to be more involved in decision making about their own lives. Having a voice in consultation processes with service providers was an issue that was raised many times throughout the research, the general feeling being that in the past too many decisions had been taken about the lives of disabled people with no reference to the views of this 'client' group:

> AB: What other (...) ways can improvement be made in the lives of disabled people?
>
> Member of C3:   In the ways services are provided – giving people greater opportunity (...) to exert their own independence, to have greater control over how services are provided, greater choice in the type of services that are available to them...creating a situation where disabled people themselves are making decisions or influencing development, so that what is available relates a bit more clearly to their actual...not just their needs, but their wants, their desires, their feeling about that. (...) I suppose to a certain extent, there's a certain idealism in that, but it's something we should work towards (...)
>
> AB: (...) What would you say were the barriers? (...)
>
> Member of C3:   (...) Oh the obvious one is that disabled people aren't a priority in terms of (...) elements of consultation – being involved. If you don't have enough disabled people working for an organization, and you're not consulting with disabled people, how can that organization, therefore, be in touch with what disabled people feel or what they need?

That this lack of consultation can be explained at least in part by the Medical Model of Disability and the traditional power of professionals and charities *for* disabled people over the lives of disabled people, was clearly identified by two respondents:

Member of L1:   (...) professionals – there are a lot of people making a lot of money out of knowing what's best for people like us. (...) I mean, it is you [*to another group member – ed.*] who is a stroke victim, and I am a cerebral palsy sufferer. (...) <u>They</u> haven't got it.

Worker at S2:   Do you think that in (...) those organizations and groups that are for people with learning disabilities (...) people with learning disabilities don't get their say?

Member of S2:   Yes, Mencap does that.

Worker at S2:   They don't let people have their say? Are there any other groups like that where people can't have their say?

Member of S2:   Yeah – in Social Services you can't...

Worker of S2:   I'm thinking about something that you said earlier [*name – ed.*] about the Down's Syndrome Association?

Member of S2:   They were talking about people with Down's Syndrome...

Worker of S2:   Who should have been doing the talking?

Member of S2:   They don't know about it really.

Worker at S2:   Who should be doing the talking more?

Member of S2:   Us! Give us a chance!

What is clear from both of these excerpts is that the power of professionals over the lives of disabled people persists both in the state and the voluntary sectors and regaining power over their lives is something that many of the respondents identified as being of great importance to them. Further, some respondents also highlighted the problem of tokenism within existing consultation processes:

Member of L1:   It's a rubber-stamping thing isn't it?

In addition to these issues of professional power and lack of consultation, disabled people in this research also routinely highlighted the barriers that they face in relation to transport and the built environment. What became clear from the discussions was that most respondents considered the inaccessible environment to be, if not the only barrier, certainly one of the *key barriers* facing disabled people today. Indeed, when asked about key issues facing disabled people, the inaccessible environment was by far the most frequently mentioned problem. The following quotations demonstrate the views of some of the respondents on this issue:

Member 1 S1:   (…) the public environment could be made accessible, also mainstream services for disabled people such as supermarkets allowing their staff to assist disabled people with their shopping. I believe this is what the disability movement is about, and I do feel part of that.

Member 2 S1:   There is still great scope for improvements in the lives of disabled people. Transport is one area where this is evident. The provision of community transport can enable a disabled person to travel a realistic number of times a week at an affordable price, but true equality, civil rights and the disability movement demands that disabled people should be able to catch a bus at any time.

Member L1:   Everyone thought it was awful that in South Africa when black people weren't allowed to use the buses for white people. But because someone cannot walk and cannot physically get on a bus, that's acceptable. I don't look at it in that way.

Member 1 C3:   But people cash in on disability as well – (…) we went to Blackpool the other weekend and we found a hotel that has wheelchair access, but we paid double for it because it had a lift and it had wheelchair access. Everywhere else we 'phoned, yes, they had steps, stairs, couldn't get up to the first floor and yet this Hotel had everything and (…) because of it they know people would have to go there, so they put the price up.

Member 2 C3:   You felt that you were exploited?

Member 1 C3:   Yes. I think people are exploited.

Member C3:   It isn't just about the physical environment, it's about people getting around as well. How many buses in Cumbria are actually accessible for disabled people? I think there's two in Carlisle (...)

Another comment which was not made directly in relation to this topic of the inaccessible environment, but is nevertheless revealing, was made by a respondent in answer to the question: *'What do you personally gain from being a part of this organization?'* In this quotation, the respondent is highlighting the fact that her experience of arthritis has made performing many tasks within the home difficult. For this respondent, one of the key benefits of the organization of which she is a member is the sharing of knowledge between members about how to overcome these problems:

Member of C1:   (...) if you can't do something in the house, people will tell you how they got round it.

Clearly this is an issue that relates to the inaccessible environment since many of the difficulties mentioned in the wider discussion from which this comment was taken relate to the design of homes, equipment, consumer good such as jars of food and so on. Interestingly, this particular group took a somewhat less 'political' stance towards the problem of the inaccessible environment, seeing it as a problem to be faced and for which solutions must be found, rather than as something that they considered to be inherently unjust.

In addition to this interesting difference between groups, two other important differences must also be highlighted within this section on structural barriers. The first relates to key differences in experiences between physically disabled people and people with learning disabilities with regard to opportunities for independent living. For many disabled respondents with physical impairments, independent living was an 'ideal' which could be achieved given the appropriate support. The main issues for these respondents were the funding shortfall in this area and the lack of availability of carers, these two issues being closely linked as is shown in the following excerpt:

Member of C2:   Independent living is a limited thing too – they've changed the rules for that now (...) because they've actually run out of the funding available. (...) It's also very difficult to recruit carers because

	unemployment is quite low and those are the sorts of jobs that people go into when unemployment is high because...
AB:	It's not the best paid job?
Member of C2:	No [*it's not – ed.*] – and it's not the nicest job in the world either...and the employment services are forcing people to do the job, so they're doing it not because they want to but because they have to. (...) whereas, if you made it lucrative enough you'd be able to recruit your own personal assistant or carers for example. But the Independent Living, I think it was the pre-1993 rules, it was almost, the ceiling was almost limitless, whereas now they've capped it to a certain amount each week.

The view of this respondent is quite clear – shortfalls in funding are the major barrier to independent living.

This was not the case for many of the respondents who had learning disabilities. The desire to 'have my own flat' was something that many of the respondents at group 'S2' mentioned as a 'hope or dream' but there was little sense that this goal was achievable for most members of this group. Discussions at group 'S2' also highlighted the fact that whilst attempts have been made to support 'quasi'-independent living for people with learning disabilities within small group homes, these living arrangements fall short of the 'ideal' of independent living. In the following excerpt from a discussion at group 'S2' one of the members of this group describes his experiences of living in a group home and the stress that this way of life causes him:

Member of S2:	I like being treated with respect
AB:	Are you (...) treated with respect?
Member of S2:	Yeah – I do, but sometimes I'm always getting blamed in that house sometimes. (...) I try to keep out of trouble...
Worker at S2:	I think that's something about living together – with a group of people. Sometimes you're bound to fall out (...)
	(...)
Member of S2:	She's [*member of shared household – ed.*] always like that, she takes it out on other people as well (...)
Worker at S2:	Who sorts it out then when it happens?

Member of S2:	We have to sort it out. So I say to her – now come on [*name – ed.*], you can stop this you know.
Worker at S2:	And do you sort it out in the end?
Member of S2:	Every time I say something she gets a face on. (...) And she storms out of the kitchen, bangs on the door on the wall – made a right mark on it and went upstairs.

The second issue relates to differences within groups between the views of members with regard to the importance of structural barriers in their lives. In the following excerpt from a discussion held at the Lancashire-based organization, what becomes clear is that there are some important differences of opinion regarding what is the central function of the organization. Whilst the excerpt may not be the most 'in-depth' of discussions on this topic, it is the only example of a discussion between members of a focus group on the topic of 'social exclusion'. One member of the group clearly states that the aim of the organization should be to combat social exclusion and to help to build a more inclusive society. The responses of the other members of the organization to this comment are interesting:

AB:	Okay – so the central hopes and aim of the organization – what might they be would you say?
Member 1 of L1:	To help build a more inclusive society. (...)
AB:	Right...to build a more inclusive society – you think that's a central part?
Member 2 of L1:	I'm not sure whether that is actually in the constitution. I think maybe it's lurking somewhere in that scatterbrain of yours [*to member 1 – ed.*].
AB:	Would you say that it should be in [*the constitution – ed.*]?
Member 2 of L1:	Yes.
Member 3 of L1:	But that is the ultimate aim, but slightly smaller than that – I mean, our aim is to give disabled people as much information, confidence, advice to live as independently as they want to live.

The first comment by member 2 about the 'scatterbrain' of member 1 was clearly this individual's *spontaneous* reaction to the idea that the chief aim of the organization is to build a more inclusive society. It was apparent at this point in the discussion that member 2 did not consider social inclusion to be a central aim of the organization, although when asked whether it should be a part of the formal constitution of the organization, member 2 agreed that it should. To what extent this second statement of agreement reflected a genuine feeling is unclear, it is possible that member 2 felt in some way obliged to agree given the current 'political' importance of the term 'social inclusion'. Most revealing, however, is the comment made by member 3, which goes some way to explaining why it might be that the organization as a whole has not embraced the idea of 'social inclusion'. Member 3 clearly indicates that 'social exclusion' is a part of a much bigger agenda, somehow 'beyond' the smaller, and more 'everyday' aims of the organization. These everyday aims member 3 identifies as 'information, confidence and advice' about independent living. Combining this comment with knowledge about the functioning of this organization, it is clear that member 3 is talking about advice regarding how to overcome structural barriers such as income inequalities, housing difficulties, employment issues and access issues.

It is proposed here that it can be inferred logically from this final comment, that for this member of the organization, 'social inclusion' is about more than combating these types of structural barriers. Indeed, the use of the term 'ultimate' may suggest that 'social inclusion' is viewed, by this member at least, as an almost *utopian* goal and one that does not reflect the everyday operations of the organization. The albeit tentative conclusion that may be drawn from this excerpt seems to be that not all disabled people feel able, or even perhaps wish, to engage in the sort of emancipatory politics that is suggested by member 1's comments about an 'inclusive society'. It would appear, therefore, that whilst not denying that there are wider issues of participation, identity and acceptance that need addressing in relation to disability, some disabled people are still choosing to focus their efforts upon helping other disabled people to remove or bypass certain key structural barriers in society.

This final point is reinforced by the comments of another respondent from a different group who admitted that fighting against the numerous structural barriers that remain in society took up so much of the organization's time, they were unable to engage in wider 'emancipatory' action:

Member C2:   (...) about being a bit more proactive and probably a bit more militant and probably raising awareness – we're so bogged down in doing what we're already doing that we find we haven't got time to do anything else.

To conclude this section of structural issues, therefore, what the evidence from this research suggests is that for many disabled people these structural issues represent some of the major, if not *the major* disabling factors in society:

> Member S1:   The environment and services – these are the two things that disable me most.

Disabling attitudes, empowering identities?

Whilst, as discussed previously, the majority of respondents identified structural barriers as being at the heart of their experience of disability, discussions relating to disabling attitudes, language and identity also formed a major part of most discussions. Indeed, many respondents demonstrated that they had very strongly held views on these matters. Several respondents described what they considered to be disabling attitudes and behaviours within society. The attitudes they described were those held by non-disabled people and ranged from unconscious acts that disempower disabled people through their unintended consequences, through widely held but influential misconceptions about certain impairments, to openly prejudiced attitudes and actions. The following excerpts point to the key power imbalances that exist between all non-disabled and disabled people. What is clear from these quotations is that such power imbalances can occur even in seemingly caring or close relationships such as between friends, and persist in the field of medicine where despite years of awareness raising, medical professionals continue to focus too heavily upon impairment and in so doing exacerbate the problem of disability.

> Member of C1:   Well, I was out and I was struggling, and I never told her, my best friend at work – it was my own fault because I ordered pizza and I couldn't cut it! And she took my plate off me – and I was mortified! Really, really mortified! – and I was: 'Oh please don't do this!' – and she was doing it and I was holding on to the plate. And she really thought she was being helpful.

> Member C1:   (...) I think it was about September that my daughter came and said 'we'll go to shop mobility in Carlisle!' – so I tried a chair and I felt awful! I really did! Because (...) people were talking to

[*name of husband – ed.*] as if I was invisible, and I was someone, you know, who was just there.

Member L1:   You get so that you can't talk as a friend to a doctor, they're just interested in you as a medical condition.

Respondents also highlighted the problem of negative assumptions that many non-disabled people make about disabled people. At one end of the scale respondents highlighted the very disempowering and offensive effects that such assumptions can have:

Member of L1:   Even now it happens that people come in assume that because there's an able-bodied in the office and assume that they're in charge.

Member of S1:   I was sitting next to a woman, she got on the bus at the Sheaf Market and she said 'Oh you're blind aren't you! My daughter's blind, and she's just had a baby! Isn't it <u>wonderful</u> what they can do!'
(...)
I was on a train once, going to Swansea from Paddington and there was an old lady, and do you know I still can't believe this story, but it happened – and I knew she wanted to talk to me, and we'd gone through Reading and Bristol and we were nearly in Cardiff and then she said – 'Young man, would you like a chocolate biscuit?' So I was doing my social bit and I said 'Oh Thank you!' and she placed this silver wrapped biscuit in my hand and there was silence whilst I unwrapped it and just as I was about to eat it, she said: 'No, stop!' and I said 'Why, what's the matter?' and she said: 'I didn't mean you to eat the biscuit, I just wanted to know if you knew where your mouth was!'.
I couldn't come back from that one, I just sat there chewing the biscuit. (...) I think she must have been in her eighties. It happens all the time and the reason for it is, we're basically excluded. I mean, I think she grew up in a school for nice 'gals' somewhere and probably they had a few Black girls – but only the very rich ones – and I

> think she'd never met a disabled person and I
> don't think she regarded me as being a human
> being, I think she regarded me as an organism that
> she could experiment with (...)

Whilst such assumptions of incompetence clearly need to be challenged very seriously, at the other end of the scale respondents at group 'S2' highlighted the even more disturbing beliefs that some people hold about disabled people, in this case people with a learning disability, that they are dangerous and 'deviant':

Member of S2:	I'm not bad, but some people think I am. I don't think much of them!
Member of S2:	(...) more able-bodied people are frightened of us.
Worker at S2:	(...) what other words have people used to describe people with learning disabilities?
Member 1 S2:	'Funny Farm'
Worker at S2:	Funny Farm?
AB:	From the Funny Farm?
Member 1 S2:	Yeah – 'cos that's what they said about us at College, 'cos we used to work at [*name – ed.*] farm – and they used to say 'Oh, here they are from the Funny Farm'.
Member 2 S2:	People call us mental as well.
AB:	Mental?
Member 3 S2:	Nutter!

According to another respondent from a different group, such attitudes are both demonstrated and perpetuated by the media. In this excerpt the respondent highlights the way in which disability is portrayed by the media in terms of crisis and incompetence:

Member of C3:	(...) like on TV – disabled people only really appear on specific disability related programmes and that becomes a bit of an extreme because they focus, I mean they do, they focus on the more extreme issues related to disability. It's not like disabled people are present in all programmes. But I suppose this is something Black people would have said a lot more a few years ago and things started

to change – but they're still saying it aren't they? And it's definitely not happening with disabled people! I mean it's usually 'issue' things that come up – if it's in the media it's like, you know (...) it'll be like, a women being pregnant and then she becomes blind and 'Ah! How will she cope with that?'. You know! And then it becomes a crisis and disability tends to be related to crises in the media and not about people like us just living their lives really.

The role of the media and the importance of preconceived ideas about the nature of disability were also considered by several other respondents during discussions about the transition from a non-disabled to a disabled identity.[2] The following excerpts demonstrate the power of disablist attitudes, and as will be discussed at greater length later, also show how understanding the extent to which most non-disabled people hold these views can, if only to a degree, help to explain subsequent differences between the attitudes of those individuals with acquired as opposed to congenital impairments:

Member of S1:   I used to work as a physio. in a rheumatism clinic and I think that my patients found (...) because they'd been able-bodied and probably their Mum or their Granny or their Dad had had arthritis before them, and when they were able-bodied they were really scornful (...) then when it goes around and comes to them, they've still got those attitudes but now they're looking at themselves like that.

AB: (...) is it important to re-identify (...) disabled people (...) in a more positive light – do you see that as something important?

C2 Member: Yes. You see prior to my accident, I was as guilty as anybody of all the stereotypical images of what disabled people are. It wasn't because I really felt like that, it was because every time you see someone on the telly, in a wheelchair, they were always stupid or something like that – you never saw them in a positive way.
(...)

You know the Tom Cruise film – the Vietnam one, when he's in the wheelchair. Again it's always about him becoming disabled, but never actually integrating or being a part. And I was as guilty as anybody else. (...) I was ignorant, like the majority of people are, of the whole disability issue – totally ignorant of what it meant, of who the people were. It's like I said, I always thought that anybody in a wheelchair, they were brain-damaged or something like that (...) and that was the perception I had at the time. It was only when I became disabled myself that my whole attitude changed.

Respondents also talked extensively about what being disabled meant to them in terms of their identities. On the whole, the majority of respondents did not perceive their disabled identity as something that was positive, or something that they felt proud about. Most of the respondents felt that their disabled identity had been imposed upon them. Of those who did not see their disabled identity as a negative thing, they nevertheless did not see it as something positive, simply as a 'fact' to be lived with. The following comments exemplify the large number of comments made on this topic throughout the research:

Member of C1: I think other people have to put the label on you [*disabled – ed.*] – I don't think that I could say myself that I'm disabled. (...) I feel that it's not my decision.

Member of C1: I think you come to accept it because you have to use it [*label of disability – ed.*] when you are claiming for this, that and the other. You accept that you've got that label.

Member of S1: We are all individuals with our own identity who have in common that we are depersonalized by barriers including attitudes.

Member of S1: (...) having part of your person not working is essentially negative. It is possible to be proud of achievements as a disabled person. To be proud to be disabled was not a concept that found support here.

AB:	Is there such a thing as a 'disability identity' and if there is, what is the image that exists – what is it like to experience it? You said that 'I'm a disabled person!' with some...well, was it pride?
Member of L1:	It was just a statement. But I think that on a practical basis, I might have needs – because of my disability – but that's a <u>fact</u>, not...it shouldn't be a <u>problem</u>. If I go into a pub and buy a lemonade, and I want to sit at a table because I'm disabled, then I need to get someone else to carry the lemonade – it's a <u>fact</u> – but it shouldn't be a problem.
AB:	When you became disabled, did you feel that you had gained a new identity?
Member of C2:	Definitely yes, without a doubt, yes.
AB:	Was it a positive identity or...?
Member of C2:	From a personal point of view – no, it's not. There are some positive things about it – but from a personal viewpoint I would say probably less than 5% – I can think of 95% more reasons of not being disabled than being disabled.

Curiously, in addition to these comments, which must bring into some doubt the idea of a positive 'disability identity' and the notion of 'celebrating' disability, some respondents expressed their reluctance to accept the 'label' of disability at all. Considering that all of the respondents were key members of a disability organization, their position in relation to this issue of identity is obviously complex:

Member of C2:	I don't always see myself as disabled (...) The only time I see myself as disabled is when someone else is having to do things for me that I can't do for myself – or I'm in bed and I obviously can't get up. And I do feel vulnerable. And I do – I am aware that I become, more passive because you are so vulnerable.
Member 1 of C3:	I get as much help as I can but I don't call that being disabled, sorry.
Member 2 C3:	Well I'm just thinking, I feel pretty normal you see. (...) I don't think of myself as disabled – I <u>am</u>, but I don't think like that. (...)

Member 1 C3:	I used to hate being called blind!
AB:	Did you? What did you prefer?
Member 1 C3:	I don't know – I probably didn't want to be called anything.
AB:	Right – which goes back to what you [*to Member 2 – ed.*] were saying – (...) that you don't want to particularly be, or feel the need to be identified as a disabled person?
Member 2 C3:	I know other people think I am, but I personally just think just 'I'm one of you'. I just have a mobility problem (...) I'm <u>me</u> you see!
Member 3 C3:	It's having a label isn't it? People seem to think that we should be labelled.
Member of S2:	We just don't want to be labelled like jars!

The important point here is that in the case of each of these respondents, the impairment that forms the 'visible' sign of their disability was clear. It is, perhaps, easy to assume that there is a greater tendency on the part of individuals with so-called 'hidden' disabilities to seek to avoid being 'labelled' as disabled. The findings of this research, however, show that this is not the case and that individuals with what might be considered by many non-disabled people to be 'profound impairments' also wish to avoid being termed 'disabled'.

Another assumption that is often made, that does not necessarily need to be rejected *completely*, but that does need to be considered more carefully, is the idea that there are fundamental differences in terms of identity between people with congenital as opposed to acquired impairments. Broadly speaking, the findings of this research do support the idea that individuals with acquired impairments have particularly negative views about their disabled identity and find the transition to such an identity very traumatic:

Member 1 of C1:	I mean, the moment I was diagnosed, I burst into tears and said to the doctor, 'Oh no! I'm going to have funny hands!' and I mean – I was in agony! I couldn't turn my wrists over I was in such pain, but all I could think about was that I was going to have these funny hands!
Member 2 of C1:	I thought the same about being in a wheelchair – I thought: 'Oh my God! I'm going to be in a wheelchair!'

These comments clearly demonstrate, as discussed earlier, the ways in which negative attitudes towards disability possessed prior to disablement can greatly affect the experience of transition from a non-disabled to a disabled identity. Other respondents commented upon the long-term effects that this transition can have upon the extent to which an individual engages in the 'politics of disability' (in the second of the two quotations below, the member of the Lancashire-based organization being discussed is an individual with a congenital impairment and the member voicing these opinions is an individual with an acquired impairment):

Member of C2:   I think that the important thing as well is whether a person has become disabled as a result of an accident or whether they were born with a disability. (...) So from a cultural point of view, I think you're going to have two cultures within one...where people are coming from...because they've not had life experience of not being disabled...whereas I have.

AB: And you think that that has an effect on how you identify yourself now?

Member C2:   Yes, (...) I think that's actually why I'm not so militant – I'm not vocal, angry, bitter, bothered about terminology.

Member 1 of L1:   Well, I've said before that [*other member of group – ed.*] is on that side of 'disability' where you have to change society, the rest of us are...we have to cope, we have to put up with things as they are and this is what we've got and we've got to do something with it.
(...)
Where [*other member of group*] would say 'This is not acceptable', I would tend to say 'Well, whether or not it's acceptable, this is the position and how do we get out of it?'

There were occasions during this research, however, when individuals made comments, or debated with each other on this topic, in such a way as to demonstrate that broad generalizations must be avoided and that the complexity of identity issues must always be acknowledged. One respondent with a congenital impairment stated that the difficult transition towards acceptance of a disabled identity is something that he has also experienced:

> Member of S1:   It is not just people who have acquired disabilities – I'm still going through it.

Equally interesting was a discussion that took place at the Lancashire-based organization between two respondents, one of whom has an acquired impairment and one of whom has a congenital impairment. In the following excerpt from this discussion the two respondents consider the differences between their identities. What becomes clear is that member 1 feels that member 2 possesses a more positive identity as a disabled person and is better adjusted to life as a disabled person. Member 1's comments reinforce the general findings of this research in terms of indicating the uneasy transition from non-disabled to disabled identities. This discussion is even more revealing, however, because the comments made by member 2 clearly bring into some doubt the idea that individuals with congenital impairments have more positive identities as disabled people. This is not to say, however, that member 2 is indicating that he does not feel positive about his identity as a disabled person, for his argument is rather more subtle than that. Member 2 suggests that the special-needs education he had received attempted to impose upon him a certain kind of identity that he considered to be essentially negative. His subsequent rejection of this negative identity and development of a more positive 'disability identity' was, therefore, not something that developed naturally because of the congenital nature of his impairment, but rather from his own determination and emancipatory thinking:

> AB: Would you say though that you had chosen your identities as 'disabled people' – or do you feel that you have been labelled by society?
>
> Member 1 of L1:   Oh it's been put on me entirely...yes (...) I do wonder though, whether there is a difference between us – you've [*to respondent 2 – ed.*] been disabled all your life and me...I wondered that?
>
> AB: So how do you think – what is it like, if I may ask you, to experience that change of identity?
>
> Member 1 of L1:   Well, this is it...you see, I think that I do rather think that it was imposed on me...whereas, you [*to respondent 2 – ed.*]...it seems to me – have had an identity of your own all your life.

Member 2 of L1:	No – not really, because...I think that at my former college, a lot of the pupils were more ready to accept what society had marked down for them...they were more likely to accept the expectations.
AB:	What were the expectations would you say?
Member 2 of L1:	Basically, to go to special school and to go to local day centre and to live in some sort of local sheltered housing. That is what is available...
Member 1 of L1:	You know...I'm shocked, in big levels about you [*to respondent 2 – ed.*] saying about disablism and about this identity thing...because you've developed your own...whereas I had one forced on me!
Member 2 of L1:	Well, I didn't choose mine!
Member 1 of L1:	Yes you did!
AB:	Okay, okay! How about me suggesting that what you are saying is that for you [*to respondent 1 – ed.*] your identity pre-existed your disability... whereas for you [*to respondent 2 – ed.*] your disability is very much a part of your sense of identity?
Members 1 and 2:	*Yes!*
	(...)
Member 1 of L1:	(...) this is one of the problems you just have to get used to...you see, when you become disabled, it just happens like that [*clicks finger – ed.*] and it took me a year to get used to it. And I think that in that year I had to develop my own identity... which came with my own reasons for wanting to be alive...it is a terribly confusing time.
AB:	Yes...this is what I've heard in other groups too – that to go from a non-disabled identity to a disabled identity, is very difficult.
Member 1 of L1:	Yes, and it is what a lot of people just can't deal with...you know the people who have strokes who are 70 or 80, and are so used to living an active life...they just can't adapt...whereas I had to adapt.
AB:	Yes, you were young...
Member 1 of L1:	I was 34...I had to adapt, or go under...and take on a new identity.

What the previous excerpt, in connection with the whole of this section of the chapter shows, is that very few respondents considered their disabled identity to be something entirely positive and several of the respondents clearly felt that their identity as disabled people was a negative factor in their lives, or something that they wished to reject, challenge or avoid. It is important at this juncture, however, to stress that whilst the findings of this research do bring into some question the idea of a positive 'disability identity' and the notion that disabled people are 'celebrating the disability identity', this is not to say that respondents entirely rejected the idea of striving for a more positive representation of disability in society.

Two respondents described how they used humour as a way of disrupting people's negative attitudes towards them:

Member of S2:   Yeah – someone says: 'There then you nutter!' I said to them: 'If I'm a nutter, they would be <u>salted nuts</u>!' And that way I got them back! If I fight back they don't like it.

Member of L1:   (...) the first time I went into the Biker's Pub in [*name of town – ed.*], I said 'Hi! I'm Wobbly [*name – ed.*]!' and after that, you know, that ended any kind of taking the piss! That meant that they had no chance to say 'Bugger Off!', you know...

Whether in defining themselves in these humorous ways these individuals are truly finding a positive 'disability identity' is unclear. There is the question, for example, of whether identities that arise as a form of 'defence' against prejudice and discrimination and are not 'about' true personal identity, are entirely 'positive', even if they are temporarily empowering. Nevertheless, the actions of these individuals do represent a definite rejection of the negative attitudes in society.

In another discussion, respondents at the Lancashire-based organization said that they felt that one of the key functions of the organization was to promote a positive image of disabled people:

Member 1 of L1:   (...) I think it also shows that disabled people can actually do it and we can be seen in a quite a positive role within the local community.

Member 2 of L1:   I actually think that is very important...too often disabled people are seen as incapable. There are not many positive roles out there.

They were also keen to reject the use of certain terms such as 'invalid' to describe disabled people because of its connotation of not being '*valid*'. Members of other organizations involved in this research put forward similar arguments against the use of derogatory language:

Member of C3:   A lot of language had a derogatory connotation didn't it? And I presume if you are trying to change things in society then I suppose a very obvious change is language, because it's something that we use and is around us all the time. If you are trying to educate, if you are trying to change, language is perhaps the most obvious way.

Of particular note was the issue of the use of the term 'sufferer' when describing individuals with certain impairments. Some of the respondents at group 'S1' explained why they disliked the term:

Member 1 of S1:   I don't like to be described as an 'MS sufferer'. [...*prefer*... – *ed.*] 'a person with MS'.
AB: What is essentially wrong with this term? (...)
Member 2 of S1:   I have a great problem with the way that society sees disabled people – they also actually assume that because we've got some sort of disability that we are all suffering, you know. (...) But it's like everything, when someone gets depressed because of their disability then they'll see themselves as suffering then. But in general I would say it's how general society sees the disabled person, rather than how the disabled person sees themselves.

Clearly for these respondents, the use of the term 'sufferer' was negative. It should be noted at this point, however, that as with many issues considered during this research, not all respondents agreed with the views of these members of group 'S1' and there was diversity of opinion even within organizations:

Member 1 of C1:   I don't think there's anything wrong with it [*term 'arthritis sufferers'* – *ed.*].
Member 2 of C1:   Because we do suffer don't we?
Member 3 of C1:   I mean, I would say 'I suffer from...' not 'I've got...'

Member 4 of C1: I think that if people say we're sufferers, it makes us sound like victims.

Member 5 of C1: Half of it is that we do want to feel in charge – it has to be <u>our</u> decision. I mean, now and again it's nice to have a bit of sympathy, or empathy.

This diversity of opinion was also evident on a number of other occasions during the research in relation to the importance of language as a way of positively 're-identifying' disabled people. For example, at the Lancashire-based organization, comments by respondents demonstrated that although they did not deny the importance of using respectful terms when talking about disabled people, they nevertheless felt that there was a limit to the importance of language when seeking to improve the overall lives of disabled people:

AB: Okay – well the next issue is about how you prefer to identify yourselves (...) I'm thinking (...) about which expression is more acceptable: 'disabled people', 'people with disabilities' and so on...?

Member 1: Oh, I think you are moving onto 'political correctness' now!

AB: Well, do you have any feelings about it yourself?

Member 2: I just find it quite ironic that there is so much discussion that is a waste of time...it has been 'academicized'. Unless the position of disabled people in society changes, saying which word is most appropriate is just tokenism.

(...)

(...) if you look at words like 'spastic' or 'Mongol', you know – then they are medical in origin. And so until we move away from seeing people in that way, and instead see people in a more positive light – then any name will become an abusive word. I mean I can imagine it in the playground now instead of saying that someone is 'spastic', they're saying 'do you have a disability?!'

Worker at L1 referring to a statement made by another member of the group [*member confirmed this statement – ed.*]:

That's the central problem (...) isn't it? – I don't care what you call me – as you said to someone when they asked you about the language of disability – you can call me a cabbage if you like, just give me the money, basically.

On the other hand, at group 'C3', another respondent thought that campaigns relating to the use of language were a vital part of the struggle to improve the lives of disabled people:

> Member of C3:   It's preferable that people either worry about it or think about it [*language – ed.*] than...even if they don't always get it right...than if they don't think about it or think it's not important.
> (...)
> But that's why, in a sense, the language becomes a kind of, not a flag-ship, but it's almost like something that stands out. If you can't change that, if you can't start to change attitudes, how do you get the support to change the other things that you need to change?

On one level these differences are quite profound. For the respondents at the Lancashire-based organization, achieving improvements in relation to the language of disability runs the risk of being a mere sop in relation to the major structural barriers still facing disabled people. The respondent at group 'C3', however, sees structural and attitudinal barriers as closely interlinked and considers, therefore, that disability campaigns need to have a dual focus. The differences between the respondents here should not be over-emphasized, however, because the comments from both groups essentially convey the same message: that the key struggle facing disabled people is still to demolish structural barriers. Their views merely differ surrounding the extent to which changing the language of disability can help in this struggle.

This is a critical finding for this research because it highlights again, that even when the respondents in this research talked about the need for changes in attitudes and language, they were not aiming to achieve cultural or identity based rights, but instead were hoping to bring about necessary 'structural' changes in their lives. Taken as a whole, the evidence from this research brings into some doubt, therefore, the idea that a unified and positive 'disability identity', as defined by proponents of 'disability politics', is at the heart of all disability campaigning. Further, the findings also have clear implications for the notion of a disability culture. This issue will be considered briefly in the following section.

Disability culture

Whilst the findings of the research referenced here bring into question the idea that all members of the disability movement are concerned with seeking recognition on the basis of a positive 'disability identity', the research also uncovered evidence that brings into some doubt the idea that the disability movement, as a whole, can be categorized as being concerned with seeking to defend a disability culture. Most respondents showed some degree of uncertainty surrounding the idea of a disability culture:

Member C3: It's hard to see that [*disability culture – ed.*] existing in very broad terms, in terms of disability as a whole.

AB: Is there such a thing as a 'culture of disabled people'? (...)

Member S1: Yes, but it is not well developed. (...) Not many cultural icons. We have our heroes and villains and jokes – some of the elements of culture, but we are fundamentally different to other cultures in that you can be proud to be a woman, proud to be black, proud to be gay – but having a part of your person not working is essentially negative.

The only 'cultural difference' that was clearly identified by a number of the respondents in this research, and is demonstrated by the following comments from a respondent at group C2, was the issue of the acceptable use of non-politically-correct language amongst disabled people in humorous contexts:

Member of C2: (...) I think that there is a culture of disability.

AB: Right – so how would you describe that then?

Member of C2: (...) for example, we tend to talk in a different language with each other than we would do with someone who is not disabled...because there is affinity (...) we can use the terms that are not PC and get away with it. (...) we can crack Christopher Reeve jokes and that.

Whilst several of the respondents suggested that this use of non-politically-correct language in humorous contexts probably represented the disability culture, it is the argument here, however, that it is questionable to what extent this amounts to an entirely separate 'culture'.

The real difficulty perhaps, when considering cultural aims as the basis of the disability movement, appears to be the assumption that there is some 'essential' cultural *difference* between disabled people and non-disabled people, and that disabled people are culturally united. Whilst the members of the Lancashire-based group largely echoed the quotations above, again identifying humour as an example of disability culture, one respondent at this organization made the following comment:

Member of L1:	It's funny...non-disabled people...if for example... in town, in a meeting area, if you are in a wheelchair, people expect you to have much more affinity to someone else in a wheelchair...and you might do...
AB:	But no more than anyone does to anyone else?
Member of L1:	Quite.

Evidently then, this respondent is not entirely convinced by the idea that to be a disabled person is to be 'different' in a way that unites all disabled individuals.

During the research, some respondents also openly voiced concerns about the activities of those engaged in Disability Arts, who they feel are 'ghettoizing' disabled people by celebrating cultural 'difference' in a manner that is exclusionary:

Worker at L1:	It's a bit like when we went to this Art's meeting, you know, what I call the Disability Arts Mafia – DAM! – sorry! – (...) they are getting too separatist (...)
Member 2 of L1:	[*Agrees – ed.*] Which I hope doesn't happen because I think it will split the movement.

Such fears are clearly related to wider issues of separatism within the disability movement that will be considered in the next section of this chapter. Before moving on to consider the disability movement, however, it is also important to note one further point about the issue of the disability culture. Included in the research questions sent in advance of each group discussion was a question about disability culture. Despite this, however, no respondent chose to focus upon or talk at length about the question. Whilst this issue of a disability culture clearly requires a fuller investigation than was possible within this research, what can perhaps be suggested tentatively is that at present *cultural issues* have yet to reach the main agenda in many organizations and further, in the case of many organizations, are unlikely ever to reach this position. To conclude this section, the principal focus of many disability organizations continues to be the dismantling of structural barriers, with identity issues being an important but somewhat complex secondary issue.

The disability movement

In *Exploring Disability. A sociological introduction*, Barnes *et al* (1999: 207) state the following:

> It is a sign of the maturity and confidence of the disabled people's movement that disabled people are able to celebrate difference, and work together to create and discuss images of their own choosing.

The purpose of this section is to consider the extent to which the evidence from this research supports this statement.

The first thing that can be said with some certainty is that, as shown in the previous discussion, there was a degree of opposition to the idea of 'celebrating difference' amongst the respondents in this research. Equally, the respondents in this research expressed views in complete contrast to Barnes *et al* in two other respects: firstly, in relation to the idea of the disability movement being characterized by disabled people 'working together'. Several respondents highlighted the major divisions that exist between disabled people, as demonstrated in the following quotations:

Member of C3: The other thing which is quite important, which we've been doing recently is trying to pull disability organizations throughout Cumbria together as a group, as a network, but that's very difficult. They're all really suspicious of each other and won't work together.
(...)
(...) one of the things we feel at the moment is that we don't have particularly strong links with the Deaf community for instance. And I don't think

that's necessarily just to do with us – it's that the Deaf community is quite self-contained as well (...)

(...) it's very fragmented the whole thing, that's why this idea of a movement is very difficult to come to terms with sometimes.

Member of S1:   Now when we set up the forum we lost all the able-bodied representatives of charities like The Spastics Society – as they were then – (...) the Multiple Sclerosis Society, the Polio Federation and all those, but we also lost a lot of disabled people from those organizations who didn't want to join the 'common pool of disability' they wanted to just stick with their impairments. Now, we said, that basically the barriers we're fighting apply to everybody – to some in one area more than others...regardless of their impairments, but maybe – I feel sure that this is an inadequacy in the Social Model, because it doesn't place sufficient, it doesn't pay sufficient attention to the specific consequences of specific disabilities and it thinks that everything can be massed together. So in a way they were right and we were wrong and in another way, we were right and they were wrong! And we actually had huge animosity from other disability groups, because when disabled people become empowered what we do is to attack each other first – I think because we see each other as weak and disempowered like ourselves and so really fairly easy targets – but useless targets! We should be taking our fight outside to the people who actually erect the barriers.

Secondly, during the course of the research other aspects of discussion also highlighted the somewhat disunited nature of the disability movement. Divisions on the grounds of impairment became apparent, the major issue being the reluctance on the part of those with physical impairments to associate themselves with people with a learning disability or a mental health problem, although this is usually explained with regard to the limits of the professional knowledge of the organization:

Member of L1:   Because none of us have a learning disability it would be very unfair of us to try to advise someone with a learning disability, depending on the inquiry. There are also quite a few organizations who deal with people with mental health problems and people with learning disabilities, so it is quite often better to signpost (...) or getting in touch with the particular organizers because they've got the expertise on whether it be mental health or learning difficulties which we do not possess.

There were some comments made, however, which show how pervasive certain images of people with a learning disability or a mental health problem can be, even amongst disabled people. In the following quotes, the first respondent demonstrates the fear she has in relation to people with a mental health problem and the second respondent, in talking about people with a learning disability, suggests that 'forbearance' is necessary when including such individuals:

Member of C3:   If you don't know them [*people with mental health problems – ed.*] you don't quite know what they're going to do (...)

Member of C1:   And we're all very <u>tolerant</u> aren't we? [*Of persons with learning disabilities – ed.*]

Whilst in many respects neither of these comments were extremely disablist in tone, nevertheless it is the suggestion here that such views may represent a major barrier to the development of an inclusive and cohesive disability movement.

Divisions on the basis of illness/disability were also apparent during the research. Members of group 'C1', for example, felt that understanding their experiences of pain was important because it helped to explain their apparent lack of politicization:

Member 3 of C1:   My achievement is getting through the day!

Another respondent, from group 'S1', although more personally 'politicized', also highlighted this issue of illness and disability:

Member 1 of S1:   I actually, personally, have – and still do to a certain extent – question whether I'm really part of it [*the disability movement – ed.*] actually, because of my impairment – because my impairment involves being ill.

Member 2 of S1:   You're not a 'fit paraplegic'?!

Member 1 of S1:   Exactly! Because I think the disability movement when it started out wanted to distance itself from people who are ill – so I sometimes feel that, okay, I'm part of it when I feel reasonably well – but when I don't feel well I don't feel part of it.

(...)

I agree quite strongly with what GLAD[3] have said – they talk about the need to bring impairment into disability (...)

What is important at this point is the manner in which this respondent identifies the underlying issue here – the inclusion of the experience of 'impairment' into definitions and understandings of disability. This respondent went on to discuss at some length her own uncertainties with regard to her position as a disabled person. She explained how, because it is unclear whether a person who is long-term 'ill', such as herself, can be a part of the disability community, she had initially found it difficult to identify herself confidently as a disabled person. Friends and colleagues had rejected the idea that she was disabled, and when the point had arrived when she felt that she could accept and embrace the 'disability identity', she then felt rejected by some elements of the disability movement. She stated that she considered the work of Jane Campbell to exemplify the attitudes within the movement which have made her feel excluded:

Member S1:   She [*Jane Campbell – ed.*] said, if somebody is ill then they deserve sympathy but that's different from disability. And I think the BCODP embodies some of that kind of attitude.

This issue is important to this research because it demonstrates that even when an individual may be keen to embrace the 'disability identity' and to be included in the disability movement, the views of dominant figures and the dominant ideologies within a movement may actually be perceived as acting to exclude that individual.

The other important division that emerged during this research was the difference between the level of 'politicization' of disabled people who live in the larger cities and traditionally more industrial areas, and disabled individuals living in more rural or isolated areas. In terms of the groups involved in this research the following organizations were city based: S1; S2; and L1. The following organizations were based in more isolated rural areas, and this includes Carlisle which, although having official 'city' status is an essentially rural centre and groups based there draw their members from the surrounding rural areas: C1; C2; and C3.

Whilst respondents particularly in groups 'L1' and 'S1' spoke in some depth about their feelings about being a part of the disability movement, respondents in the more rural based organizations considered themselves to be somewhat removed from the movement:

Member of C3:   We kind of live outside that world for the moment (...) in terms of voluntary sector organizations I would say Cumbria is still behind, lags behind especially (...) the urban areas. But is that about pace of development? It would be quite surprising to see a rural area moving well in advance of an urban area because of the way they can organize – they've got a smaller area, they can pull people together far more easily.

AB: Do you feel a part of the disability movement?

Member of C2:   I don't, no. (...)

I think it's difficult to mobilize people, and motivate... (...) 'I can't do anything as a single voice' you know – there's not enough of us in the local area.

(...)

AB: So it's isolation?

Member of C2:   To come out and shout...yes, the feeling of isolation...it might not be particularly isolated...

AB: But you feel that you are?

Member of C2:   Yes, but you feel a lone voice a lot of the time... and then you become accepting of things that you should never really accept.

These discussions would suggest that there is a rural/urban divide between disabled people in terms of the activities of their organizations.

The final, and perhaps most important, issue that divides disabled people, and which was greatly evident in this research, is the extent to which disabled individuals see the need for a 'separatist' movement, strong on 'internal bonding' amongst members of the group, and with a clear separation between 'insiders' and 'outsiders' to the movement. As has already been discussed within Chapter 1, all of the groups that participated in this research were run by and for disabled people, and all place limits upon the involvement of non-disabled people. None of the groups, however, excluded non-disabled people *entirely*. In most of the groups there were non-disabled workers, and some groups chose to include a non-disabled worker in their group discussion. Further, at groups 'C2' and 'L1', helping the carers of disabled people is included in the work of the organization:

Member of C2:   Well, because carers have needs as well.

Several respondents also expressed their concerns surrounding moves being made by one of the most important 'umbrella' organizations of disabled people, the BCODP, towards a '100% disabled' rule, whereby all BCODP member groups are required to be run entirely by disabled people, with no non-disabled people on their management committees:

Member of L1:   I think they [*BCODP – ed.*] may be going too far for
                [*group L1's – ed.*] liking.
                (...)
                I've already said my biggest concern about the
                '100%' issue is that RADAR[4] will look like a more
                reasonable option!

AB: (...) I don't know if you are aware that there are
                moves within some organizations to become,
                totally, 100% controlled by disabled people. Is that
                a positive step, is it something you could see...

Member of C2:   It's a negative step! (...) It's segregation again isn't
                it?

In a related comment, a respondent at group 'C3' expressed concerns over the extent to which separatism in general, both in terms of the 'disability identity' and within the disability movement, is a positive step:

Member of C3:   But there are situations where, for whatever reason,
                whether it's social, political or both, people do
                need to identify together and form some sort of
                grouping. And it may be more appropriate in cer-

tain circumstances or localities than it is in others. (...) In a political sense that is – there may be greater strength, well, some people may feel there's greater strength in grouping with a clear identity to put forward (...) ideas (...)

AB: So you can see times when people would need, or want to identify themselves, firmly, as 'disabled'?

Member of C3: There may be. How far they could do that successfully and in terms of separating themselves off completely – creating a totally separate identity is very difficult because as I said earlier, we live in a mixed society. (...) So there is a danger in grouping (...) that also allows the wider, non-disabled society the opportunity (...) to say, well, 'There they are, that group – let them get on with it!'

To return then to the quotation from Barnes *et al* (1999) that began this section, a consideration all of these different divisions between disabled people and between different disability organizations, clearly suggests that there are limits to the extent to which there is a unified disability movement in which disabled individuals are 'working together'. Equally, as the previous discussion demonstrates, the implications of these important divisions between disabled people suggest that the idea of a 'mature disability movement' must also be questioned. Indeed, precisely on this point, several respondents commented on the fact that they considered the disability movement to be in its fairly 'early stages':

Member of S1: My feeling is that it is realistic to talk about a disability movement but it is still very young and it is not coherent and it is in danger of falling apart.

Member of L1: (...) if you look at when the suffragettes started, they were just a handful of 'extreme' women. (...) They did not represent, you would not have said that they were a 'Woman's Movement.' (...)

AB: Would you say it was as embryonic as that? – that the Disability Movement is in a very embryonic stage in that case then?

Member of L1: Yes, I mean, maybe not at the very beginning.

AB: No.

Member of L1: But a long way off any kind of movement.

In the light of such disunity and the agreed lack of 'maturity' of the disability movement, the question of what kind of movement it is, and what it means to be a part of the existing movement, was an issue much discussed between respondents. In terms of locating the movement, discussions at groups 'S1' and 'L1' revealed that although respondents unquestionably believed that the BCODP was a major part of the disability movement, that it could not be said to *be* the disability movement:

Member of L1:	(...) I think the closest we've got to a movement is the BCODP. (...) But it's a long way off being a movement, simply because the numbers don't add up.
Member of L1:	Well, we are quite willing to leave it [*BCODP – ed.*] if necessary.
AB:	Yes? So you don't think...we can't equate the Disability Movement with the BCODP?
Member of L1:	No.
Member of S1:	I'm against being hide-bound by one organization. The BCODP is not the movement.

In saying such things, these respondents were aware that they were going against some of the orthodoxies of Disability Studies that place considerable emphasis on the BCODP as the site of the movement. This is a key point, because quite apart from the issue of which organization is the most important within the disability movement, it also raises the issue of what it means to be a part of the movement. Is it necessary to be affiliated to any organization to be a part of the disability movement? Here again, there were interesting differences of opinion between disabled people, as demonstrated by this excerpt from discussion at the Lancashire-based organization where the issue of what constitutes involvement in the movement was debated:

Member 1 of L1:	But if you get from the house to the pub and people see you, you are immediately representing disabled people.
Member 2 of L1:	*I hope not!*
Member 1 of L1:	Oh I hope you are – well, I hope people will stand in the street and go 'Oh look! There's [*name – ed.*] on his bike, going to the pub like a normal human being!'

The idea that a broader definition of what constitutes involvement in the disability movement is needed was also raised by a respondent from group 'C3':

Member of C3: (...) So, it is strange isn't it – with saying we don't think there's a great, necessarily a movement, and it is giving the impression that we're not particularly political in a sense – especially with a big 'P'! Yet at the same time, we've got involved in a disability organization – why aren't we involved in a childminding organization! You know what I mean?

To conclude this section of analysis, therefore, it is plain that there are some important problems with the views of certain leading academics and activists in the field of disability with regard to their theorizing on the coherence, location and functioning of the disability movement. Whilst the evidence from this research does not, overall, bring into doubt the existence of the disability movement, it does suggest that the definition of the disability movement provided by mainstream Disability Studies may not be entirely accurate. Before embarking, within the following chapter, upon a more theoretical consideration of these findings, there is one final section to this chapter:

Deafness and disability[5]

As previously explained within Chapter 1, during the process of the research an issue arose surrounding the absence from any of the participating organizations, of Deaf/deaf people, or people with mental health problems. This absence led to inevitable questioning of whether this was a chance occurrence, or whether these groups were, for some reason, not a part of the disability community. Since the most striking theme arising from the first round of group discussions surrounded the issue of identity, it was thought to be important to establish whether the absence of such individuals was because they did not feel themselves to be welcome within the disability movement, or because they did not regard themselves to be disabled people. Since research time was limited, it was decided that further investigation would be made into the apparent absence of Deaf/deaf people from such disability organizations. To achieve this, a letter and series of questions was posted onto the web-based mail group: 'Deafmail'. In this section, the findings of this part of the research will be considered.

Before considering the comments of the three Deafmail respondents, it is important to note one key fact about each of these individuals: that each person identified themselves as 'deaf' or 'deafened' and made it clear that they were not a part of the 'Deaf' community. Despite the fact that 'Deafmail' is a mail-based group used by both deaf and Deaf people, no Deaf individuals chose to respond to the research questions posted on this website. Therefore, whilst it is not possible to gauge the views of the Deaf community on these matters, it may be possible to surmise from this absence of response that the Deaf community either did not wish to address the issue of their association with the disability movement, or simply did not find the question of 'disability' relevant to their experiences. Either way, what can be concluded is that there is some uncertainty about whether Deaf people are, or wish to be, a part of the disability community/movement.

That key divisions between deaf/deafened and Deaf communities exist, is something that all of the respondents identified, but was most clearly identified by respondents 1 and 2.

Deafmail respondent 1: I do not feel part of the Deaf BSL community. I've my deaf friends from boarding school [*name of school – ed.*] but do not identify with Deaf culture or feel I am part of a linguistic minority. This is despite having spent several years in the London Deaf scene and having Deaf boyfriends.

AB: Is there a Deaf identity and/or a Deaf culture that is different from those of hearing people?

Deafmail respondent 1: Yes, but I don't identify with it. It is about as accessible to me as a culture like Australian aborigines or African Bushmen. (...)

I wish the Deaf world would stop bickering and in-fighting. Deaf BSL users look down on SSE[6] deaf people and the deafened. It's just stupid. We all need to accept that everyone is different. (...)

I do feel excluded from the Deaf Community. And yes I did expect to become part of it. When I left school, I started going down the deaf club and learnt to sign – but never felt accepted. In London I was very involved in the Deaf world for about 4–5 years but gradually grew to feel that my face didn't fit and that the way I saw life was different. So I just started fading out of the picture. Incidentally two school friends, who are both fluent in BSL and who have been very involved in the Deaf community, both say they don't feel they are 'real' Deaf people.

Deafmail respondent 2: The Deaf have their own identity and culture based on their use of BSL. The deafened do not have a separate identity or culture. (...)

As things are at present, I have absolutely no wish to be part of the 'D' community. It is a very bitchy and back-stabbing group. People within it seem to take offence very quickly because they are unaware of the nuances that one can place on one's voice to create irony or something else. (...)

I would very much like to see the different sections of the deaf (i.e. *ALL* sections of the deaf community) (...) find common ground. That is achievable as we do co-operate within the Telecommunications Action Group (TAG). But I very much doubt whether we'll see agreement on all issues that will allow us to be presented as a homogeneous group of people.

Clearly these divisions run deep and are the basis of some conflict between groups of deaf/Deaf people.

In relation, however, to the question of whether deaf people are 'disabled' and whether they consider themselves to be a part of the disability movement, there was less agreement between the respondents.

All respondents said that they did identify themselves as disabled people. The interesting point about their comments, however, is that they define their disability only in terms of impairment. This suggests that these respondents may not be as aware of the Social Model of disability as some of the members of the disability organizations that took part in this research.

AB:	Are deaf people disabled? [*Respondents all replying to same question – ed.*]
Deafmail Respondent 1:	Yes, from my point of view. My ears don't work. Outside the deaf world, only family and 2–3 close friends can understand what I am saying. Of course I'm disabled. But it is a sensory handicap rather than a physical mobility issue.
Deafmail Respondent 2:	Deafened people like myself are prepared to accept we are disabled since we don't have full access to communication via our auditory senses.
Deafmail Respondent 3:	In my view absolutely yes but some would not see it that way. Indeed it took me many years before I would recognize the position. It is because the deafness is hidden unlike a physical disability.

The tone of these comments clearly suggests that for these respondents the disabled identity is something that is essentially negative since it is associated with loss, in this case of hearing. The comments also suggest that these respondents have not embraced their identities as disabled people, but rather it is something that they have come to 'accept/recognize'. That they would prefer not to be deaf and cannot, therefore, be seen to be 'celebrating' their deafness is shown by following comments:

Deafmail Respondent 1:	Being deaf is just something that I am. I get on with life and try to live the life I want to have. I'd just prefer not to be deaf.
Deafmail Respondent 2:	I am aware that Deaf people (i.e. the born deaf) have some concerns that medical progress e.g. cochlear implants may even-

tually lead to the reduction in size of the Deaf Community particularly if Genetic Engineering identified the faulty gene that causes loss of hearing in inherited deafness. Some of the more extreme Deaf campaigners see medical advances as a means of committing genocide on the Deaf Community. I hasten to add that is NOT my view nor the view of the majority of deaf people but some people genuinely do hold that belief.

(...)

I would personally welcome advances in genetics that led to deafness being eradicated. No one who has not been deaf themselves will be aware of how isolating the problem can be.

Clearly these types of view echo the rejection of the idea of a positive 'disability identity' expressed by some members of the disability organizations that participated in this research. Interestingly, the final comment from respondent 2 above, about genetics, stands in stark contrast to the concerns of some leading disability activists and academics in relation to this matter. Whilst it must be stated that the attitudes of these individuals towards such issues as advancements in genetics may not represent the views of all deaf people, and certainly cannot be said to represent the views of the Deaf community, such opinions must not be ignored by mainstream Disability Studies. That such 'diverse' opinions have been largely ignored with Disability and Deaf Studies is something that respondent 1 clearly identified:

Deafmail Respondent 1:   Nearly all social science work is around Deaf language and culture, you don't often get anything analysing the world of those who have hearing loss and the divisions between the deaf.

Further, respondent 2 expressed how powerless he felt in relation to his views on genetic engineering when faced with the powerful opposition to these new technologies being voiced by key activists and academics in the field:

Deafmail Respondent 2: I think it will be difficult to put forward reasoned debate to those who are opposed to genetic engineering. I think we have to reluctantly accept their viewpoint.

This comment highlights some important disparities of power between leading figures in the field and 'ordinary' deaf individuals. This comment also clearly resonated with the views of some of the disabled respondents in the research in relation to the power of dominant voices within a community. Respondent 1 also highlighted the tendency on the part of some key figures in the field to hold a 'your either with us or against us' attitude when facing differences of opinion within the deaf community. She talked about the 'exclusive' nature of the Deaf identity and how some deaf people feel that they are not 'real' Deaf people and that they have not been 'accepted' by the Deaf community. She also stressed her own concerns about the way in which certain deaf voices have been silenced in favour of the voices of the dominant few and of the negative implications of this:

Deafmail Respondent 1: One of the reasons I'm not terribly keen on this Deaf Community approach is that it's so limiting. The world is full of hearing people.
(...)
The Deaf BSL user community is a tiny minority; they just happen to be extremely vocal.

This quotation clearly echoes the views of several of the disabled respondents in this research in relation to fears they had about separatism in the movement and the potential for 'ghettoization'.

Moving to the issue of the disability movement, having stated that they each felt themselves to be disabled people, the deafmail respondents did, however, have mixed feeling about whether they were a part of the disability movement:

Deafmail Respondent 1: Deaf people are cut off from the disability movement because of the communication barrier. I do, however, identify with the disability movement because the idea is to remove barriers, whether physical or not.
(...)

	If you put me in a room full of people with physical disabilities, I still can't talk to them without communication support. For me, they are hearing people. To them, I am able bodied.
Deafmail Respondent 2:	Some Deaf people are a part of a campaign to obtain recognition of British Sign Language in its own right but would probably not see that as part of a disability movement. Other deafened people are campaigning for equal access to things and do recognize that their campaigns are part of the wider disability movement. I'm not actively campaigning though.
AB:	Do you personally feel a part of a disability movement?
Deafmail Respondent 3:	I am not as I prefer to work positively in the hearing world (...) I am basically a part of the hearing world.

Thus, for these respondents, the disability movement is not something that they feel strongly connected with. This is interesting considering that, during the email correspondence with these individuals, they each mentioned that they were facing the same sort of structural and social barriers identified by many of the members of the disability organizations involved in this research. In the case of respondent 1, the similarities in barriers faced between deaf and disabled people is something that she herself acknowledges:

Deafmail Respondent 1:	Do you know about deaf education? The Oralism versus Total Communication debate?
AB:	Yes (...) – what are your views on this issue?
Deafmail Respondent 1:	I could go on for hours on this one! To put it very baldly, oralism works fine for kids with enough hearing to support their lipreading and speech. Lipreading is 90% guesswork on its own. But oralism has been implemented as a blanket method of educating ALL deaf children to be as normal as possible. Unfortunately

the end result of oralism applied to very very deaf children is nearly always illiteracy (reading age of 7 at most) plus speech no one can understand. There's a parallel here with other disabled children being educated to 'pass' and it not working at all well. Total communication at least means deaf children leave school with language and skills.

Other respondents commented about experiences in the workplace and public attitudes towards deaf people and, whilst not making direct comparisons with the experiences of other disabled people, such comparisons are nevertheless obvious:

Deafmail Respondent 2:   There does need to be some education on the part of hearing people to understand how isolating the invisible handicap of being deaf can be. How that can be addressed I am not sure. I know there are several Deaf Awareness Courses but I'm not sure whether hearing people would welcome them if there was some compulsion to attend them. (...)
People are much more helpful now but I do find that people still have doubts that deaf people can be intelligent and reliable workers.

Deafmail Respondent 3:   (...) there is still much that could be improved in deaf awareness. (...) The willingness to provide support under the DDA also needs to be pressed. Many public services do not provide or understand the need to provide support.

Despite these obvious similarities between the experiences and concerns of deaf people and disabled people, however, the overall conclusion to this section must, nevertheless, be that there is some uncertainty about the position of deaf/Deaf people in relation to the 'disability identity' and the disability movement. This picture is made considerably more complex by the internal divisions between deaf/Deaf people.

Conclusion

This chapter has highlighted the fact that, for many disabled people, breaking down structural barriers remains of central importance. Respondents in this research identified a range of problems facing disabled people in the public sphere, for example in relation to the institutions of government, education and in the labour market. They routinely stressed the role of the state and/or society in relation to their disempowerment. In this respect, the views of respondents in this research clearly supported the idea of the 'disabling society'.

In other central respects, however, the respondents' comments often stand in some contrast to the views of a number of key activists and academics who argue for the exclusion of impairment from the Social Model of disability and who also espouse the idea of a 'politics of disability' based upon a celebration of a 'disability identity'. Whilst the findings of this research do not bring into serious question the existence of a disability movement *per se*, they do highlight the fractured nature of this collective. The views of the respondents in this research also bring into doubt the idea that a unified and positive 'disability identity' lies behind all disability campaigning or that the idea of a celebration of a separate 'culture of disability' is part of the main agenda for all disability organizations.

As will be discussed in the following chapter, it is the argument in this book that these findings have clear implications for contemporary theorizing on citizenship, social movements and for the approach taken by mainstream Disability Studies to disability politics.

6
Reconsidering Theorizing on Citizenship and Social Movements in the Light of Disability

Introduction

As previously discussed within Chapter 2, despite centuries of theorizing, citizenship remains a contested concept. Whilst a widely agreed definition of what exactly 'citizenship' entails remains largely elusive, certain themes are recurrent within contemporary theorizing. As shown in the discussion in Chapter 2, issues of 'identity' and 'difference' are now at the heart of most contemporary citizenship theorizing. That these two issues have become of major importance must largely be the result of successful campaigning by a variety of pressure groups. Consequently, such things as class, ethnicity, employment status and sexuality are now routinely considered by citizenship theorists and have greatly affected thinking in this field. Disability, however, has been largely ignored and yet the findings of the research referenced in this book suggest that this omission may be unwise, for what a consideration of disability tells us does not always sit comfortably with recent citizenship theorizing. Indeed, it is the argument here that a consideration of disability related issues is invaluable for it provides useful insights into the shortcomings of many key theories of citizenship and demonstrates the need for ongoing theorizing in this field.

The very ancient origins of the citizenship debates have already been discussed at some length in Chapter 2. The first thing that must be stated, therefore, is that the focus of this chapter is upon the more modern/contemporary approaches. These approaches include a variety of theories that have been developed after World War II and move from the frequently criticized, but nevertheless influential, Social-Liberal perspectives exemplified in the work of Rawls, Marshall and

Berlin, through the pluralist accounts of writers such as Kymlicka and Young, to the reflexive account of Habermas and finally to the post-structuralist critiques provided by authors such as Mouffe.

The second point that should be noted is that it is not the intention within this chapter to revisit the critiques of the various citizenship theories as considered in Chapter 2. For this reason, the reader is asked to consider the arguments that have been made there alongside the discussion within this chapter. The aim of this chapter is to relate the necessarily particular findings of the research referenced in this book to key aspects of existing theories of citizenship. These aspects are, therefore, 'selective'.

Social-Liberalist accounts

As previously stated, the Social-Liberal view of citizenship is probably best exemplified in the work of Rawls, Marshall and Berlin. Whilst some authors might question Marshall's position as a Social-Liberal, since he is often considered to be more of a social-democrat, his credentials as a modern proponent of the older liberal tradition have, nevertheless, been discussed at some length in Chapter 2. It is on the basis of the argument made there, that he is considered within this section.

For Rawls, citizenship is best viewed as a system of co-operation. He describes this system as rational individuals co-operating on the basis of mutual respect for one another. The first thing to note here, therefore, is that the attitudes of non-disabled people towards disabled people are clearly not always rational. Several quotations from the respondents cited in Chapter 5 demonstrate the ignorance of, or fear felt by, non-disabled people about disabled individuals. Equally, however, divisions between disabled people, for example between individuals with physical impairments and those with mental health problems, may also be due partly to beliefs, arguably both rational and irrational, held by some physically disabled people about the 'risks' involved in working or associating with such individuals. In the light of this, and the other divisions that have been demonstrated both within the disability community and in relation to the position of disabled people in wider society, the idea that Rawls' 'system of co-operation' exists, or is easy to achieve, is clearly problematic.

Of course, it can be argued that Rawls' system of co-operation is still a useful ideal and one that although not currently in place, is nevertheless something that we should be striving to achieve. Equally, however, it can be argued that Rawls' theory is unrealistically utopian in that he appears to ignore the seemingly 'natural' tendency on the part of human beings to categorize, stigmatize and disadvantage certain groups. Theorists in the area of 'race' and ethnicity, from as seemingly 'diverse' standpoints as the functionalist (Patterson, 1963), Marxist (Cox, 1970, Miles, 1982, 1993) and Weberian (Rex and Tomlinson, 1979) perspectives have all highlighted the fact that conflict is at the heart of society. Further, arguably, when considering the position of disabled people in society, the functionalist views on 'scapegoating', the Marxist theories of exploitation and the divisive impact of 'scapegoating' on the working class, and the Weberian approach to prejudice as a form of ideology which is used to disadvantage a supposedly 'inferior' group, can *all* be used to question the feasibility of Rawls' notion of co-operation.

In relation to the findings of the research upon which this book is based, it must also be stated that there is a problem with Rawls' ([1985] 1998: 60) account of citizenship in that it rests upon the idea of 'competency':

> (...) persons as citizens have all the capacities that enable them to be normal and fully co-operating members of society.

There is a great deal here that needs 'unpacking', for the construction of society being put forward here by Rawls is clearly a normative one. It is the argument here that this is also a view of society shared by Marshall in his famous work: *Citizenship and Social Class*. Although the extent to which Marshall was proposing a normative or an empirical outline of citizenship is much debated, it is the argument within this book that it was clearly both. In this respect the argument here owes much to Delanty's (2000: 17) analysis, for he states that although Marshall's work '*was primarily a description of the development of citizenship in England*' it was '*one that had a strong normative edge to it*'. This 'normative edge' is demonstrated by Marshall's ([1963] 1998: 102 [my emphasis]) definition of citizenship as a 'status', for he writes that:

> All who possess the status are equal with respect to the rights and duties with which the status is endowed. There is no universal principle that determines what those rights and duties shall be, *but societies in which citizenship is a developing institution create an image of an ideal citizenship against which achievement can be measured and towards which aspiration can be directed.*

The theories of both Rawls and Marshall therefore clearly rest upon an image of an 'ideal/good citizen' against which the achievements of individuals can be measured. This has implications for all groups whose beliefs or actions do not conform to the dominant group's notions of 'normality' or 'civilization'. Alternatively, such normative views also have implications for individuals or groups who may be unable to 'live up to' this image of 'ideal citizenship', for they are judged to be failing in what clearly amounts to an important aspect of the status of *'personhood'*.

Explanations for the concept of 'personhood' and who is termed a 'proper person' and who is *not* appear, therefore, to underlie both Rawls' and Marshall's approaches to citizenship. There is a tendency in such Social-Liberalist accounts, therefore, to view citizenship as a 'status' in which respect is given to those who take up the role and perform it competently. In relation to the position of disabled people in society, as Marks (2001) states, the manner in which society constitutes disabled people as 'racialized others' positions them outside the category of 'personhood' and this impacts upon their perceived competency with regard to citizenship. As has already been discussed in Chapter 4, (in)competence must, therefore, be seen as a social construction (Jenkins, 1998). As Goodey (1995) has commented, by defining who is *fit* to exercise the responsibilities of citizenship, citizenship as a concept has traditionally been *about* exclusion. In other words, a vicious circle emerges in that where there is stigma, there is also an assumption of 'incompetence' with regard to citizenship. The implications of this assumption of incompetence then prevent those experiencing this stigmatized identity from achieving those goals associated with being a 'good citizen', thus perpetuating their image as 'failures' within society.

As a society we appear to regard such things as living an independent life, achieving paid employment and 'responsible' parenting as being central to the image of the 'good citizen'. It has been well documented, however, by research in the field of disability and within the findings of this research, that many disabled people continue to face major structural barriers when it comes to gaining proper employment, living their lives independently, and having relationships and family lives. Further, in relation to what Marshall clearly believed to be the 'backbone' of citizenship – *education* – the comments of respondents in the research upon which this book is based clearly demonstrate that there have been in the past, and still are, serious failings in terms of the life opportunities provided by special-needs education. Also, as discussed in Chapter 4, despite key attempts to improve the educational opportunities and attainment of disabled children and young people, important questions remain surrounding the success of more recent moves towards 'mainstreaming'.

According to the Social Model of Disability, the reasons why the provision of a range of services for disabled people fails to *enable* disabled people to 'live up' to this image of a 'good citizen', rest upon the views held by non-disabled people about disabled people. The vicious circle previously described thus emerges in the lives of disabled people, for the 'stigma' attached to the identity of a disabled person can be seen to be both the result of, and the reason for, their continuing position in society. The 'stigma' attached to the identities of disabled people with different impairments does differ, and it may be easier to fight against the stigma associated with certain impairment than others, but nevertheless the assumption of incompetence with regard to citizenship applies to the majority of disabled people, to a certain extent.

Ironically, of course, one of Marshall's other interests, apart from theorizing British citizenship, was the historical and global comparison of different types of citizenship and social structure. When considering the effects of social status upon citizenship, he considered the caste system of India and the manner in which it is underpinned by notions of purity and impurity. It is clear that Marshall did not consider the British system of social structure and citizenship to have any similarities with this caste system and yet it can be argued, perhaps somewhat controversially, that this connection does exist. Shakespeare (1994: 294), for example, draws upon Mary Douglas' (1966) notion of purity and impurity when he comments that: '*When boundaries are breached, and identities seem threatened, behaviour is devoted to re-establishing the fixates, reinforcing categories and power relations*'. It is, perhaps, possible to suggest therefore, that the fact that the identities of disabled people have been stigmatized and that their overall position in society is not entirely based upon personal wealth but upon other more psychosocial reasons, means that the position of disabled people in Britain today bears more relation to the caste system than to the class based analyses that are more usually employed when considering the UK.

In short, what Marshall, like Rawls, did not adequately resolve within his early work, was the problem of *persistent and unjust social inequality*. If citizenship is to be about *justice*, then unequal status must be *fairly* apportioned according to unequal abilities. In reality, power differentials within society ensure that certain groups remain disadvantaged. Images of the 'ideal citizen' may be socially and culturally determined and in societies in which power inequalities exist, it is likely that the dominant group will determine the image of the 'ideal citizen'. In the same way that host societies tend to deny their own ethnic identities, however, the powerful group are also likely to think that their image of the 'ideal citizen' is non-group-specific. In this way, it can be argued that if the dominant group comprises non-disabled, middle-class, white men, then the image of an 'ideal citizen' is likely to reflect the characteristics of this distinct group. The effect of this is to 'legitimize' rather than reduce social inequality as more and more people are seen to 'fail' to live up to the image of the 'ideal citizen' and the 'official' status of equal citizenship then becomes meaningless as it fails to compensate for that social inequality.

This critique of the early work of Marshall, along with the work of the earlier liberals was, of course, advanced convincingly by feminist writers during the 1980s (see for example, Pateman, 1988). It does not tend to be widely acknowledged, however, that at about the same time, Marshall re-visited his earlier theorizing. In his 1981 work *Reflections on Power*, Marshall discussed the civil rights movement in America and argued that what was being claimed by this movement was not 'power over' or 'redistribution', but rather an effective share in the total power of society. In other words as Isin and Wood (1999: 31) have stated, Marshall perceived such movements as being about the *'power to escape anomie, disrespect and alienation to achieve legitimate goals by the use of legitimate means'*. The goal, Marshall believed, was a new kind of multicultural society, or if that should prove impossible, then a society composed of independent and equal ethnic communities. In this way, Marshall quite clearly anticipated the pluralist accounts of citizenship.

Having stated the above, however, it is the argument here that Marshall's dominant contribution to the citizenship debates, no matter how unfair this may be to his wider thinking, is still that of his earlier theorizing. Furthermore, whilst his later work is interesting in the way in which it can be seen as an important pre-cursor of the pluralist accounts, the work of Marshall's contemporary Isaiah Berlin, has clearer pluralist credentials.

Before considering the work of Berlin and the pluralist thinkers, it must be stated, however, that there are a number of arguments in favour of the idea that there is nothing inherently wrong with this Social-Liberalist definition of citizenship, particularly as it appears in the work of Marshall, and that perhaps what is needed is to ensure that all groups, including disabled people, experience full rights in every sphere. For example, in relation to the lives of disabled people – as has been discussed in Chapter 4 in relation to education – improvements could be made in terms of a range of social rights for these individuals. In addition, as has been well documented elsewhere, improvements within the civil sphere could be made to the Disability Discrimination Act (DDA) with its numerous 'let-out clauses'. Although improvements to the DDA have been made under the current Labour government, it will be some time before the legal changes that can be enforced have positive effects in reducing the numerous disabling barriers and discrimination experienced by disabled people.

As was discussed in Chapter 5, respondents in this research identified the importance of enabling disabled people to 'participate' in decision-making. Within the political sphere, access to decision-making processes could be further improved at the most basic level by ensuring that all disabled people can exercise their right to vote. In reality there are several obstacles, in addition to issues of access, which prevent disabled people from participating. Barnes *et al* (1999) list some of these barriers as: traditional assumptions about disabled people's inability to make independent decisions; legalized barriers such as the Representation of the People Act 1983 that codifies an assumption of incompetence on the part of people with learning disabilities resident in institutions, and only permits such individuals to vote once they have proved themselves capable to do so; finally, the right to be entered onto the electoral register is often determined by the awareness and integrity of those who are 'in charge' of the lives of the disabled person, be that within the family or in an institution. In addition to voting, more genuine consultation with disabled people on a range of policy issues, in particular issues relating to welfare provision, is also needed in combination with an assurance that this consultation advances beyond what respondents in the research upon which this book is based described as mere 'rubber-stamping'.

It can be argued, however, that the most fundamental flaw in Marshall's definition of civil, political and social rights is that he assumes the possession of certain freedoms and powers on the part of each individual 'citizen'. What, for example, is the benefit of *liberty* without *choice*? It is often the case that disabled people are denied the right to make basic choices about their everyday lives because they rely upon local authority provision; or they experience, as many disabled people do, a life in poverty; or they have not got the confidence to speak out about their preferences. The growing number of self-advocacy and empowerment based groups of disabled people, including and akin to those that participated in the research referenced in this book, is a reaction to this historical reluctance by disabled people to speak out about the issues in their lives.

Ultimately, then, despite the appeal of some aspects of Marshall's work, these problems and the normative, monistic nature of his famous early work, and that of other Social-Liberal thinking, continue to be viewed as a major stumbling block when advancing this concept of citizenship as a way of tackling the inequalities faced by many disadvantaged groups, including disabled people. As has already been discussed at some length in Chapter 2, these theoretical problems were clearly identified by Isaiah Berlin (1958), who, although a contemporary of Marshall and a liberal thinker himself, arguably advanced beyond Marshall in terms of his theoretical understanding of the need broadly to reject the idea of a 'universal' definition of 'ideal citizenship'. It is proposed here, however, that despite this, the great value of Berlin's work on value-pluralism has been largely overlooked by sociologists. This is unfortunate, for it can be argued that his work avoids many of the pitfalls of other Social-Liberals. It is also proposed here that whilst Berlin's work can be seen as an important pre-cursor of the pluralist accounts of citizenship, his ideas may in fact be more useful than the subsequent pluralist theorizing. For this reason, a brief discussion of the value of Berlin's theorizing will appear at the end of the following section.

Pluralist accounts

Pluralist accounts of citizenship suggest that any contemporary definition of citizenship must include the realm of 'culture' in addition to the *civil, political and social*. For Stevenson (1997a: 42):

> (...) cultural citizenship can be said to have been fulfilled to the extent to which society makes commonly available the semiotic and material cultures necessary in order to make social life meaningful, critique practices of domination, and allow for the recognition of difference under conditions of tolerance and mutual respect.

According to Stevenson, the recognition of difference is only one part of cultural citizenship and it is also important to guarantee democratic institutions and to provide protection from the excesses of the free market. Nevertheless, the pluralist accounts do appear to place a large emphasis on the *politics of difference*. This would seem to be essential to the development of the concept of cultural citizenship.

Both Kymlicka and Young take as the basis of their theorizing a critical stance towards universalist, normative notions of citizenship. Both theorists perceive that in pluralist societies it is essential to consider group rights within the citizenship framework. In developing this alternative approach, however, an important problem faced both theorists, namely how to determine, in a non-arbitrary way, which groups 'deserve' such special provision. Answering this question has, arguably, led to one of the key difficulties with regard to this account of citizenship, for there would seem to be an underlying assumption with the work of both Kymlicka and Young that disadvantaged groups possess distinctly different identities/traits, or are part of a distinctive culture and that it is on the basis of these differences that group rights should be granted. The problem with this approach, as previously mentioned in Chapter 2, is that:

> (...) to assert that one simply knows that another person is defined predominantly by their culture or specific group traits rather than other factors seems as oppressive as refusing to believe that cultural characteristics are important at all.   (Fierlbeck, 1998: 99)

It is the argument here that individuals often have very complicated feelings about their own identities and that not everyone agrees about the existence of cultural differences between supposedly distinct groups. As was demonstrated in the research referred to in this book, this issue is much in evidence within the UK disability movement. Whilst Young does tackle some of these issues, as will be discussed later, Kymlicka's ideas are somewhat more problematic.

Drawing upon Rawls' (1971, 1996) 'social bases of self-respect', Kymlicka (1991: 192–3) treats cultural membership as being a precondition for the appreciation of other goods, not as a means of achieving those goods:

> But cultural membership is not a means used in the pursuit of one's ends. It is rather the context within which we choose our ends, and come to see their value, and this is a precondition of self-respect, of the sense that one's ends are worth pursuing. And it affects our very sense of personal identity and capacity. When we take cultural identity seriously, we'll understand that asking someone to trade off her cultural identity for some amount of money is like expecting someone to trade off her self-respect for some amount of money. Having money for the pursuit of one's ends is of little help if the price involves giving up the context within which such ends are worth pursuing.

In other words, in relation to disability, if disability culture is being used to *achieve* ends not as a context within which to *choose* ends then, according to Kymlicka's argument, the idea of a distinct cultural context of disability must be questioned. The evidence from this research suggests that this *achievement-orientation* is precisely what characterizes the activities of many members of the disability community, whose goal – be they using 'cultural' practices such as humour to achieve it – nevertheless continues to be their acceptance as part of the mainstream 'normal'[1] world. Equally, the evidence did not support the idea that there is a 'culture of disability' that differs from more 'mainstream' culture in any significant way or is experienced widely amongst all/ most disabled people. Instead evidence emerged that some disabled people are concerned about the risks associated with reinforcing 'difference' in a manner that is separatist.

In the light of Kymlicka's theorizing, the only logical conclusion that can be drawn from the views of the respondents in this research is that they do not consider their self-respect to be connected with a strong 'cultural identity' as a disabled people. Hence for these individuals, achieving the resources necessary to become assimilated into the 'normal' world does not mean a loss of 'true' identity. That many disabled people do not feel that the issue of 'trading off' cultural identities in order to achieve resources applies to them is exemplified in the comment made by one respondent: *'you can call me a cabbage if you like, just give me the money'* (Member of group L1, please see Chapter 5). Whilst it is possible that this member of the Lancashire-based group quoted here was intentionally using inflammatory language when making this comment in order to make his point more forcibly, the comment nevertheless reflected his overall opinion that calls for 'representation rights' to be given to disabled people should not take precedence over calls for more 'structural' improvements in the lives of these individuals.

In this way Kymlicka's analysis is, to a certain extent, helpful when seeking to *understand* the position and views of many disabled people, but a problem then arises, for if by his very construction, disabled people cannot be considered to be engaged in the struggle for cultural citizenship, then what alternative theory should be employed to explain the aims of the disability movement? Kymlicka's theorizing is clearly of value when considering the citizenship aims of groups that are unambiguously defined by cultural context but it is unclear how he would accommodate into his theory of group rights, groups that have a less clear cultural context. The need to advance theory in this area is all the more urgent not just in the light of disability, but also because of the increasing importance of the post-modern approaches to 'ethnicity'. Such approaches propose a more fluid understanding of cultural contexts and, further, have identified certain situations in which identities may be 'created' rather than originating in historical cultural contexts.

It is the – admittedly somewhat controversial – argument here that there is a clear sense in which the ideas of a political 'disability identity' and disability culture, being hailed by some of the key activists in the disability movement, represent a form of 'defensive engagement' akin, if not as well developed, to the defensive identities that have emerged amongst some ethnic minority groups in the face of racism (see, for example, the post-modernist account of Modood, 1997). The real difficulty, therefore, when considering cultural aims as the basis of the disability movement, appears to lie with the assumption that there is some 'essential' cultural *difference* between disabled people and non-disabled people. As discussed in Chapter 5, this is an issue identified as of some importance by respondents in the research upon which this book is based.

Further, whilst there are undoubtedly differences between all people, the manner in which the concept of 'difference' can be manipulated in an essentialist manner in order to categorize some groups as 'other', needs to be problematized. This point applies as much to the manner in which the dominant group – for example in relation to disability, non-disabled people – defines certain groups as 'different', as it does to the manner in which in prioritizing group solidarity, or *'marching to the beat of a single drum'* to use Shakespeare and Watson's phrase, dissident voices within a group are silenced and 'incarcerating identities' can be created. Further, in relation to the last issue, as one respondent from group C3 commented, there is a danger associated with the 'creation' of clearly defined separate group identities by minority groups themselves, in that it allows those in dominant positions external to the group to ignore the views of the minority systematically. In other words it: *'allows the wider, non-disabled society the opportunity (...) to say, well, "There they are, that group – let them get on with it!"'* (Member of C3. Please see Chapter 5)

It is at this point that it is useful to add in some further words of caution relating to these issues of group identity, arising from Bourdieu's work on the nature of *groups and categories*. For Bourdieu, whilst it is not an easy task to classify discretely the great variety of individuals that make up the real world, differences do nevertheless exist. He argues, however, that: *'it is possible to deny the existence of classes as homogenous sets of economically and socially differentiated individuals objectively constituted into groups, and to assert at the same time the existence of a space of differences based on a principle of economic and social differentiation'* (Bourdieu, 1987: 3). Bourdieu also proposes that it might be possible to do this by making a distinction between two types of collectivity, the *probable group* and the *practical group.*

In defining these two types of group, Bourdieu is clearly drawing heavily upon Marx's notion of *Klasse an sich* (class in itself) and *Klasse fuer sich* (class for itself), in which potentiality is turned into actuality, a class in itself into a class for itself, only when individuals occupying similar positions become involved in *'common struggles, a network of communication develops, and they thereby become conscious of their common fate'* (Coser, 1971: 49). Marx, however, somewhat *assumed* the practical existence of theoretical classes. Bourdieu (1987) questions this assumption and claims that it is only ever possible, at the outset, to talk with confidence about the existence of *probable groups*, whose constituent individuals are likely to form networks and mobilize on the basis of their similar dispositions, but may not in fact do so.

Bourdieu then provides a useful definition of a *practical group* against which to compare *probable groups*. For Bourdieu (1987: 15), a practical group exists when:

> (...) there are agents capable of imposing themselves, as authorized to speak and to act officially in its place and in its name (...)

He claims, however, that a paradox then arises, for whilst individuals who so identify themselves with a group may become empowered and gain recognition, at the same time they are relegating their individual powers to those who claim to speak on behalf of the group. Further, Bourdieu warns that the development of practical groups also involves a process by which the group begins *'to represent themselves as real as opposed to constructed via social struggles'* and in so doing *'they tend to essentialize properties of individuals that make up such groups by appealing to nature, God or science'.* (Isin and Wood, 1999: 38)

In relation to the findings of the research upon which this book is based, Bourdieu's theorizing therefore clearly resonates with the concern respondents expressed about the risks associated with embracing a political 'disability identity'. As previously discussed, respondents were clearly worried that such activity might lead to the essentializing of the 'disability identity' as 'other'. They also expressed fears about relegating their individual powers to the more vocal members of the disability movement who claim to speak on behalf of disabled people, and who are most closely involved in making claims on the basis of this political 'disability identity'.

The implications of Bourdieu's warnings for citizenship theorizing is therefore clear, for it demonstrates the importance of not taking 'at face value' the claims of group advocates as representing the views of all constituent members of a group and instead also to consider the views of the group's constituent members, lest they have somewhat conflicting opinions. In other words, to relate this discussion to Bourdieu's notion of *habitus*, citizenship theorists need to be careful to acknowledge that whilst the formation of a group does involve the conditioning of members into particular ways of being in, and understanding, the world – more so in fact than members would perhaps be aware, or wish – it is not true that all individuals displaying the same habitus are identical. For Bourdieu, the relationship between the habitus of the individual and the habitus of the group will always be homologous, but not identical. For this reason, citizenship theorizing should, perhaps, be concerned not with either the individual, or collectivities as seen as concrete groups of individuals, but rather with the '*mutual conditioning between group and individual habitus*'. (Bourdieu and Wacquant, 1992: 126–7)

Relating this discussion back to the matter in hand – the adequacy of the pluralist notion of citizenship that proposes that groups be given specific rights on the basis of their perceived cultural differences – in the light of Bourdieu's theorizing, therefore, it is important to be cautious about the idea of 'differentiated citizenship' when applied to any apparently distinct group. The fact that it is difficult to apply Kymlicka's notion of 'differentiated citizenship' to disabled people does not, therefore, mean that the position of disabled people represents the 'exception to the rule'.

To a degree, Young also assumes greater homogeneity within groups than may in fact exist. She does, however, acknowledge the need for a more contextualized understanding of difference and in this respect her theorizing is significantly unlike Kymlicka's. As has already been discussed at some length in Chapter 2, what sets Young apart from Kymlicka is her theorizing on the need for a more fluid and contextualized understanding of difference that rejects the tendency on the part of the dominant group to essentialize differences whilst denying their own specificity. Further, Young (1990) points to what she terms the 'dilemma of difference'. She defines this as a dilemma facing some socially excluded groups as they find that they have to deny that they are different from others since citizenship rights are so often based upon the equal moral worth of each individual, and yet simultaneously have to affirm their difference from other groups since formal equal treatment has placed them in a position of disadvantage.

Young's theorizing here on the construction of difference is useful when considering the position of disabled people, a group which she herself, in a somewhat rare move by a citizenship theorist, actually considers. Her argument, that depending upon the groups being compared and the context, differences may become more or less salient, echoes clearly with the findings of the research upon which this book is based. Her use of the following example also relates to these findings:

> (...) in the context of athletics, health care, social service support, and so on, wheelchair-bound people are different from others, but they are not different in many other respects. Traditional treatment of the disabled entailed exclusion and segregation because the differences between the disabled and the able-bodied were conceptualised as extending to all or most capacities.   (Young, 1990: 171)

Young considers that traditional politics has excluded or devalued people by suggesting that there are such things as essential differences. 'Difference' is therefore best viewed as the result of social processes, as a *social construction*. According to Davis (1999) it is precisely this notion of essential difference that has been perpetuated by the highly criticized Medical Model of Disability. For those who are involved in the construction of welfare policy there has been a convenient tradition of assuming that disabled people are 'different'. This has had two results: firstly, the development of a number of often disempowering apparatuses of welfare for disabled people, based upon assumptions about their 'special needs' and their dependency. Secondly, it further supports the notion of 'bodily perfection', in which disabled people are viewed as the imperfect 'other' and the non-disabled community refuse to accept their own, perhaps less visible, bodily imperfections or vulnerabilities. As Davis (1999) has commented, this attachment to the Medical Model and associated notions of ab/normality has been heavily criticized by the disability movement. Further, a number of campaigns by organizations of disabled people have taken place that have been based upon the notion that all people are vulnerable and interdependent to some extent during their lifetimes, and that therefore strike at the very heart of widely held beliefs about 'difference'.

The difficulty when considering the disability movement, however, is that, as previously stated, campaigns such as these that seek to break down assumptions about differences between disabled and non-disabled coexist with other campaigns that seek 'recognition' on the basis of a distinctly 'different' 'disability identity' and culture. That the latter type of campaign activity may not result in the 'positive' outcomes intended is something that it starting to be acknowledged within Disability Studies – the debate probably starting in earnest with the publication of the book *Exploring the Divide: Illness and Disability* edited by Barnes and Mercer (1996). This edited collection includes an important chapter by Tom Shakespeare (1996b) in which he begins the process of addressing this issue.

Adding to this debate, and drawing upon the findings of the research upon which this book is based, it is the assertion here that whilst all disabled people are keen to achieve recognition and respect, they are not all seeking to be recognized as having essentially *different* identities from those of non-disabled people, or as being a part of a *different* culture, but rather, as equal *persons*. In other words, there is then a risk of lapsing into a 'false consciousness' when considering identity and culture amongst disabled people. Everyone has an identity, and everyone has the right to have that identity respected by others. Further, it would be inaccurate to state that the imagery of 'identity', 'difference' and what Fraser (1995b) terms 'recognition', do not play a part in the disability movement's campaigns. There may be, however, misconceptions about the true nature of disability identity politics.

Whilst Young's work on 'essentialism' is key to this argument, further analysis of the disability movement highlights an issue that she has, arguably, not yet theorized adequately – namely the possibility that individuals may be 'labelled' inaccurately as 'different' not only by dominant 'outsiders', but also by dominant voices internal to the group. The maintaining of a unified political identity in this way by dominant members of the collective then becomes too reductive of the complexities of social identities (Fawcett, 2000). Disability is thus better viewed as a contested concept and issues of unity surrounding the homogeneity of the disability movement need to be considered carefully.

Equally, the manner in which Young utilizes her understanding of difference to develop a model of democracy and citizenship is also, arguably, somewhat problematic. This issue has already been discussed at some length in Chapter 2, but whilst it is not the intention here to repeat the critique of Young's theorizing that appears there, it is important to consider how the evidence from the research upon which this book is based relates uneasily to some important aspects of her work.

The first way in which the evidence from this research does not appear to correspond with Young's analysis is in relation to the idea that the self-organization of group members in order that they achieve collective empowerment is not only possible, but it is also *desirable*. As has previously been discussed in this chapter, both the views of the respondents in this research and the arguments put forward by Bourdieu bring into question Young's views in this regard. The findings of this research suggest that disabled people are far from being a *practical group* and many disabled individuals have profound concerns over the effects that a transition towards such a group may have in relation to the abdicating of individual powers. This is a particularly thorny issue for disabled people in the light of the obvious divisions between disabled people and the lack of a unifying 'disability identity'.

The second way in which evidence from this research challenges Young's (1990) work is in relation to her reliance upon the idea that the only collectivities that should be given specific representation are what she defines as 'social groups' that are culturally determined. Whilst she acknowledges the existence of collectivities such as interest groups that are based on other factors, she nevertheless appears to prioritize cultural issues over any other. As has already been discussed in relation to Kymlicka's work on cultural citizenship, the evidence from this research suggests that there are potential problems with Young's approach at this point when it is used to consider the concerns of the disability movement, and perhaps other movements as well. Firstly, disabled people along with many other disadvantaged groups within society still face major structural inequalities. For disabled people at least, these issues form the major focus of their campaigns. Further, as the previous discussion here and in Chapter 5 has indicated, the 'culture of disability' is not a uniting factor amongst disabled people. According to Young's theory, this means that disabled people as a collective would not be considered to be a 'social group' and would not require specific representation. It is hard to see, therefore, how Young's notion of democracy is likely to improve the position of groups who are concerned more with redistribution than recognition.

Of course, as discussed in Chapter 2, in response to similar criticisms directed towards her work by Fraser (1997), Young (2000) has now restated her position somewhat, emphasizing that her notion of a primarily structural politics of difference should not be confused with that of a primarily cultural politics of identity (Lister, 2003). She thus claims that groups are not constituted by the substantive attributes of their members, but rather relationally according to '*cultural forms, practices, special needs or capacities, structures of power or privilege*'

(Young, 2000: 90). Further, she argues that mechanisms designed to increase group representation must not act to rigidify groups and group relations.

Despite Young's clarification on this point, however, the problem, as Lister (2003) has commented, is that it is difficult to see how such mechanisms can genuinely capture the fluidity and differentiation within groups. This leaves us in a 'Catch-22 situation' as Aziz (1992: 299–300) has described, in which the very assertion of 'difference' tends to create *'fixed and oppositional categories which can result in another version of the suppression of difference'*. The fluidity and differentiation within the disability movement and the 'risks' associated with asserting a 'distinct' 'disability identity' that have already been discussed, demonstrate that this difficulty associated with Young's approach is particularly pertinent in relation to disability.

Further, despite Young's restatement of her definition of the 'politics of difference', it is the argument here that the notion of 'cultural difference' continues to be a central aspect of her theorizing on the need for group representation. As the previous discussion in this chapter and throughout this book demonstrates, however, the problem of how to determine the existence of a 'culture' persists and this has implications for the notion of the 'politics of difference'. It is unclear, for example, whether Young would give representation rights to 'defensive cultures' which do not exist historically but have developed in the face of prejudice. Would Young give disabled people specific representation rights according to a 'culture of disability' that is based not upon an essential cultural difference between disabled and non-disabled people, but upon a process of defensive engagement in an unjust society? Additionally, since many disabled people reject the idea of a positive 'disability identity' and culture or are ambivalent about it, giving them the identity/culturally based representational rights that are key to Young's pluralist model of citizenship may have implications for any individuals who may appear to be members of that collective but who do not share the cultural identity. For any groups, such as disabled people, where their identities are often clearly *embodied*, giving such a group representational rights on the basis of a purportedly shared identity/culture runs the risk of locking all members of the group into an alleged shared identity which bears no relation to their own true sense of identity. That is to say, if you are *obviously a disabled person*, then clearly you must also be a part of that 'other' culture. The risks associated with granting these types of rights should, therefore, be of grave concern.

Given this apparent disjuncture between some important aspects of both Young and Kymlicka's theories and the findings of this research, it must be concluded that in relation to disability at least, the pluralist accounts of citizenship do not appear to be entirely satisfactory. Of course, it must be stated that some of these problems have been acknowledged within even more recent pluralist accounts by authors such as Stevenson (1997a/b). As was mentioned previously, Stevenson writes about the need for a multi-layered notion of citizenship in which 'cultural citizenship' is viewed as a model in which a diversity of rights, both structural and identity-based, can be guaranteed. Whilst Stevenson's account may be a more convincing approach, the intractable problem of his and other pluralist thinkers' continuing focus upon 'culture' and the idea that social groups can be 'clearly' defined by their need for cultural recognition, nevertheless remains in relation to disability.

It is at this point that it is interesting to return to the work of Berlin, and to propose that whilst undeniably a liberal thinker, elements of his theorizing may form the basis of a more convincing pluralist approach. Where Berlin differs from pluralist thinkers such as Kymlicka and Young is in the way that his particular *brand* of pluralism is not about seeking recognition for disadvantaged groups on the basis of respect for different cultures *per se*, although he would consider this to be entirely necessary under certain circumstances and for particular groups, but rather is about ensuring that all individuals are regarded as 'fully human'. In this respect, Berlin's work is clearly an important part of the human rights debate. Whilst some critics have pointed out that Berlin's adherence to the principle of a 'minimal moral horizon', common to all human societies and cultures, is an essentially universalistic concept and therefore stands somewhat in tension to his anti-monistic theorizing, it is proposed here that this aspect of his work is of considerable importance and merits reconsideration. In particular, the importance of Berlin's thinking is clear when it is compared with the writings of both Habermas and Mouffe, both of whom have provided important alternatives to both the liberal and pluralist accounts of citizenship.

Beyond the pluralist accounts

The argument here is that the reflexive and post-structuralist accounts of citizenship may well provide some way out of this apparent disjuncture between pluralist accounts of citizenship and the true nature of the disability movement's 'struggle'. In this respect it must therefore be stated that there is some similarity between the argument put forward here and that made by Shakespeare (1996b) who suggests that Disability Studies might find it useful to engage with more post-structural theories of identity.

Shafir (1998) highlights the way in which the journey from modernity to late/post-modernity has resulted in an increasingly complex set of frameworks within which individuals construct their citizenship identity. It is in the light of these changes that Habermas developed his reflexive account of citizenship, and Mouffe her more post-structuralist account. Whilst both authors are firmly opposed to the liberal approach to citizenship, some interesting links can nevertheless be seen between their work and that of Berlin.

Berlin's (1958) notion of a 'minimal moral horizon' is clearly echoed by Habermas when he proposes a form of citizenship as a 'minimal shared identity' in which consensus is reached between members of society by striving for a 'reflexive position'. Such a 'reflexive position' Habermas describes as being the critical appropriation of competing positions. Whilst essentially 'macro' in approach, the strength of Habermas' thinking in this regard is in his lack of focus upon the 'politics of difference' as the 'end goal' of citizenship and instead upon processes of reflexive engagement which involve individuals and groups from a variety of different positions striving for shared interests.

There are two problems with this approach, however: the first relates to the fact that Habermas appears to have over-looked the importance of power when considering the ability of individuals to engage reflexively. Differentials of power, often flowing from differential control of resources of one type or another, still affect the degree of autonomy individuals have as actors. As the findings of this research show, it is clear that disabled people in the UK still experience profound problems in what Habermas would term the 'pre-discursive' space in terms of lack of resources within, or access to, the public sphere. These problems have clear implications in terms of limiting the ability of disabled people to participate actively in this process of reflexive engagement.

The second problem is clearly articulated by Mouffe (1992, 1993) in her consideration of the fragmentary effects of multiple identities upon the public sphere. Whilst Berlin's notion of a 'minimal moral horizon' and Habermas' notion of a 'minimal shared identity' are also clearly echoed in terms of the end goal of Mouffe's 'radical democracy', Mouffe highlights the difficulties associated with achieving such a goal within a polity defined as a 'societas' of individuals with shared interests, but with very different ideas about the meanings and definitions of these shared interests. Her ideas about the 'multiple self' are also key here, for she explains that the multiple subject positions individuals inhabit will further complicate the processes within a radical societas as members of particular groups are likely to have very different ideas about the meanings and definitions of their shared interests. In the light of this complexity, achieving a 'minimal moral horizon' is likely to be increasingly difficult but all the more necessary if society is not to become dangerously fragmented.

The considerable worth of Mouffe's thinking on this point is clear when used as a point of departure for considering the disability movement because, as previously discussed in this chapter and in Chapters 4 and 5, divisions between members of the disability movement on the basis of additional factors of oppression and/or important differences of opinion regarding the nature of the 'cultural' aims of the movement, are clear. Subsuming this diversity under the banner of a positive 'disability identity' within a distinct disability culture, and using this as something around which to rally is, therefore, unlikely to be successful within the disability movement. Clearly then, the pluralist notion of citizenship is brought into further question since, in the light of such complexity, identity politics and the 'politics of difference' are unlikely to achieve consensus. In the light of this, the idea that individuals such as disabled people should be joining, according to their *particular* subject positions, in a wider political struggle for a 'minimal moral horizon', along with individuals from other subject positions might, therefore, be a more empowering option, even if in reality difficult to achieve.

That the nature of citizenship is changing in the light of the progressive fragmentation of the public sphere and that new forms of engagement may be emerging is something that Ellison (1997, 2000) has clearly identified and his theorizing represents an interesting new development in this field. In some respects interesting parallels can be drawn at this point between his work and that of Castells (1997) on identity and new social movements. Ellison's approach, however, is more specifically focused on the issue of citizenship as he is concerned with combining a more convincing reflexive/post-structural account of citizenship that acknowledges the effects of 'power differentials' between individuals with different identities – an issue that, as previously stated, has been overlooked somewhat by Habermas – with an understanding of current forms of protest and social movements. In doing this, he proposes that citizenship is now best understood as a process of defensive and/or proactive engagement in the context of a society characterized by increasingly complex social and political identities.

The argument here is that rapid change transforms the nature of citizen participation and 'encourages' engagement, willing or not, in the pursuit, or defence, of particular interests and/or social rights. In short, both the capacity to engage, and the differential nature of engagement itself, are rapidly becoming the most significant features of a citizenship conceived as a series of fractured 'contiguous belongings' (...) (Ellison, 2000: para. 1.1).

Ellison's (2000: para. 1.4) definition of *defensive engagement* is particularly useful when considering the position of disabled people because he defines it as being the activity of *'those lacking access to relevant power networks who find themselves engaged in efforts – perhaps to maintain a status quo, or to develop new arrangements – simply to preserve existing interests and entitlements'*. In other words, if the context in which a group engages is one in which power is concentrated in the hand of the 'opponent', then the group may only be able to engage defensively. In terms of understanding citizenship this is a useful model because it explains why some disempowered groups, including for example the respondents in the research upon which this book is based, may appear to be more concerned with claiming or protecting existing rights than with claiming 'new' rights. In other words, the concept of 'defensive engagement' is a useful way of explaining why it is that many disabled people are more concerned about achieving *real* equal treatment in spheres where they are already 'officially' equal (for example in relation to equal opportunities legislation in employment), than they are about claiming 'new' rights on the basis of 'identity politics'.

Whilst providing a useful way of *understanding* the aims and activities of movements such as the disability movement, the really interesting aspect of Ellison's (2000: para. 7.3) approach is that he questions the extent to which, ultimately, *'defensive forms of engagement'* which are *'likely to be organised around social divisions already shaped by existing discourses'* enable true *agency*. In defending particular sets of interests, he argues, a group may utilize identities such as the 'disability identity' as a way of appealing to a supposedly pre-existing sense of solidarity. Quite apart from the problems associated with whether or not such identities are true representations of solidarities, Ellison states that this approach does not give the same scope for agency that more pro-active engagement might provide. A more genuinely pro-active approach could move beyond existing discourses such as disabled/non-disabled and allow instead for the challenging of *'established assumptions about social divisions'* (Ellison, 2000: para. 7.3). New and differently conceived solidarities might then emerge which by the very nature of their formation will be inherently unstable.

Having stated that Ellison considers proactive engagement to enable agency more than defensive engagement, that is not to say that he is overtly proposing that proactive engagement is the *preferable* form of engagement. Indeed, he states clearly that it is the hallmark of contemporary citizenship that individuals are able to engage defensively *and/or* proactively and that the two forms of engagement are not mutually exclusive. It might, however, be necessary to go one step further than Ellison and suggest that proactive engagement *is* likely to bring about the best long term results for disadvantaged groups since it is about *transforming* rather than working *within* existing social relations and in so doing is more likely to be able to tackle the assumptions that may be underpinning social exclusion.

Further, arguably, the very act of defensive engagement only becomes necessary in the absence of previously successful proactive engagement. In other words, defensive engagement becomes necessary when disadvantaged groups have been excluded from decision-making processes and have thus been unable to influence the development of structures or policies that impact upon them. The hallmark of contemporary citizenship then becomes the ability to engage *proactively* and without the need to engage *defensively*. Whilst this idea may be slightly at odds with Ellison's theorizing, it nevertheless remains true to his understanding of citizenship as a *process*.

Whilst the types of issues that may form the bases of this proactive engagement will be considered in the final chapter of this book, it is important to note that although Ellison's approach clearly represents an important new development in terms of our understanding of *citizenship*, by defining citizenship as a *process of engagement,* it is, therefore, also a vital new development in terms of social movement theorizing. As has already been discussed at some length in Chapter 3, important issues remain as yet unresolved within social movement theorizing.

Implications for social movement theorizing

As has been discussed in Chapter 3, the current debates in the field of social movement theorizing focus upon the key differences that exist between what have been termed here the *first* and *second phase* theories, between the American and European traditions and over which of these theories provides the most convincing account for the aims and activities of contemporary social movements. In relation to the 'case study' upon which this book is based – the UK disability movement – how this movement is best defined continues to be debated, of particular 'issue' being whether or not the disability movement can be defined as a 'new' social movement (see for example Oliver and Zarb, [1989] 1997, Shakespeare, 1993).

In many respects, however, the most curious thing about this ongoing debate is its very existence. The debate appears to have resulted from and be framed according to a particular underlying assumption – that it would be a 'good thing' if the disability movement was a 'new' social movement. Thus, whilst to be fair to the writings of Shakespeare, Oliver and Zarb it must be stated that their claims that the disability movement is a 'new' social movement tend to be *tentative*, it is nevertheless difficult to avoid reaching the conclusion from their writing that they would probably *like* the disability movement to be defined in this way. There may be understandable reasons for this. One possible explanation is that there appears to be a 'popular' assumption, not always supported in actual theorizing on the topic, that 'new' social movements possess greater emancipatory potential. Since many of the key academics writing about disability and the disability movement are also key disability activists, it is understandable that they might wish to give the disability movement impetus by claiming that it is a 'new' social movement. A different stance is taken here to this issue, however.

For the disability movement to be a 'new' social movement, the type of citizenship underlying the disability movement would *clearly* reflect the pluralist account of citizenship. As the previous discussion has demonstrated, however, it is not easy to locate the type of citizenship underlying disability campaigns in any one of the modern/contemporary models of citizenship, but it is especially difficult to analyse the goals of the movement in terms of the 'politics of difference' of the pluralist account.

By way of explaining the argument here, whilst in no way disregarding all of Touraine's contributions to social movement theorizing, his focus upon identity and culture as the basis of contemporary social movement activity is brought into question by the findings of the research upon which this book is based. As is evident from the views of the respondents in this research (please see Chapter 5) the disability movement is not, as a whole, concerned with defending the cultural parts of private life as are, he suggests, other contemporary social movements. Further, the disability movement does not appear to be about redefining culture and lifestyle, the *'grammar of forms of life'* as Habermas (1981: 33) suggests, or seeking a *'space for difference'* as Melucci (1985: 810) believes. In the light of these problems and those associated with the essentializing of difference and the rejection by many disabled people of the idea of a positive 'disability identity', there would appear, therefore to be some important questions remaining in relation to the adequacy of these theories of 'new' social movements when used to understand all contemporary movements.

Further still, Melucci argues that contemporary social movements are positioned outside the established boundaries of political systems and are characterized by 'alternative' behaviour such as deviance and 'cultural experimentation'. Again, very little evidence emerged during this research to support the idea that there is a 'culture of disability' being *widely* celebrated by disabled people or that disabled people wish to be seen as 'deviant' from the 'norm'. Indeed, quite on the contrary, most respondents in this research questioned the notion that disabled people are 'different' from non-disabled people in any *essential* way. Further, several respondents, as discussed in Chapter 5, highlighted what they considered to be the importance of establishing a firm place for disabled people in the established boundaries of political systems and of ensuring that the views of such individuals are taken seriously.

Having stated what they did not consider to be the main focus of the disability movement, respondents were even clearer about what truly concerned the movement. When asked a variation on the question *'what, if any, barriers or problems are disabled people facing today?'* most respondents showed a marked tendency to identify structural issues only, or before any other issues. These findings therefore echo a concern voiced by Oliver and Zarb ([1989], 1997), who although proposing that the disability movement may be considered to be a 'new' social movement 'generally', nevertheless acknowledge that there is a lack of 'fit' between the disability movement and models of 'new' social movements because the disability movement cannot be said to be prioritizing 'post-materialist' or 'post-acquisitive' values over concerns about income, material needs or social security. It is the argument here, however, that it is necessary to go one step further than Oliver and Zarb and argue that the disability movement's continuing focus on a range of persistent social inequalities means that it is *very unlikely* to be a 'new' social movement.

This view of the movement is, of course, likely to be considered to be 'controversial' by many people within Disability Studies and the movement, especially by individuals whose personal sense of empowerment is firmly connected with their embrace of the idea of a positive 'disability identity' and disability culture. It is not in any way the intention here to deny the views or equally valid experiences of these individuals. Nevertheless, the rejection by the respondents in this research of the idea of a truly 'positive' 'disability identity' and their uncertainty with regard to the existence of a 'disability culture' make it difficult to analyse the goals of the disability movement, as a whole, in terms of the 'politics of difference' and logically therefore, as a 'new' social movement. The important point to make, however, is that it is the argument here that this is *not a 'bad thing'*, and clearly the disability movement is not some sort of social movement 'dinosaur' – far from it – but rather that what is needed is a new approach to understanding many contemporary social movements, including the disability movement.

Whilst it is not possible within the confines of this book to develop such an alternative approach, it is nevertheless interesting to consider where the point of departure might be for this new theorizing. One question raised by the findings of this research is the extent to which it is either necessary or desirable to reject completely the first-phase theories when seeking to understand contemporary movements such as the disability movement. In other words, is it time to re-visit theories of social movements that existed before the '1960s watershed'? Blumer's ([1951] 1995) understandings of social movements, for example, seem very useful when seeking to understand the disability movement. According to his theorizing, the 'career path' of all movements concerned with social change involves a transition from a 'general', only loosely united movement to a 'specific' social movement characterized by unity, locational focus and aim. Although he lists a number of factors involved in this transition, he identifies the ideology of a movement as playing an important role, for it must carry respectability and prestige and answer to the genuine wishes and hopes of the members of the movement.

That respondents in this research clearly disagree with the views of many of the key academics/activists in the field demonstrates that such a unanimously agreed upon 'populist' ideology is absent within the disability movement. Disagreements, highlighted by this research, relating to issues such as the nature of the 'disability identity' and disability culture plus other issues evident in the literature such as the extent to which non-disabled people should be excluded from participating in the disability movement or disability research, or the nature of the relationship between illness and disability, have prevented the formation of a shared ideology. It can, perhaps, be concluded from this that the disability movement is a long way from becoming a specific social movement and that it is best defined as a 'general social movement'. Defining it in this way, as being at a fairly early stage of development, may thus be a useful way of understanding the disability movement.

There are, however, problems with Blumer's approach, as discussed in Chapter 3, for he somewhat assumed the natural 'career path' of social movements from 'general' to 'specific'. This is a problem that was identified by later theorists such as Tilly. A further question posed by the findings of this research, therefore, is to what extent the later American Tradition of social movement theorizing may be helpful when seeking to understand the disability movement. Tilly's (1993: 6) much more fluid definition of social movement activity sees them as: *'dragons living continuously somewhere in the social underground, but emerging recurrently from their labyrinths to stomp around roaring'*. In this way he does not give social movements the progressive life histories implied by the collective behaviour approach of Blumer. Instead, he proposes that social movements are best understood as varying in nature according to the effects of four main factors: the nature of the claims being made by the movement; the prevailing political opportunity structure; the shared understandings of the participants; and the social structure from which members are drawn (Tilly, 1993: 19). This is an appealing approach because in terms of this research it explains how factors such as the continuing focus of many disabled people upon structural issues and the lack of a shared identity amongst all members of the disability movement, shape the nature of the movement. This approach also avoids the old/new distinction that may not be entirely justified or productive.

Tilly's approach therefore avoids the underlying *implication* within Blumer's work: that the ultimate goal of a social movement *should be* to become homogenous. According to Tilly's schema it would, therefore, be entirely possible for a movement to comprise separatist and non-separatist factions, factions based upon differing ideological beliefs and factions based upon the addition of further factors of inequality. Such divisions, according to Tilly's schema, do not necessarily bring into doubt the existence of a movement, but do alter its structure. Thus, to understand the disability movement in the light of Tilly's theorizing, it is vital to *acknowledge* divisions within the movement, for example between the separatist and non-separatist factions, for such divisions will affect the nature of the movement.

Tarrow furthers Tilly's theorizing by adding into the equation the idea that social movements must also be understood according to the level at which they are able to sustain collective action. Tarrow appears to share Tilly's definition of social movements as 'dragons' which emerge only sporadically to struggle against particular foes and particular threats. He adds to Tilly's definition, however, the idea that movements have inherent problems in relation to *'co-ordinating un-organized, autonomous and dispersed populations into common and sus-tained action'* (Tarrow, 1994: 9). As the evidence from this research demonstrates, the disability movement does indeed experience these collective action problems. Tarrow's analysis is therefore of considerable use in this regard. His work on 'mobilizing structures' can also be employed profitably when considering movements such as the disabil-ity movement. Although many key activists and writers in this field see organizations such as the British Council of Disabled People (BCODP) as a 'mobilizing structure', the evidence from this research demonstrates that not all disabled people agree on the importance of the BCODP to their lives or to the disability movement as a whole. It can be argued, therefore, that the very absence of such 'mobilizing structures' within the 'embryonic disability movement' accounts for the latter's problems in relation to activating and sustaining collective action.

A problem does arise in relation to both of these approaches, however, for if a social movement is significantly divided in terms of its constituent groups, and has mobilizing difficulties, then how is it possible to state categorically that it is a social movement as opposed to a political coalition or a loosely structured protest event? It is the argument here that Della Porta and Diani (1999: 19) provide the most convincing answer to this question:

> The aspect which enables us to discriminate is the present of a vision of the world and a collective identity which permit particip-ants in various protest events to place their action in a wider perspective. In order to be able to speak of social movements it is necessary that single episodes are perceived as components of a longer-lasting action, rather than discrete events; and that those who are engaged feel linked by ties of solidarity and of ideal com-munion with protagonists of other analogous mobilizations.

This is a useful quote because it explains how despite the apparently heterogeneous nature of the disability movement, it can still be cat-egorized as a social movement: firstly, whilst the evidence from this research suggests that it is important to treat with caution the idea that a collective identity based upon a *positive 'disability identity'* exists throughout the disability movement, this is not necessarily the type of collective identity implied by Della Porta and Diani. It is the argument here that, according to this approach, the existence of such a collective identity may amount simply to the acknowledgement by constituent members that they have been labelled as being the *same* in some way. In the case of this research the collective identity is, therefore, the experience of the label of 'disability'. More importantly, despite the heterogeneity within the disability movement, it is still possible to see that constituent members share an overall vision of the world as 'disabling'. This may be one of the only views behind which all respondents in this research would unite, but it is of fundamental importance to the disability movement. Finally, the evidence from this research also suggests that whilst total agreement does not exist amongst the various factions of the movement, an overall solidarity does exist. This solidarity was demonstrated by the reluctant way in which certain respondents criticized leading organizations, such as the BCODP. Such respondents clearly felt sufficient affinity with, and perhaps even 'loyalty' to, this organization to be reluctant to criticize the organization to any great extent.

Despite the appeal, however, of these aspects of previous models of social movements, in particular of their explanations for both 'how' and 'when' social movements can be seen to exist and mobilize, these theories still do not provide adequate explanation for 'why' social movements come into being in the first place. In the light of this problem, it is proposed here that any new theory of social movements, whilst building upon some aspects of older traditions, would need to focus upon this 'why' aspect of movements. As has already been discussed, in the light of this research, the second phase European theorists' focus upon culture and identity as being at the heart of the campaigns of 'new' social movements does not explain satisfactorily the activities and aims of the disability movement, and arguably therefore of *all* contemporary social movements. This aspect of the approach is, therefore, unlikely to provide the best starting point for this new theorizing.

That having been stated, there are some strands of thinking within the second phase European approach that may prove to be more fruitful. Both Habermas (1981) and Melucci (1993) write that the important role of social movements is to prevent the system from closing in upon itself and in Melucci's (1993: 190) view to expose the *'shadowy zones of invisible power'*. Both theorists are therefore calling for a more radical sense of democracy and engagement. Although Melucci is probably the chief proponent of this approach to social movement theorizing, what is often termed the Reactive/Defensive Model can also be seen in the work of Foweraker (1995). Foweraker (1995) echoes much of the work of Melucci when he states that 'new' social movements are the result of major changes in society, changes in particular to the boundary conditions of the social system. Reflecting Melucci's (1993: 190) theorizing on the *'shadowy zones of invisible power'*, Foweraker draws upon the work of Foucault (1979) when he comments that 'new' social movements challenge the 'microphysics of power'. Thus, the role of these movements becomes one of reaction to negative aspects of these changes in the social system and to the 'microphysics of power', in defence of the position of the group. Whilst, as the work of Bourdieu (1987) has demonstrated, care must always be taken when using the term 'group', Foweraker's overall conclusion, that 'old' or 'new', in the end the central focus of all social movements is therefore citizenship, is nevertheless an important contribution to this debate.

It is at this point, therefore, that the focus returns again to Ellison's (2000) notion of engagement since the links between his work and that of the Reactive/Defensive model are clear, for both approaches consider understanding 'citizenship' to be at the heart of understanding contemporary social movements. Ellison argues that it is necessary to understand not only the process of engagement, but also the kind of rights that are in need of 'defence' or are being 'proactively' sought. To this end he seeks to combine a more convincing reflexive account of contemporary citizenship with an understanding of current forms of protest and social movements. In this respect his ideas represent as significant a new development in this field of social movement theorizing, as they do in relation to citizenship theorizing.

Conclusion

As stated, one of the departure points for understanding the true nature of contested citizenship, not only for disabled people but also for many other vulnerable groups, may be Ellison's understanding of the difference between the goals of those engaging *defensively* or *proactively*. As has also been discussed, the work of Berlin on the 'minimal moral horizon' and Habermas on the 'minimal shared identity' combined with Mouffe's understandings of 'radical democracy' and the nature of the 'societas' are also theoretically important in the quest for a model of citizenship that seeks to avoid some of the difficulties associated with the pluralist accounts. There may be other areas of theorizing that need to be considered along side of these, however, and it is the argument here that such areas include: *human rights discourses; theories of personhood; and theories of embodiment.* In the final chapter that follows, these issues will be considered in more depth and the future of citizenship will be considered.

7
Conclusion

The future for citizenship theorizing

In Chapter 4, new trends in Medical Sociology were discussed which stress the need for a more *embodied* understanding of disability (Bendelow and Williams, 1995, Hughes and Paterson, 1997). There are thus calls for a more highly developed theory of impairment and for Disability Studies to engage actively with the sociology of the body. These calls have not gone entirely unheeded, yet many authors from within Disability Studies continue to believe that considering issues of embodiment will result in a weakening of the Social Model of Disability. It is the argument here, however, that the costs in terms of questioning the Social Model of Disability may be outweighed by the benefits that can be gained by placing disability firmly at the centre of contemporary theorizing on the embodied self.

As has already been discussed in Chapter 2, Turner has developed a sociology of the body which places theorizing about the *embodied* nature of human life at the heart of many of the central sociological debates. It is not possible within the limits of this book to consider in any great depth the implications of all of Turner's theorizing on these issues. It is important, however, to note how his concerns with the ethical implications of medical interventions into people's lives impact upon debates surrounding vulnerability in terms of the experience of attacks upon 'self' and 'personhood' felt by certain individuals in relation to the eradication of congenital disabilities *via* genetic screening and other new techniques. His ideas about the cultural formation of the body also have implications for understanding the effects of powerful images, such as the 'body-beautiful', on both the lives of disabled people and perceptions of disability amongst non-disabled people.

192

At this point in Turner's theorizing, the links between his ideas and those of Goffman (1968) on stigmatized bodies and Foucault (1979) on 'abnormal' bodies and stigma is clear. As has already been discussed earlier in this book, Goffman's work in particular remains central to understanding both the attitudes of non-disabled people towards disabled people and the divisions that exist among disabled people and which account, at least in part, for the somewhat disunited nature of the disability movement. Further, Turner appears to have been greatly influenced by the work of Foucault (1979) in relation to his understanding of the manner in which the body has become increasingly governed by the state and is firmly connected to systems of domination and oppression. Understanding the ways in which the body is both governed and oppressed is of great value when considering the lives of disabled people and many other vulnerable groups.

Where Turner departs from both Goffman and Foucault, however, is in his rejection of the earlier theorists' views of the body as being almost entirely socially constructed. According to Turner, the central problem with this view is that it ignores the *materiality* of embodiment. In this respect, as has already been discussed in Chapter 2, there are clear links between Turner's work and that of a number of feminist authors (for example Butler, 1993, Yeatman, 1994, Lister, 1997a, Weeks, 1998, Richardson, 2001 and others). Thus, for Turner ([1996] 2000: 492):

> There is a phenomenology of the life-world as a lived experience, about which cultural relativism and structuralism have no interest or purchase.

In relation to disability, the links between Turner's work and current moves within Medical Sociology – with regard to developing a more embodied notion of disability – are also clear. The frequent use of his work within contemporary Medical Sociology reflects this. The strong point of his approach is that it appears to provide a way of closing the divide between impairment and disability. This is important, because despite arguments by authors such as Oliver (1996) in favour of the development of a *separate* model of impairment that *together with* the Social Model of Disability may produce a *Social Theory of Disability*, my argument here is that *closing, not redefining* this divide is essential. It is no longer possible to ignore or bracket off into a separate 'category' the experiences of such things as pain and the effects that such experiences have upon the 'self' and identity.

Further, according to Turner, there should be an equal focus upon the 'materiality of embodiment' as upon the historical controls that have been placed for example upon disabled bodies by non-disabled medical professionals – the issues, in other words, that have been the traditional focus of Disability Studies. It is understandable, given the level of importance Turner gives to the materiality of embodiment, that some proponents of the Social Model find this approach threatening. Turner's views should not be seen in this way, however, for his ideas do not threaten the central tenet of the Social Model – that society 'disables' individuals with impairments. Rather, his ideas are of considerable assistance in dealing with the real threat to the Social Model – that many disabled people who are not 'able-disabled', or who experience illness or pain, have felt that their experiences fall 'outside' the Social Model. If the Social Model of Disability is to be truly inclusive of the experiences of all disabled people then it must engage with issues of embodiment or it will risk losing validity.

Having established his Sociology of the Body, Turner then turns his attention to the implications of this embodied understanding of personhood for discourses of citizenship and human rights. He proposes that: *'given frailty and precariousness, human beings need a universalistic legal framework in which to seek protection'*. (Turner, [1996] 2000: 496). In other words, Turner is proposing a theory of personhood that perceives it as inherently fragile and a corresponding theory of human rights that rests upon the awareness, of every individual, of his/her own vulnerability. Thus:

> Human beings will want their rights to be recognised because they see in the plight of others their own (possible) misery.   (Turner, 1993b: 506)

Clearly there is some way to go before the majority of people become so 'enlightened', but this is an appealing idea.

There is, as yet, however, an unresolved problem in Turner's work and this is whether or not such a notion of human rights removes the need for citizenship rights. Turner (1993b) suggests that human rights debates are beginning to replace citizenship debates and that achieving proper human rights for all would mark the end of the need for citizenship. I am uneasy about this argument, however, for the problem of *governance* remains. Even if a universally agreed set of non-culturally specific human rights could be devised – and this is itself likely to be a utopian aim – individuals would still remain the 'citizens' of a given state. The apparatuses of that state would remain central to the lives of individuals and be the main context within which individuals seek support against potential and actual vulnerabilities. Under such circumstances the idea that human rights 'exist' somehow beyond the boundaries of the state is problematic.

By way of tackling this problem, I therefore propose that a new approach to citizenship is required and suggest the following 'working model' as a starting point for future theorizing. According to this model, citizenship is defined as a process of proactive engagement in a radical democracy, the aim of this engagement being *the achievement of human rights for all citizens*, and these rights being determined on *the basis of a universal acceptance of vulnerability*.

Rather than rejecting Turner's theory of human rights, therefore, I suggest that the way to overcome this problem of governance is to position human rights at the heart of citizenship, with citizenship acting as an 'umbrella' for Human Rights rather than the other way around. In this way, human rights can be viewed as representing what Berlin termed the 'minimal moral horizon' and citizenship becomes a process that occurs within a radical democracy, as imagined by Mouffe, and is akin to Ellison's notion of proactive engagement, but with the goal being to achieve this 'shared horizon'.

Such a notion of citizenship as a *process* also avoids overly emphasizing rights as opposed to responsibilities, for if the nature of the 'minimal moral horizon' is an understanding of personhood as vulnerable and contingent, then each individual in claiming his/her right to be protected from the effects of potential vulnerabilities is also defending the rights of others to receive support in the light of their *actual* vulnerability. Such a notion of citizenship is one that avoids marking out certain groups as 'other' and in so doing makes it clear that we are all vulnerable in terms of disability, racism, sexism, poverty or other forms of social exclusion. Such a concept of citizenship also removes the need to make a distinction between structural and identity based rights, for since cultural identity may be an important part of an individual's sense of personhood, then they must also be protected from forces which might attack this aspect of their person. Dominant groups must acknowledge their own cultural specificity and that their own cultural identities are potentially precarious and need to be defended. In so doing, as argued above, they guarantee that those whose cultures may *actually* be vulnerable receive protection in this regard.

Concluding comments: implications for future research and theorizing

In writing this book my aim has been to demonstrate that by placing disability at the heart of citizenship debates, valuable insights can be gained into both the strengths and the weaknesses of a number of modern/contemporary theories of citizenship. My argument in the previous chapter and throughout the book is also that analyses of contemporary social movements such as the disability movement must go hand in hand with the development of new theories of citizenship, for it is clear that if citizenship is to be seen as a process of engagement, then social movement activity is likely to be a major part of that engagement. Further, it is my contention that whilst competency, personhood, embodiment and human rights are becoming important areas of debate within Medical Sociology, Disability Studies must not avoid such issues for it seems likely that they will be key to the citizenship debates of the future. It is important that theorists concerned with disability both engage and find a way to position their subject matter in a more prominent place in these debates. In proposing the starting point for a new approach to citizenship that does take account of disability, albeit an approach that has clear theoretical antecedents, I hope that I have begun the process of doing this.

In proposing this model of citizenship, whilst making some suggestions at a fairly abstract level, I do not profess to have provided an account of how such a model could be 'operationalized'. Space does not permit me to do this adequately within this book. In leaving the theorizing at this abstract level there is always the risk that the model proposed here will be criticized on the basis that it is as utopian as previous models. Clearly, then, in order to increase its validity, it is important that it is 'operationalized'. Future research and theorizing is needed, therefore, to support the argument put forward in this book and it seems to me that there are several likely avenues that this might take.

The important role that education, for example, could play in fostering the idea of active citizenship proposed here amongst 'citizens-to-be', is something that might be considered. This issue is of particular pertinence in the light of the ongoing debate surrounding the adequacy and theoretical merits, or otherwise, of the current national curriculum for citizenship education in England. One problem that emerges from even a most cursory examination of the current approach to education for citizenship is the fact that whilst the current curriculum (as set out within the Crick Report, 1998) stresses the importance – and rightly so – of encouraging children to respect the different identities of individuals within society, the model of 'active citizenship' proposed is one in which citizens engage in 'reasoned debate' in order to reach a consensus.

The problems posed by incommensurate views does not appear to have been considered within the teaching framework – one possible conclusion that can be drawn from this being that underlying the citizenship curriculum is an assumption that views that cannot be accommodated within a majority 'consensus' are 'unreasonable' and can thus be disregarded. In other words, echoing Kymlicka's views in many respects, according to the current policy for citizenship education one of the key 'sentiments' that each citizen must possess is an ability to negotiate 'reasonably' with their fellow citizens. It seems likely, however, that the intractable problem of majority-minority relations means that the definition of 'reasonable' will continue to be determined culturally by the dominant group.

On the basis that the model of citizenship proposed within this book is concerned with avoiding this sort of problem, amongst other issues, by suggesting a basis for uniting people in a shared understanding of 'vulnerability' and the need for proactive engagement, it might be interesting, therefore, to consider whether this model might provide a useful alternative account of citizenship upon which to base citizenship education – in other words, whether there might be benefits associated with encouraging young people to see themselves as proactive citizens, concerned with negotiating the establishment/maintenance of a range of mechanisms designed to protect each individual from both potential and actual vulnerabilities.

There are, of course, other implications in relation to the model of citizenship proposed here, not least in relation to a range of other social policies, for if citizenship is understood as a process of citizen engagement and this engagement is concerned with seeking protection from potential and actual vulnerabilities, then the institutions of the welfare state must, surely, be the most obvious mechanisms for securing such protection. The model of citizenship proposed in this book, therefore, implies both the need for the existence of a welfare state and at the same time highlights the importance of citizen participation in establishing the level and type of welfare provision required by a society. Whilst it is not my intention to consider these implications in any great depth here, nevertheless it is interesting to hypothesize about the type of welfare state that would result from citizen participation of the type proposed within this book. I suggest, for example, that on the basis of a widespread understanding of 'vulnerable personhood', many societies might opt for 'robust' welfare states, despite the higher costs in terms of taxation that this would entail.

In reality, of course, the political will to foster or act according to such a model of citizenship does not appear to exist at present within the UK. In many respects this is understandable, because the universal acceptance of 'vulnerability' is far from widespread in UK society. Any government that sought to implement policies directly on the basis of this notion of citizenship is therefore likely to experience resistance in relation to the additional costs required to develop truly adequate mechanisms of protection against a range of potential vulnerabilities. The possible solution to this problem, however, may lie with the activities of a wide range of 'grass-roots' organizations. It is these organizations that may be best placed to promote the idea that we are all vulnerable to some extent over our lifetimes and to encourage citizens to engage more proactively on this basis.

Further, for such groups, embracing the concept of citizenship proposed in this book might provide an empowering basis from which to challenge a number of disempowering discourses and binaries. For the disability movement, for example, this type of proactive engagement might involve challenging a number of key assumptions about disabled people, especially the notion that there is something *fundamentally* different about disabled people and, as previously mentioned, bringing into focus the reality that we are all vulnerable to experiencing impairment and disability at some point during our life-time.

Further, these organizations and protest groups may find that there are benefits to joining with other groups from different subject positions in a shared 'struggle' against disempowering practices and to achieve the 'minimal moral horizon' previously discussed. They may find such joint activity more empowering, not least because it would help to overcome some of the problems that have been considered in this book in relation to the 'politics of difference'.

That it is time to abandon the focus on the 'politics of difference' and instead look towards forming 'bridging ties' and temporary alliances between groups of individuals with *different* identities, is an idea that is being increasingly voiced (see for example Yuval-Davies, 1997) – even by those who have previously espoused the 'politics of difference'. Peter Tatchell (1999) in an article in the Guardian about gay/lesbian politics entitled *'Let us cease these gay campaigns'* has said that it is time to leave the *'self-centred ghetto'* and that the key to freedom for gay/lesbian people *'is a new, comprehensive, transformative politics for the emancipation of everyone'*. Clearly, this argument is pertinent in relation to many other groups, including disabled people and the potential that such new forms of 'proactive engagement' may have for challenging existing power imbalances is, I propose, considerable.

Notes

Chapter 1   Introduction

1 In this way, I am making no distinction between episodes of collective action such as the disability rights campaigns/movement of the 1970s and more contemporary expressions of collective action by disabled people. According to this somewhat 'loose' framework for defining a social movement, the fact that the nature and basis of collective action may alter somewhat over time, does not mean that successive action by a recognized collective should not be considered to be a part of a larger phenomenon – a social movement.

2 That this issue of the need for disability organizations to be run *by* disabled people not *for* disabled people remains central to the campaigns of the disability movement is shown by criticisms directed against the Disability Rights Commission:

> The Disability Rights Commission (DRC) was a positive outcome of Labour's review of disabled people's rights, to help to enforce the DDA. However, the commission is not the voice of disabled people – commissioners are appointed by the government, not by disabled people, and some bodies who should consult disabled people consult the DRC instead, believing that is sufficient.   (Rickell, 2003: http://www.guardian.co.uk/comment/story/0,3604,1053066,00.html viewed on 8 February 2004)

Chapter 2   Citizenship

1 For more information on this debate please see: http://www.deafgene.info/designer.htm and related links.

Chapter 3   Social Movements

1 For readers who may be interested to read further about this approach, please see: Parsons (1961, 1969); Smelser (1963); and Eyerman and Jameson (1991).

Chapter 4   Issues in Disability

1 For example, see Finkelstein (1996) who argues that to consider impairment is to dilute the effectiveness of the Social Model.

2 See Swain and French (2000) for a useful discussion on the disempowering aspects of the 'tragedy model'.

3 This report can be viewed on the web at: http://www.teachers.org.uk/resources/pdf/within_reach.pdf Date: 30 April 2005.

4 The Welsh Assembly and Scottish Parliament have chosen not to implement the value added measure.

5 Figures from Department of Work and Pensions (2003) *Autumn Performance Report*.

6 Figures from Burchardt, T. (2000) (JRF Findings)

7 http://www.connexions-cw.co.uk/employers/ Date: 18 September 2003.

8 http://fast-forward.scope.org.uk/employers/buscase.shtml Date: 18 September 2003.

9 Please see http://www.statistics.gov.uk/STATBASE/Expodata/Spreadsheets/ D6467.xls Figure 8.1 'Expenditure on social protection benefits in real terms by function, 1990/91 and 2000/01.' Date: 18 September 2003.

10 The following definitions are used throughout this chapter and book: 'Disability identity' – is used to denote the political identity of disabled people that is key to *disability politics*. 'Disabled identity' – is used as 'shorthand' for: individuals who have been categorized or 'labelled' as being disabled.

11 Readers may note that no reference is made within this section to the particular experiences of those people with congenital hearing impairments who self-define as **D**eaf, rather than **d**eaf, who use Sign Language and who consider themselves to be a part of a cultural minority. This omission was not unintentional. Clearly the Deaf culture does constitute a separate culture on the basis of a shared language and Deaf people's arguments in favour of viewing them as a cultural minority analogous to other minority ethnic groups is convincing.

The reason why this group has not been considered in more depth within this chapter, however, is because Deaf people have long resisted identification as disabled or impaired people and this has proved to be a major stumbling block to developing links between Deaf people and the disability movement. Since this is a very specific issue applying to only a very small proportion of the 'disabled population', and does not reflect the views of the many deaf people who do not identify themselves with the Deaf culture, or who do clearly define themselves as disabled people, it was not considered necessary to go into any depth with regard to this debate. For those who wish to know more about these issues, however, a good introduction to the debate has been provided by Mairian Corker (1998).

Chapter 5   The Views of Disabled People

1 Since respondents in this research are being kept anonymous, quotations in this chapter have been coded as 'members of a particular group'. In excerpts in which more than one member is speaking the quotations have been coded according to the order in which the respondents speak in each excerpt – i.e. member 1 for the first speaker and so on. *There is no connection between the coding of each excerpt*, so the code 'member 1 of C3' for example may refer to more than one individual. This is part of a system of coding which aims to avoid accidentally identifying certain individuals. In the case of the Deafmail respondents, the coding 'respondents 1/2/3' does refer to the same individuals throughout this chapter. This was considered to be justifiable

since the membership of Deafmail is extensive and the respondents replied privately to my questions, therefore making it unlikely that other users of Deafmail will identify them easily. In all excerpts 'AB' refers to the author.

Within the text (...) refers to a pause or a break in the flow of the conversation. (...) on a separate line is used to denote that these are two separate quotations from the same respondent.

2   Please see Chapter 4, note 10 for definitions of the two terms 'disabled identity' and 'disability identity'.

3   Greater London Action on Disability (GLAD).

4   RADAR stands for the Royal Association for Disability and Rehabilitation. RADAR's constitution currently states that there must be sufficient disabled members of the association for them to have a controlling vote. RADAR does not, however, exclude non-disabled people from becoming members. It would seem likely, however, that implied in the comment of this respondent is a criticism of RADAR that goes beyond the issue of membership of the organization. Unfortunately, this respondent did not expand upon this comment and so the exact details of the wider criticism of RADAR, implied by this comment, is unknown.

5   Throughout this research, the word 'deaf' is used to refer to those people who experience the physical impairment of deafness, but who do not regard themselves as being a part of the culture of Deaf people. The word 'Deaf', therefore, refers to those individuals who aspire to British Sign Language usage and its related cultural heritage.

6   Sign Supported English (SSE).

Chapter 6   Reconsidering Theorizing on Citizenship and Social Movements in the Light of Disability

1   This is a term that was used by respondents in this research.

References

Abberley, P. (1993) 'Disabled people and normality', in J. Swain *et al* (eds) *Disabling Barriers – enabling environments*. London, Sage in association with the Open University.

Abberley, P. (1997) 'The limits of classical social theory in the analysis and transformation of disablement – (can this really be the end; to be stuck inside of Mobile with the Memphis blues again?)', in L. Barton and M. Oliver (eds) *Disability Studies: past, present and future*. Leeds, The Disability Press.

Ablon, J. (1981) 'Stigmatised health conditions', *Social Science and Medicine*, 15B, 5–9.

Acklesberg, M. (1997) 'Rethinking anarchism/rethinking power: a contemporary feminist perspective', in M.L. Shanley and U. Narayan (eds) *Reconstructing Political Theory. Feminist Perspectives*. Cambridge, Polity Press.

Albrecht, G. (1992) *The Disability Business: rehabilitation in America*. London, Sage.

Arendt, H. (1958) *The Human Condition*. Chicago, The University of Chicago Press.

Aziz, R. (1992) 'Feminism and the challenge of racism: deviance or difference?', in H. Crowley and S. Himmelweit (eds) *Knowing Women*. Cambridge, Polity/ Open University Press.

Barbalet, J.M. (1988) *Citizenship*. Milton Keynes, Open University Press.

Barber, B. (1984) *Strong Democracy: participatory politics for a new age*. Berkeley, CA, University of California Press.

Barnes, C. (1992a) For the British Council of Organizations of Disabled People, *Disability and Employment*. Viewed on web at: http://www.leeds.ac.uk/ disability-studies/archiveuk/archframe.htm Date: 25 July 2003.

Barnes, C. (1992b) For the British Council of Organizations of Disabled People, *Disabling Imagery and the Media: an exploration of the principles for media representations of disabled people*. Halifax, Ryeburn Publishing. Viewed on the web at: http://www.leeds.ac.uk/disability-studies/archiveuk/Barnes/disabling% 20imagery.pdf Date: 3 September 2003.

Barnes, C. (1996) 'Disability and the myth of the independent researcher', *Disability and Society*, 11, (1), 107–10.

Barnes, C. and Mercer, G. (eds) (1996) *Exploring the Divide: illness and disability*. Leeds, The Disability Press.

Barnes, C. (1997) Introduction to article by Rae, A. 'Bolton data for inclusion: survivors from the special school system'. Bolton, Bolton Institute. Viewed on web at: http://www.leeds.ac.uk/disability-studies/archiveuk/ Date: 21 July 2003.

Barnes, C. (1999) 'Disability studies: new or not so new directions?', *Disability and Society*, 14, (4), 577–80.

Barnes, C. *et al* (1999) *Exploring Disability. A Sociological Introduction*. Cambridge, Polity Press.

Begum, N. (1992) *Something to be proud of: the lives of Asian disabled people and carers in Waltham Forest*. Waltham Forest, The Race Relations Unit of Waltham Forest.

Begum, N. (1994) 'Mirror, mirror on the wall', in N. Begum *et al*, *Reflections: the views of black disabled people on their lives and community care*. London, CCETSW.

Bendelow, G. and Williams, S. (1995) 'Transcending the dualisms: towards a sociology of pain', *Sociology of Health and Illness*, 17, 139–65.

Berlin, I. (1958) 'Two Concepts of Liberty'. An inaugural lecture delivered before the University of Oxford on 31 October 1958. Oxford, Clarendon Press.

Blaikie, N. (1993) *Approaches to Social Enquiry*. Cambridge, Polity Press.

Blair, Tony (1996*) New Britain: my vision of a young country*. London, Fourth Estate.

Blumer, H. [1951] (1995) 'Social movements', in S.M. Lyman (ed.) *Social Movements. Critiques, Concepts and Case-studies*. Basingstoke, Macmillan.

Booth, T. and Booth, W. (1994) *Parenting Under Pressure: mothers and fathers with learning difficulties*. Buckingham, Open University Press.

Bourdieu, P. (1987) 'What makes a social class? On the theoretical and practical existence of groups', *Berkeley Journal of Sociology*, 32, 1–18.

Bourdieu, P. and Wacquant, L.J.D. (1992) *An Invitation to Reflexive Sociology*. Chicago, University of Chicago Press.

Burchardt, T. (2000) (JRF Findings) *Enduring Economic Exclusion: disabled people, income and wealth*. Viewed on the web at: http://www.jrf.org.uk Date: 18 January 2003.

Burchell, D. (1995) 'The attributes of citizens: virtue, manners and the activity of citizenship', *Economy and Society*, 24, (4), 540–58.

Bury, M. (1997) *Health and Illness in a Changing Society*. London, Routledge.

Butler, J. (1993) *Bodies that Matter: on the discursive limits of sex*. London, Routledge.

Butler, J. (1995) 'Contingent foundations: feminism and the question of post-modernism', in L. Nicholson (ed.) *Feminist Contentions: a philosophical exchange*. London, Routledge.

Byrne, D. (1999) *Social Exclusion*. Buckingham, Open University Press.

Calhoun, C. (1994) 'Social theory and the politics of identity', in C. Calhoun (ed.) *Social Theory and the Politics of Identity*. Oxford, Blackwell.

Caminada, K. and Goudswaard, K. (2000) 'International trends in income inequality and social policy'. Paper given at the Year 2000 International Research Conference on Social Security, Helsinki.

Campbell, J. (2002) 'Diversity: the disability agenda – we've only just begun', *Disability and Society*, 17, (4), 471–8.

Castells, M. (1997) *The Information Age: economy, society and culture. Vol. II. The Power of Identity*. Oxford, Blackwell.

Clarke, P. (1996) *Deep Citizenship*. London, Pluto Press.

Cohen, J.L. (1985) 'Strategy or identity: new theoretical paradigms and contemporary social movements', *Social Research*, 52, (4), 663–716.

Corbett, J. (1994) 'A proud label: exploring the relationship between disability politics and gay pride', *Disability and Society*, 9, (3), 343–57.

Corker, M. (1998) *Deaf and Disabled, or Deafness Disabled?*, Buckingham, Open University Press.

Corker, M. (1999) 'Differences, conflations and foundations: the limits to "accurate" theoretical representations of disabled people's experience?', *Disability and Society*, 14, (5), 627–42.

Coser, L.A. (1971) *Masters of Sociological Thought. Ideas in Historical and Social Context*. New York, Harcourt Brace Jovanovich.

Cox, O. (1970) *Caste, Class and Race*. New York, Monthly Preview Books.

CRICK REPORT. Department for Education and Employment. Advisory Group on Education and Citizenship and the Teaching of Democracy in Schools (1998) *Education for Active Citizenship and the Teaching of Democracy in Schools*. London, QCA.

Daone, E. and Scott, R. (2003) *Ready, Willing and Disabled – executive summary and recommendations for employers*. Viewed on the web at: http:www.scope.org.uk/downloads/work/RWDsummery.pdf Date: 23 July 2003.

Davis, K. (1999) 'The disability movement: putting the power back in empowerment', in M. Barnes and L. Warren (eds) Paths to Empowerment. Bristol, The Policy Press.

Dean, H. *et al* (1999) *Poverty, Riches and Social Citizenship*. Basingstoke, Macmillan.

Delanty, G. (2000) *Citizenship in a Global Age. Society, Culture, Politics*. Buckingham, Open University Press.

Della Porta, D. and Diani, M. (1999) *Social Movements. An Introduction*. Oxford, Blackwell.

Douglas, M. (1966) *Purity and Danger*. Harmondsworth, Penguin.

Duncan Smith, I. (2002) *Defeating the Five Giants*. Speech given at Toynbee Hall on Iain Duncan Smith's first anniversary as Party Leader 13/09/02. Viewed on the web at: http://www.conservatives.com/news/article.cfm?obj_id=38954& speeches=1 Date: 22 February 2004.

Dwyer, P. (2000) *Welfare Rights and Responsibilities. Contesting Social Citizenship*. Bristol, The Policy Press.

Ellison, N. (1997) 'Towards a new social politics: citizenship and reflexivity in later modernity', *Sociology*, 31, (4), 697–717.

Ellison, N. (2000) 'Proactive and defensive engagement: social citizenship in a changing public sphere', *Sociological Research Online*, 5, (3). Viewed on web at: http://www.socresonline.org.uk/5/3/ellison.html Date: 4 June 2003.

Erevelles, N. (1996) 'Disability and the dialectics of difference', *Disability and Society*, 11, (4), 519–37.

Eyerman, R. and Jameson, A. (1991) *Social Movements. A Cognitive Approach*. Cambridge, Polity Press.

Faulks, K. (2000) *Citizenship*. London, Routledge.

Fawcett, B. (2000) *Feminist Perspectives on Disability*. Harlow, Essex, Pearson Education Ltd.

Fierlbeck, K. (1998) *Globalizing Democracy: power, legitimacy and the interpretation of democratic ideas*. Manchester, Manchester University Press.

Fine, M. and Asch, A. (1988) *Women with Disabilities: essays in psychology, culture, and politics*. Philadelphia, Temple University Press.

Finkelstein, V. (1980) *Attitudes and Disabled People*. New York, World Rehabilitation Fund.

Finkelstein, V. (1996) 'Outside, "inside out"', *Coalition*, April.

Foucault, M. (1970) *The Order of Things*. London, Tavistock Publications.

Foucault, M. (1979) *Discipline and Punish*. Harmonsdworth, Peregrine.

Foucault, M. (1980a) *A History of Sexuality*. New York, Vintage.

Foucault, M. (1980b) *Power/knowledge: selected interviews and other writings, 1972–1977*. New York, Pantheon.

Foweraker, J. (1995) *Theorizing Social Movements*. London, Pluto.

Fraser, N. (1989) *Unruly Practices*. Cambridge, Polity.

Fraser, N. (1995a) 'False antithesis: a response to Seyla Benhabib and Judith Butler', in L. Nicholson (ed.) *Feminist Contentions: a philosophical exchange*. London, Routledge.

Fraser, N. (1995b) 'From redistribution to recognition? Dilemmas of justice in a "post-socialist" age', *New Left Review*, 212, 68–93.

Fraser, N. (1997) *Justice Interruptus: critical reflections on the 'postsocialist' condition*. New York, Routledge.

Galipeau, C. (1994) *Isaiah Berlin's Liberalism*. Oxford, Clarendon Press.

Giddens, A. (1982) 'Class division, class conflict and citizenship rights', in A. Giddens *Profiles and Critiques and Social Theory*. London, Macmillan.

Giddens, A. (1984) *The Constitution of Society*. Cambridge, Polity Press.

Giddens, A. (1993) *Sociology*. 2nd edition. Cambridge, Polity.

Gilson, S.F. *et al* (1997) 'Ethnographic research in disability identity: self-determination and community', *Journal of Vocational Rehabilitation*, 9, 7–17.

Gilson, S.F. and Depoy, E. (2000) 'Multiculturalism and disability: a critical perspective', *Disability and Society*, 15, (2), 207–18.

Goffman, E. (1968) *Stigma: notes on the management of spoiled identity*. Harmondsworth, Penguin.

Goodey, C.F. (1995) 'Mental retardation: social section – section I', in G. Berrios and R. Porter (eds) *A History of Clinical Psychiatry: the origins and history of psychiatric disorders*. London, Athlone Press.

Gray, J. (1995) *Berlin*. London, Fontana.

Guigni, M. (1999) 'Introduction. How social movements matter: past research, present problems, future developments', in M. Giugni *et al* (eds) *How Social Movements Matter*. Minneapolis, University of Minnesota Press.

Gussow, Z. and Tracey, G. (1968) 'Status, ideology and adaption to stigmatised illness', *Human Organisation*, 27, 873–84.

Habermas, J. (1981) 'New social movements', *Telos*, 49, 33–7.

Habermas, J. (1984) *The Theory of Communicative Action. Volume 1. Reason and the rationalization of society*. Trans. T. McCarthy. Boston, Beacon Press.

Habermas, J. (1987) *The Theory of Communicative Action*. Cambridge, Polity Press.

Habermas, J. (1992) 'Citizenship and national identity: some reflections on the future of Europe', *Praxis International*, 12, 1–19.

Habermas, J. (1996) *Between Facts and Norms: contributions to a discourse theory of law and democracy*. Cambridge, Polity.

Habermas, J. *et al* (1998) *The Inclusion of the Other: studies in political theory*. Cambridge, MA, MIT Press.

Hall, S. *et al* (1988) 'New Times', *Marxism Today*, October.

Haraway, D. (1991) *Simians, Cyborgs and Women: the reinvention of nature?* London, Free Association Books.

Hayek, F. (1944) *The Road to Serfdom*. London, Routledge.

Hearn, K. (1988) 'Oi! What about us?', in B. Cant and S. Hemmings (eds) *Radical Records: thirty years of lesbian and gay history*. London, Routledge.

Heenan, D. (2002) 'It won't change the world but it turned my life around: participants' views on the personal advisor scheme in the New Deal for disabled people', *Disability and Society*, 17, (4), 383–401.

Heywood, A. (1994) *Political Ideas and Concepts*. London, Macmillan

Hobbes, T. (ed.) (1973) *Leviathan*. London, Dent.

Hughes, B. and Paterson, K. (1997) 'The social model of disability and the disappearing body: towards a sociology of impairment', *Disability and Society*, 12, (3), 325–40.

Hunt, P. *et al* (1966) *Stigma: the experience of disability*. London, Geoffrey Chapman.

Hurd, D. (1988) 'Citizenship in Tory democracy', *New Statesman and Society*, April, 29.

Isin, E.F. and Wood, P.K. (1999) *Citizenship and Identity*. London, Sage.

Jenkins, R. (1998) 'Culture, classification and (in)competence', in R. Jenkins (ed.) *Questions of Competence. Culture, Classification and Intellectual Disability*. Cambridge, Cambridge University Press.

Jones, A. and Longstone, L. (1990) *A Survey of Job Centre Vacancies*. Employment Services, Sheffield, Department of Employment.

Jordan, B. (1996) *A Theory of Poverty and Social Exclusion*. Cambridge, Polity.

Karpf, A. (1988) *Doctoring the Media*. London, Routledge.

Kenny, M. (2000) 'Isaiah Berlin's contribution to modern political theory', (Review Article), *Political Studies*, 48, (5), 1026–39.

Kymlicka, W. (1991) *Liberalism, Community, and Culture*. Oxford, Clarendon Press.

Kymlicka, W. and Norman, W. (1994) 'Return of the citizen: a survey of recent work on citizenship theory', *Ethics*, 104, 352–81.

Kymlicka, W. [1995] (1998) 'Multicultural citizenship', in G. Shafir (ed.) *The Citizenship Debates. A Reader*. London, University of Minnesota Press.

Lister, R. (1997a) *Citizenship: feminist perspectives*. Basingstoke, Macmillan.

Lister, R. (1997b) 'Citizenship: towards a feminist synthesis', Feminist Review, 57, 28–48.

Lister, R. (2003) *Citizenship: feminist perspectives*, 2nd edition. Basingstoke, Macmillan.

Lloyd, M. (1992) 'Does she boil eggs? Towards a feminist model of disability', *Disability, Handicap and Society*, 7, (3), 207–21.

Locke, J. (ed.) (1965) *Two Treatises of Government*. New York, New American Library.

MacFarlane, A. (1994) 'On becoming an older disabled woman', Disability and Society, 9, (2), 255–6.

Macleod, A.M. (1998) 'Instrumental rationality and the instrumental doctrine'. Paper given at the Twentieth World Congress of Philosophy, Boston, Massachusetts. Viewed on the web at: http://www.bu.edu/wcp/papers/Teth/TethMacl.htm Date: 25 June 2003.

Mann, M. (1987) 'Ruling class strategies and citizenship', *Sociology*, 21, (3), 339–54.

Marks, D. (2001) 'Disability and cultural citizenship: exclusion, "integration" and resistance', in N. Stevenson (ed.) *Culture and Citizenship*. London, Sage.

Marshall, T.H. [1963] (1998) 'Citizenship and social class', in G. Shafir (ed.) *The Citizenship Debates. A Reader*. London, University of Minnesota Press.

Marshall, T.H. (1972) 'Value problems of welfare capitalism', *Journal of Social Policy*, 1, (1), 15–32.

Marshall, T.H. (1981) 'Reflections of power', in *The Right to Welfare and Other Essays*. London, Heinemann.

Martell, L. (1994) *Ecology and Society. An Introduction*. Cambridge, Polity Press.

McAfee, N. (2000) *Habermas, Kristeva and Citizenship*. New York, Cornell University Press.

Mead, L.M. (1997) 'Citizenship and social policy: T.H. Marshall and poverty', *Social Philosophy and Policy Foundation*, 14, (2), 197–230.

Meehan, J. (ed.) (1995) *Feminists read Habermas: gendering the subject of discourse*. New York, Routledge.

Meier, C. (1990) *The Greek Discovery of Politics*. Cambridge, Harvard University Press.

Melucci, A. (1985) 'The symbolic challenge of contemporary movements', *Social Research*, 52, (4), 789–816.

Melucci, A. (1989) 'Movements as messages', in J. Keane and P. Mier (eds) *Nomads of the Present. Social Movements and the Individual Needs in Contemporary Society*. London, Hutchinson Radius.

Melucci, A. (1993) 'Paradoxes of post-industrial democracy: everyday life and social movements', *Berkeley Journal of Sociology*, 38, 185–92.

Melucci, A. (1994) 'A strange kind of newness: what's "new" in new social movements?', in E. Larana *et al* (eds) *New Social Movements. From Ideology to Identity*. Philadelphia, Temple University Press.

Melucci, A. (1996) *Challenging Codes. Collective Action in the Information Age*. Cambridge, Cambridge University Press.

Merleau-Ponty, M. (1962) *Phenomenology of Perception*. Trans. C. Smith. London, Routledge.

Michels, R. (1959) *Political Parties*. New York, Dover.

Miles, R. (1982) *Racism and Migrant Labour*. London, Routledge.

Miles, R. (1993) *Racism after 'Race Relations'*. London, Routledge.

Modood, T. (1992) *Not Easy Being British: colour, culture and citizenship*. London, R.T. Trentham.

Modood, T. (1997) *Ethnic Minorities in Britain: diversity and disadvantage*. London, Policy Studies Institute.

Morris, A. (1993) 'Centuries of Black protest – its significance for America and the world', in H. Hill and J.E. Jones Jr (eds) *Race in America – the struggle for equality*. Madison, University of Wisconsin Press.

Morris, J. (1989) *Able Lives: women's experience of paralysis*. London, Women's Press.

Morris, J. (1991) *Pride Against Prejudice*. London, Women's Press.

Morris, J. (ed.) (1996) *Encounters with Strangers: feminism and disability*. London, Women's Press.

Mouffe, C. (1992) 'Democratic politics and the question of identity', in Mouffe, C. (ed.) *Dimensions of Radical Democracy: pluralism, citizenship, community*. London, Verso.

Mouffe, C. (1993) *The Return of the Political*. London, Verso.

Murray, C. (1990) *The Emerging British Underclass*. London, IEA.

Murray, C. (1994) *Underclass: the crisis deepens*. London, IEA.

Narayan, U. (1997) 'Towards a feminist vision of citizenship: rethinking the implications of dignity, political participation, and nationality', in M.L. Shanley and U. Narayan (eds) *Reconstructing Political Theory. Feminist Perspectives*. Cambridge, Polity Press.

Norwich, B. (2002) *LEA Inclusion Trends in England, 1997–2001: statistics on special school placements and pupils with statements in special schools*. Bristol, CSIE.

Nozick, R. (1974) *Anarchy, State and Utopia*. Oxford, Blackwell.

Oakeshott, M. (1975) *On Human Conduct*. Oxford, Oxford University Press.

Oberschall, A. (1973) *Social Conflict and Social Movements*. Englewood Cliffs, New Jersey, Prentice Hall.

Offe, C. (1984) *Contradictions of the Welfare State*. London, Hutchinson.

OFSTED (2004) *Special Educational Needs and Disability. Towards Inclusive Schools*. London, OFSTED.

Oldfield, M. (1990) *Citizenship and Community: civic republicanism and the modern world*. London, Routledge.

Oliver, D. and Heater, D. (1994) *The Foundations of Citizenship*. London, Harvester Wheatsheaf.

Oliver, M. and Zarb, G. [1989] (1997) 'The politics of disability: a new approach', in L. Barton and M. Oliver (eds) *Disability Studies: past, present and future*. Leeds, The Disability Press.

Oliver, M. (1990) *The Politics of Disablement*. Basingstoke, Macmillan.

Oliver, M. (1992) 'Changing the social relations of production?', *Disability, Handicap and Society*, 7, (2), 101–14.

Oliver, M. (1995) *Defining Impairment and Disability: issues at stake*. Unpublished paper.

Oliver, M. (1996) 'A sociology of disability or a disablist sociology?', in L. Barton (ed.) *Disability and Society: emerging issues and insights*. London, Longman.

Oliver, M. (1997) 'The disability movement is a new social movement!', *Community Development Journal*, 32, (3), 244–51.

Pakulski, J. (1997) 'Cultural citizenship', *Citizenship Studies*, 1, (1), 73–86.

Parsons, T. (1951) *The Social System*. New York, Free Press.

Parsons, T. *et al* (1961) *Theories of Society. Vol.1*. New York, The Free Press of Glencoe.

Parsons, T. (1969) *Politics and Social Structure*. New York, Free Press.

Pateman, C. (1988) *The Sexual Contract*. Cambridge, Polity Press.

Patterson, S. (1963) *Dark Strangers*. Harmondsworth, Penguin.

Peters, S. (1996) 'The politics of disability identity', in L. Barton (ed.) *Disability and Society: emerging issues and* insights. London, Longman.

Phillips, A. (1993) *Democracy and Difference*. University Park, Penn State University.

Pinder, R. (1997) 'A reply to Tom Shakespeare and Nicholas Watson', *Disability and Society*, 12, (2), 301–5.

Priestley, M. (1995) 'Commonality and difference in the movement: an "Association of Blind Asians" in Leeds', *Disability and Society*, 10, (2), 157–69.

Prioetto, R. (1995) 'New social movements: issues for sociology', *Social Science Information*, 34, (3), 355–88.

Putnam, R. (1993) *Making Democracy Work: civic traditions in modern Italy*. Princeton, NJ, Princeton University Press.

Rawls, J. (1971) *A Theory of Justice*. Cambridge, Cambridge University Press.
Rawls, J. [1985] (1998) 'Justice as fairness in the liberal polity', in G. Shafir (ed.) *The Citizenship Debates. A Reader*. London, University of Minnesota Press.
Rawls, J. (1993) *Political Liberalism*. New York, Columbia University Press.
Rawls, J. (1996) 'Priority of the rights and ideas of the good', *Political Liberalism*. New York, Columbia University Press.
Reed, G.F. (1980) 'Berlin and the division of liberty', *Political Theory*, 8, (3), 365–80.
Rex, J. and Tomlinson, S. (1979) *Colonial Immigrants in a British City: a class analysis*. London, Routledge and Kegan Paul.
Rhodes, M. (1996) 'Globalization and West European welfare states: a critical review of recent debates', *Journal of European Social Policy*, 6, (4), 305–27.
Richardson, D. (2001) 'Extending citizenship: cultural citizenship and sexuality', in N. Stevenson (ed.) *Culture and Citizenship*. London, Sage.
Rickell, A. (2003) 'Our Disability is Political', *Guardian*, October 1, 2003. Viewed on the web at: http://www.guardian.co.uk/comment/story/0,3604,1053066,00. html Date: 8 February 2004.
Roche, M. (1987) 'Citizenship, social theory, and social change', *Theory and Society*, 16, 363–99.
Roche, M. (1992) *Rethinking Citizenship: welfare, ideology and change in modern society*. Cambridge, Polity Press.
Roche, M. (1995) 'Citizenship and modernity', (Review Article), *British Journal of Sociology*, 46, (4), 715–33.
Roche, M. (2002) 'Social citizenship: grounds of social change', in E.F. Isin and B.S. Turner *Handbook of Citizenship Studies*. London, Sage.
Ross, K. (1997) *Disability and Broadcasting: a view from the margins*. Cheltenham, Cheltenham and Gloucester College of Higher Education.
Roulstone, A. (2000) 'Disability, dependency and the New Deal for disabled people', *Disability and Society*, 15, (3), 427–43.
Rousseau, J.-J. (ed.) (1913) *The Social Contract and Discourses*. Trans. G.D.H. Cole. London, Dart.
Scambler, G. and Hopkins, A. (1986) 'Being epileptic and coming to terms with stigma', *Sociology of Health and Illness*, 8, 26–43.
Scope/NUT (2001) *Within Reach 3: an evaluation of the schools access initiative*. Viewed on the web at: http://www.teachers.org.uk/ Date: 18 September 2003.
Shafir, G. (ed.) (1998) 'Introduction: the evolving tradition of citizenship', *The Citizenship Debates. A Reader*. London, University of Minnesota Press.
Shakespeare, T. (1993) 'Disabled people's self-organisation: a new social movement?', *Disability, Handicap and Society*, 8, (3), 249–64.
Shakespeare, T. (1994) 'Cultural representation of disabled people: dustbins for disavowal?', *Disability and Society*, 9, (3), 283–99.
Shakespeare, T. (1996a) 'Rules of engagement: doing disability research', *Disability and Society*, 11, (1), 115–21.
Shakespeare, T. (1996b) 'Disability, identity and difference', in C. Barnes and G. Mercer (eds) *Exploring the Divide: illness and disability*. Leeds, The Disability Press.
Shakespeare, T. and Watson, N. (1997) 'Defending the social model', *Disability and Society*, 12, (2), 293–300.
Shakespeare, T. (1998) 'Choices and rights: eugenics, genetics and disability equality', *Disability and Society*, 13, (5), 665–81.

Sharma, A. and Love, D. (1991) *A Change in Approach: a report on the experience of deaf people from black and ethnic minority communities.* London, Royal Association in Aid of Deaf People.

Silver, M. (2002) 'Reflections on determining competency', *Bioethics*, 16, (5), 455–68.

Smelser, N.J. (1963) *Theory of Collective Behavior.* New York, Free Press.

Soysal, Y.N. (1994) *Limits of Citizenship: migrant and postnational membership in Europe.* Chicago, University of Chicago.

Stevenson, N. (1997a) 'Globalisation, national cultures and cultural citizenship', *The Sociological Quarterly*, 38, (1), 41–66.

Stevenson, N. (1997b) 'Global media and technological change: social justice, recognition and the meaningfulness of everyday life', *Citizenship Studies*, 1, (3), 365–88.

Strauss, A.L. and Glaser, B. (1975) *Chronic Illness and the Quality of Life.* St Louis, Mo, C.V. Mosby and Co.

Stryker, S. *et al* (2000) 'Introduction. Social psychology and social movements: cloudy past and bright future', *Self, Identity, and Social Movements.* Minneapolis, University of Minnesota Press.

Stuart, O. (1992) 'Race and disability: just a double oppression?', *Disability and Society*, 7, (2), 177–88.

Stuart, O. (1993) 'Double oppression: an appropriate starting point?', in J. Swain *et al* (eds) *Disabling Barriers, Enabling Environments.* Buckingham, Open University Press.

Stuart, O. (1994) 'Journey from the margin: black disabled people and the antiracist debate', in N. Begum *et al* (eds) *Reflections: the views of black disabled people on their lives and community care.* London, CCETSW.

Swain, J. and French, S. (2000) 'Towards an affirmation model of disability', *Disability and Society*, 15, (4), 569–82.

Tarrow, S. (1989) *Democracy and Disorder. Protest and Politics in Italy, 1965–1975.* Oxford, Oxford University Press.

Tarrow, S. (1994) *Power in Movement. Social Movements, Collective Action and Politics.* Cambridge, Cambridge University Press.

Tatchell, P. (1999) 'Let us cease these gay campaigns', *Guardian*, 24 June.

Thatcher, M. [1988] (1989) 'Speech to the Church of Scotland', in J. Raban *God, Man and Mrs Thatcher.* London, Chatto and Windus, May.

Thomas, A. (1997) *Exam Performance in Special Schools.* Bristol, Bristol Centre for Studies on Inclusive Education.

Tilly, C. (1978) *From Mobilization to Revolution.* Reading, MA, Addison-Wesley.

Tilly, C. (1993) 'Social movements as historically specific clusters of political performances', *Berkeley Journal of Sociology*, 38, 1–30.

Tilly, C. (1999) 'Conclusion. From interactions to outcomes in social movements', in M. Giugni *et al* (eds) *How Social Movements Matter.* Minneapolis, University of Minnesota Press.

Touraine, A. (1985) 'An introduction to the study of social movements', *Social Research*, 52, (4), 749–87.

Touraine, A. (1987a) 'Social movements: participation and protest', *Scandinavian Political Studies*, 10, (3), 207–22.

Touraine, A. (1987b) *The Workers' Movement.* Cambridge, Cambridge University Press.

Turner, B.S. (1984) *The Body and Society. Explorations in Social Theory.* Oxford, Blackwell.

Turner, B.S. (1986) *Equality.* London, Tavistock.

Turner, B.S. (1992) *Regulating Bodies: essays in medical sociology.* London, Routledge.

Turner, B.S. (1993a) 'Outline of a theory of human rights', in B.S. Turner (ed.) *Citizenship and Social Theory.* London, Sage.

Turner, B.S. (1993b) 'Outline of a theory of human rights', Sociology, 27, (3), 489–512.

Turner, T. (1994) 'Bodies and anti-bodies: flesh and fetish in contemporary social theory', in T. Csordas (ed.) *Embodiment and Experience: the existential ground of culture and self.* Cambridge, Cambridge University Press.

Turner, B.S. [1996] (2000) 'An outline of a general sociology of the body', in B.S. Turner (ed.) *The Blackwell Companion to Social Theory* 2nd edition. Oxford, Blackwell.

UPIAS (1976) *Fundamental Principles of Disability.* London, UPIAS.

Vernon, A. (1999) 'The dialectics of multiple identities and the disabled people's movement', *Disability and Society*, 14, (3), 385–98.

(Warnock Report) Committee of Enquiry into the Education of Handicapped Children and Young People (1978) *'Special Educational Needs: report of the committee of enquiry into the education of handicapped children and young people'.* London, HMSO.

Warren, L. (1999) 'Conclusion: empowerment: the path to partnership?', in M. Barnes and L. Warren (eds) Paths to Empowerment. Bristol, The Policy Press.

Weeks, J. (1998) 'The Sexual Citizen', *Theory, Culture and Society*, 15, (3–4), 35–52.

Williams, F. (1996) 'Postmodernism, feminism and the question of difference', in N. Parton (ed.) *Social Theory, Social Change and Social Work.* London, Routledge.

Williams, R. (1980) *Problems in Materialism and Culture.* London, New Left Books.

Williams, R. (1981) *Culture.* Glasgow, Fontana.

Wolfensberger, W. (1989) 'Human service policies: the rhetoric versus the reality', in L. Barton (ed.) *Disability and Dependence.* Lewes, Falmer Press.

Yeatman, A. (1994) *Post-modern Revisionings of the Political.* London, Routledge.

Young, I.M. (1990) *Justice and the Politics of Difference.* Princeton, NJ, Princeton University Press.

Young, I.M. [1989] (1998) 'Polity and group difference: a critique of the ideal of universal citizenship', in G. Shafir (ed.) (1998) *The Citizenship Debates. A Reader.* London, University of Minnesota Press.

Young, I.M. (2000) *Inclusion and Democracy.* Oxford, Oxford University Press.

Yuval-Davies, N. (1997) *Gender and Nation.* London, Sage.

Zarb, G. and Oliver, M. (1993) *Ageing with a Disability: what do they expect after all these years?* London, University of Greenwich.

Index

Abductive Research, 5

Barnes, C.
  disabling imagery, 109–11
  institutional discrimination, 106
Berlin, I., 43–5, 169, 179
  desire for recognition, 44–5
  value pluralism, 45
Blumer, H., 67–71
Bourdieu, P.
  habitus, 174
  on groups, 52–3, 172–4

Citizenship
  active, 30–3, 196–7
  Ancient, 24–5
  and competence, 37, 62, 165
  Conservative Neo-Liberalist, 31–2
  education for, 196–7
  Liberal, 26–8
  Liberal Republican, 28–30
  Neo-Republican, 33–4
  Pluralist/Multicultural, 46–54,
    169–79
  Post-structural, 59–61, 179–81
  Reflexive, 55–8, 180, 181
  Social-Liberal, 30, 34–45, 163–9
  and vulnerability, 1–4, 194, 195,
    197–8
Competency, 36–7, 62, 93–4, 164–6
  and disability, 130–1, 165–6

Deafness, 153–60
Disability, *see also* disability movement
  and competency, 130–1, 165–6
  culture, *see under* disability culture
  and deafness, *see under* deafness
  definition, 13–14
  and education, *see under* education
  and employment, *see under*
    employment
  identity, 111–15, 133–9, 148,
    150–1, 172–4, 176

  and impairment, 13–14, 94–8,
    162–3, 192–4
  and the inaccessible environment,
    124–5
  and income, *see under* income
  and independent living, 125–7
  language of disability, 140–2
  in the media, 109–11, 131–2
  Social Model, 13, 95–9, 192–4
  and vulnerability, 3–4, 175
Disability Culture, 115–17, 143–5,
  171–2, 186
Disability Movement, 145–53
  definition, 17–18
  and Disability Studies, 6–7
  as a 'new' social movement,
    112–13, 184–6
Disability Studies, 95–9
Disabling attitudes, 129–32
Disabling imagery, 109–11
Discursive democracy, 56–7

Education
  for citizenship, 196–7
  and disability, 100–3, 119–21
  legislation, 102–3
  and meritocracy, 37
Ellison, N.
  proactive and defensive
    engagement, 181–3, 190
Employment
  and disability, 103–8, 120–1
  legislation, 107–8

Goffman, E.
  stigma, 91–2

Habermas, J.
  discursive democracy, 56–7
  minimal shared identity, 58, 180
  'new' social movements, 80–2
Hobbes, T., 27
Human Rights, 194–5

Identity
  and disability, 111–15, 133–9, 148,
    150–1, 172–4, 176
Impairment
  and disability, 13–14, 94–8, 162–3,
    192–4
Income
  and disability, 108–9

Kymlicka, W., 46–9, 170–4
  differentiated citizenship, 147–9, 174

Marshall, T.H., 37–43, 164–9
  educational meritocracy, 37
Marxism
  and social movements, 72
Medical Sociology, 92–5
Melucci, A., 84–7
Mouffe, C., 59–61, 180–1
  radical democracy, 60, 195

'New' Social Movements, 80–7, 184–6

Oberschall, A., 75–6
Oliver, M., 96–7

Parsons, T.
  sick role, 90–1
Politics of difference, 51–4, 177–8, 198
Proactive engagement, 195
  and defensive engagement, 181–3

Radical Democracy, 60, 195
Rawls, J., 34–6, 163–4
Rousseau, J.-J., 28–9

Shakespeare, T.
  on emancipatory research, 6–7
  new genetics, 111
Social Exclusion, 14–15
Social Model of Disability, 13, 95–9,
  192–4
Social Movement Theory
  Collective Behaviour, 67–71,
    186–7
  'New' Social Movements, 80–7,
    184–6
  Resource Mobilization and Political
    Process, 74–9, 187–8
  Social Democratic, 71–3

Tarrow, S., 78–9, 188
Tilly, C., 76–8, 187
Touraine, A., 82–4
Turner, B.
  human rights, 194–5
  sociology of the body, 63–4,
    193–4

Vulnerability
  and citizenship, 1–4, 194, 195,
    197–8
  definition, 1–4
  and disability, 3–4, 175
  and personhood, 3

Weber, M., 72–3

Young, I., 51–4, 174–8
  politics of difference, 51–4,
    177–8